# Using
# TECHNOLOGY
## *to Enhance*
# Writing

Innovative Approaches *to* LITERACY INSTRUCTION

EDITED BY RICHARD E. FERDIG,

TIMOTHY V. RASINSKI, AND KRISTINE E. PYTASH

*Contributors*

Natalie Bernasconi, Monica T. Billen, Tammy B. H. Brown, Ashley Callan, Laurie O. Campbell,
Gail Desler, Jooyoung Do, Sally Valentino Drew, Sarah T. Dunton, Carol Wade Fetters,
Deborah-Lee Gollnitz, Lisa Holmes, Jeremy Hyler, Robin D. Johnson, Julia Kara-Soteriou,
Gilda Martinez-Alba, Ewa McGrail, J. Patrick McGrail, Michael S. Mills, Renee M. R. Moran,
Paul Morsink, Sue Nash-Ditzel, Timothy C. Pappageorge, Youngmin Park, Matthew T. Pifer,
Sharon M. Pitcher, Dawn Reed, Juan M. Ruiz-Hau, Andy Schoenborn, Victoria Seeger,
Katie Stover, Jenifer Salter Thornton, Charles A. Vogel, Amber White, Lynda Williams, Chase Young

Solution Tree | Press

a division of

Solution Tree

555 North Morton Street
Bloomington, IN 47404
800.733.6786 (toll free) / 812.336.7700
FAX: 812.336.7790
email: info@solution-tree.com
solution-tree.com

Visit **go.solution-tree.com/technology** to download the reproducibles in this book.

Printed in the United States of America

18  17  16  15  14        1  2  3  4  5

Library of Congress Cataloging-in-Publication Data

Using technology to enhance writing : innovative approaches to literacy instruction / Editors: Richard E. Ferdig, Timothy V. Rasinski, Kristine E. Pytash [and 36 contributors].

    pages cm

  Includes bibliographical references and index.

  ISBN 978-1-936764-97-6 (perfect bound)  1.  English language--Composition and exercises--Study and teaching--Computer network resources. 2.  English language--Composition and exercises--Study and teaching--Computer-assisted instruction.  I. Ferdig, Richard E. (Richard Eugene). II. Rasinski, Timothy V. III. Pytash, Kristine E., 1979–

  LB1576.7.U85 2014

  808'.042071--dc23

                    2014015997

---

**Solution Tree**
Jeffrey C. Jones, CEO
Edmund M. Ackerman, President

**Solution Tree Press**
*President:* Douglas M. Rife
*Editorial Director:* Lesley Bolton
*Managing Production Editor:* Caroline Weiss
*Senior Production Editor:* Edward M. Levy
*Copy Editor:* Sarah Payne-Mills
*Proofreader:* Elisabeth Abrams
*Text and Cover Designer:* Laura Kagemann

This book is dedicated to the educators who work daily with
students to foster and encourage a love of writing.
"We write this to make our joy complete."
(1 John 1:4 New International Version)

# Acknowledgments

We commend the thirty-six chapter authors for their enthusiasm and dedication in sharing their knowledge of writing instruction and technology. Each of them could have written more extensively about their classroom experiences; however, they all worked to meet our goal of succinctly providing the most critical research-based, pedagogical strategies. In the spirit of collaboration, the authors also participated in a peer review process, in which they provided feedback to one another. This book is thus itself a cohesive example of how technology can be integral to writing instruction. We would like to thank Kari Gillesse and Ed Levy for their generous support and encouragement in bringing this book to print. —Richard E. Ferdig, Timothy V. Rasinski, and Kristine E. Pytash

Amber White and Paul Morsink would like to acknowledge the talented teachers and students of Ruth Fox Elementary School for their contributions to developing and fine-tuning the "Wonder project" described in chapter 4. In particular, they would like to acknowledge Ruth Fox colleagues Cindy Lewis and Anne Sherrieb, together with Michigan State University colleague Michelle Hagerman, for their contributions to the initial piloting of the project in the summer of 2012.

Ewa and J. Patrick McGrail would like to acknowledge Anne Davis, a co-researcher and a teacher in the blogging project described in chapter 11. Anne's passion and commitment to blogging at school made this project possible and successful. We thank Lani Ritter Hall for sharing with us Harley's blog, which features a dog who took to blogging. And we thank, too, the student bloggers who participated in the project, their teachers, and the many kind readers who contributed their valuable time and made comments on student blogs.

Solution Tree Press would like to thank the following reviewers:

Erin Cuartas
Instructional Supervisor, Department of Language Arts/Reading
Miami-Dade County Public Schools
Miami, Florida

Troy Hicks
Associate Professor and Chippewa River Writing Project Director
Department of English Language and Literature
Central Michigan University
Mt. Pleasant, Michigan

Jessica Sands
Writing Lecturer
Cornell University
Ithaca, New York

Jack Zangerle
English Language Arts Teacher and Department Chair
Dover Middle School
Dover Plains, New York

Visit **go.solution-tree.com/technology** to
download the reproducibles in this book.

# Table of Contents

# About the Editors

**Richard E. Ferdig, PhD,** is the Summit Professor of Learning Technologies and professor of instructional technology at Kent State University, where he works in the Research Center for Educational Technology and the School of Lifespan Development and Educational Sciences. He has served as researcher and instructor at Michigan State University, the University of Florida, the Wyzsza Szkola Pedagogiczna (Kraków, Poland), and the Università degli studi di Modena e Reggio Emilia (Italy). At Kent State, his research, teaching, and service focus on combining cutting-edge technologies with current pedagogic theory to create innovative learning environments. His research interests include online education, educational games and simulations, and what he labels a deeper psychology of technology. In addition to publishing and presenting in the United States and internationally, Rick has also been funded to study the impact of emerging technologies, such as K–12 virtual schools.

Rick was the founding editor-in-chief of the *International Journal of Gaming and Computer-Mediated Simulations*. He is the associate editor-in-chief of the *Journal of Technology and Teacher Education* and serves as a consulting editor for the Development Editorial Board of *Educational Technology Research and Development* and is on the review panel of the *British Journal of Educational Technology*. Rick earned his PhD in educational psychology from Michigan State University. To learn more about Rick's work, visit his website, www.ferdig.com, or follow him on Twitter @rickferdig.

**Timothy V. Rasinski, PhD,** is a professor of literacy education at Kent State University. As a researcher, author, consultant, and presenter, he focuses on reading fluency and word study, reading in the elementary and middle grades, and readers who struggle. His research on reading has been cited by the National Reading Panel and published in *Reading Research Quarterly*, *The Reading Teacher*, *Reading Psychology*, and the *Journal of Educational Research*. He has also taught literacy education at the University of Georgia and was an elementary and middle school classroom and literacy intervention teacher in Nebraska for several years.

Tim served a three-year term on the board of directors of the International Reading Association and for seven years was coeditor of *The Reading Teacher*, the world's most widely read journal of literacy education. He has also served as coeditor of the *Journal of Literacy Research*. Tim is former president of the College Reading Association, and he has won the A. B. Herr and Laureate awards from the College Reading Association for his scholarly contributions to literacy education. In 2010, he was elected to the International Reading Hall of Fame.

Tim has written more than two hundred articles and authored, coauthored, or edited over fifty books or curriculum programs on reading education, including the best-selling *The Fluent Reader*. To learn more about Tim's work, visit his website, www.timrasinski.com, or follow him on Twitter @TimRasinski1.

**Kristine E. Pytash** is an assistant professor in teaching, learning, and curriculum studies at Kent State University's College of Education, Health, and Human Services, where she codirects the secondary Integrated Language Arts Teacher Preparation Program. She is a former high school English teacher. Kristine's research focuses on using disciplinary writing, understanding the literacy practices of youth in alternative schools and juvenile detention facilities, and preparing teachers to teach writing. Her work has appeared in the *Journal of Adolescent and Adult Literacy*, *English Journal*, *Voices from the Middle*, and *Middle School Journal*. Visit her online at www.literacyspaces.com, and follow her on Twitter @kpytash.

To book Richard E. Ferdig, Timothy V. Rasinski, or Kristine E. Pytash for professional development, contact pd@solution-tree.com.

# Introduction

We work in a variety of educational settings with a range of teachers and students. Despite the differences in focus, we have all been asked, "Why is writing relevant, and why, in the era of tweeting, texting, and video blogging, should we bother to teach it?"

Writing is important for several reasons. Writing allows us to communicate information, feelings, and ideas with others. Poetry, song lyrics, speeches, and novels express our emotions, beliefs, and values. Business reports, legal briefs, research articles, and editorials enable people to fully participate in economic and civic life. Written expression allows people to be self-reflective. Writing is a vital tool for learning and processing information.

Yet, teaching writing has often been overshadowed in school. Many educational programs have focused on reading rather than writing instruction. Even though evidence, such as the National Assessment of Educational Progress (NAEP) scores, highlights students' continued struggles with writing, the emphasis on reading prevails (National Center for Education Statistics [NCES], 2012). The adoption and implementation of the Common Core State Standards (CCSS), however, have led policymakers, school representatives, and teachers to concentrate efforts on writing instruction across all K–12 classrooms (National Governors Association Center for Best Practices [NGA] & Council of Chief State School Officers [CCSSO], 2010).

Coupled with this increased focus on writing instruction is teachers' and students' increased access to new technologies. Many districts are implementing one-on-one programs and blended and online courses. Teachers are examining their current writing instruction and considering how to integrate it with digital and technological tools. School districts, curriculum directors, principals, and teachers are learning how certain technologies can meaningfully and effectively contribute to writing instruction. They are asking how technology can strengthen and further develop what they already know about effective best practices.

This book is meant to be a handbook for educators interested in using technology to teach writing. While examining and answering questions that the integration of technology with writing poses, it also provides practitioners with research-based approaches effective for K–12 classrooms.

## How This Book Is Organized

We group the chapters in this book into the following eight parts.

- I. Prewriting and Introduction to Writing
- II. The Reading and Writing Connection
- III. The Process Approach
- IV. Awareness of Audience and Purpose
- V. Collaborative Writing
- VI. Grammar Instruction
- VII. Editing and Revising
- VIII. Assessment

We created these parts to highlight how technology can support specific approaches throughout the writing cycle. Each focuses on effective, research-based pedagogical practices. In creating each part, we consulted three resources: (1) research documents, such as *Writing Next* (Graham & Perin, 2007c), a large-scale meta-analysis that identifies instructional approaches effective for teaching adolescent writers; (2) the Institute of Education Sciences (IES) practice guides (for example, Graham et al., 2012); and (3) academic journals from leading professional organizations, such as the International Reading Association (IRA), the National Council of Teachers of English (NCTE), the Literacy Research Association, and the Association of Literacy Educators and Researchers. Each part begins with an introduction that provides background information about its theoretical perspectives and research base, indicating evidence-based practices. Each part consists of three chapters, which are in turn divided into three sections, as follows:

1. **How Do I Do It?**—A description of the specific pedagogical practice associated with this approach

2. **Classroom Example**—Specific examples highlighting how the instructional approach advances students' knowledge, writing instruction, and the use of technology

3.   **Your Turn**—An exploration of how readers can adapt this pedagogical practice for their own classrooms

Because the authors use these instructional approaches in their own classrooms, the chapters provide firsthand accounts of how particular instructional approaches work and include suggestions for how to adapt them to other settings. Exemplary educators, many of whom have conducted their own research, have penned all the chapters. Many have also published work in leading journals, such as *English Journal, The Reading Teacher, Voices from the Middle*, and *Journal of Adolescent and Adult Literacy*.

We have collected the references for all chapters at the end in one section.

## Important Considerations

Writing is a recursive and ongoing process. The continual cycle of brainstorming, drafting, and revising is critical to students' development as writers. For example, revision might compel writers to begin a new draft or make significant changes to a previous draft. Additionally, genre studies must happen throughout the writing process, not only at the beginning. As you read this book, we encourage you to consider how these instructional practices might inform your instruction before, during, and after writing. We recognize that we could have divided the book by grade bands, but despite the fact that writers in first grade will have different instructional needs than writers in a tenth-grade English course, we felt it was important to show how teachers can implement certain approaches across grade levels. It is also important to note that the approaches and tools of some chapters could fit into other parts or span multiple parts.

## Conclusion

In order to effectively teach writing with technology, teachers must have conceptual knowledge of the writing process, pedagogical knowledge about the teaching of writing, and knowledge about how technology can facilitate growth and development. There is thus much for them to know and consider. As students engage in creating multimodal compositions with video, images, and audio, teachers must continue to explore what these new forms and formats mean for the teaching of writing. Additionally, as the tools students use continue to change and advance, teachers must have extensive knowledge of why certain tools promote particular instructional approaches. We hope this book can provide a deeper understanding of the theoretical perspectives and research base as well as a practical exploration of how teachers can implement instructional approaches in the writing classroom.

# PART I | Prewriting and Introduction to Writing

At the outset, teachers need to consider ways that instruction can foster a learning environment that will support, nurture, and develop writers. This can mean everything from how we teach specific strategies for building background, brainstorming, and organizing to creating and fostering a community of writers. This requires teachers and students to have frequent discussions about how they can support and offer each other feedback during the writing process in order to develop and grow as writers.

When students learn specific strategies to help them brainstorm, plan, and organize their writing, the quality of their writing improves (Graham & Perin, 2007c). Prewriting, for example, helps students create effective plans for their writing. Brainstorming activities, such as free writes and graphic organizers, help students in the initial stages of writing. An evidenced-based approach for introducing students to a new task—such as the gradual release of responsibility model of instruction (Pearson & Gallagher, 1983)—can be particularly important during the prewriting stage. Teachers should begin by articulating the purpose of an activity and explaining the ways the strategy will assist students. It is not enough to simply give directions; rather, teachers must model the prewriting strategy. During modeling, teachers should explain their thinking as they move through the stages of the strategy. Students must then have opportunities to work collaboratively and independently.

As teachers and writers, we have our own strategies that work best for us in crafting a written piece. However, we need to ensure we provide students with a variety of strategies, so they will have a range of tools to assist them, and we should articulate why certain strategies may be effective for certain tasks. The goal is not for students to have one strategy that they use each time they write; rather, we want them to have a wide repertoire as they engage in making meaning through writing.

Technology supports students' prewriting in at least three key ways. First, technology can give teachers access to multiple models of successful writing behavior; second, educators can use technology to show finished publications, existing writing communities, and videos of authors describing their practice; and third, technology can serve as an environment where student authors share writing artifacts that become part of the larger community of practice.

At all stages of writing, technology influences the ways we help students plan and organize their thinking. New innovations allow students to easily create or draw visual representations of their ideas. This may include brainstorming tools with which students can type and then move and manipulate their ideas and images on virtual paper, or it may include gaining access to materials to use while writing, such as artwork from an international gallery or images from a war-torn country.

However, the introduction of technology into writing comes with its own challenges: educators must convey the proper use of technology. At the prewriting stage, the focus should be on rules for interacting with others online and on rules and suggestions for dealing with the indefinite shelf life and therefore potentially long-lasting impact of the printed or digital word.

Natalie Bernasconi and Gail Desler begin this section by exploring how to develop digital citizenship, including how to address issues of cyberbullying and intolerance. In chapter 2, Gilda Martinez-Alba and Sharon M. Pitcher describe how to create a digital language experience approach. Carol Wade Fetters concludes this section by discussing the use of interactive graphic organizers for expository writing.

 **Gail Desler** is a technology coach at Elk Grove Unified School District, Elk Grove, California, where she focuses on promoting digital literacy and digital citizenship with K–12 students and staff. Her passion for supporting students in becoming digital change writers stems from her longtime association with the National Writing Project. To learn more about Gail's work, visit http://blog walker.edublogs.org, or follow her on Twitter @GailDesler.

 **Natalie Bernasconi** is a middle and high school English language arts, English learner, and Advanced Placement Via Individual Determination teacher at Salinas Union High School District, Salinas, California. She also teaches an online educational technology course for the University of California, Santa Cruz. Her doctoral dissertation and professional work focus on leveraging collaborative leadership to advocate for equity and access to technological literacy for English learners. You can also follow Natalie on Twitter @nbernasconi.

To learn more about Gail and Natalie's work, visit http://digital-id.wikispaces.com.

# CHAPTER 1

# Driving Without a License:
# Digital Writing Without Digital Citizenship

By Gail Desler and Natalie Bernasconi

Through the lens of our combined forty-five-plus years of teaching experience and in our respective teaching capacities, we have come to see the critical role that digital citizenship plays in developing strong, confident, and ethical writers, a position the National Writing Project (www.nwp.org) firmly supports. In addition, the U.S. Children's Internet Protection Act (CIPA) has added a legal mandate for any districts utilizing federal funding for technology to teach principles of digital citizenship. Clearly, any book with the title *Using Technology to Enhance Writing* must include the fundamental concept of digital citizenship as an integral part of its exploration.

What exactly *is* digital citizenship? We drew from Ribble and Bailey (2007) and Jason Ohler (2010) to collaboratively develop the framework for our not-for-profit Digital ID Project (http://digital-id.wikispaces.com) and arrived at our own working definition of what it means to be a digital citizen.

> As upstanding "Citizens," we need to participate positively in our physical communities—our schools, neighborhoods, cities, states, countries and the world. Likewise, as exemplary "Digital Citizens," we must learn how to participate positively in a variety of digital/cyber/online communities. It is only by developing a clear sense of both our rights and our responsibilities that we can become fully engaged, contributing "Citizens" of all the communities in which we find ourselves. (Bernasconi & Desler, n.d.)

We've identified four specific foci that together comprise the quintessential digital citizen.

1.  **Stepping up:** Saying "I do" to respecting all people and "I don't" to cyberbullying and risky online behaviors

2.  **Building identities:** Saying "I do" to maintaining a responsible digital footprint and "I don't" to inappropriate online behavior

3.  **Respecting boundaries:** Saying "I do" to respecting others' intellectual property and "I don't" to pirating and plagiarism

4.  **Protecting online security:** Saying "I do" to taking precautions to protect my computer and personal information and "I don't" to jeopardizing privacy

As can be seen from these four foci, we've come a long way from the olden days of the 20th century, when teachers only needed to focus on teaching students proper "netiquette," which included such helpful communication rules such as, "Don't type in all CAPS or people will think you are shouting." While still useful and important, we consider netiquette to be just one small component—akin to learning how to use the blinkers when learning how to drive a car—among the many skills required of a digital citizen. These four foci and the overall concept of 21st century citizenship can be introduced to students in a Prezi (a cloud-based presentation using software of that name) we created, *Digital ID: Citizenship in the 21st Century* (Desler, 2013b). We urge all teachers, but especially those who actively engage their students in digital writing, to integrate these four foci into their pedagogy and daily instructional practices.

## How Do I Do It?

The first and most essential step for the digital writing teacher is to recognize that despite your excellent preparation and anticipation of potential issues, one of your students will inevitably make a bad decision that will challenge your commitment to fostering a digital writing community. Students can and will test the boundaries. It's what they do. It might be something as benign as using Google Docs to chat instead of for collaborative commentary, or it could be perhaps a more egregious violation, like deleting another student's work and just leaving the word *sucka* in its place (true story). Regardless, every teacher needs to know that just as transgressions occur in the pencil-and-paper world, they will also arise in the digital world. Just as you wouldn't permanently forbid the student who writes a bad word on a piece of paper to ever have paper again, you wouldn't permanently banish a student who posts something inappropriate from ever using a digital device again, nor would you ban digital devices for the whole class because of one student's transgression. Kids grow up riding around in cars, but that doesn't mean they have the maturity and judgment to get behind the wheel without adult guidance and training. Similarly, in the digital world, students need our modeling and guidance in order to put the rules of the road into practice on their journey to becoming full-fledged digital citizens.

We have developed our Digital ID Project's policy resources page (http://digital-id .wikispaces.com/Policy+Resources) as a repository for a variety of documents to help policymakers and teachers cover all the bases, including district-level acceptable-use agreements; parent letters explaining rules, safeguards, and expectations; netiquette guidelines; and student guidelines for respectful online academic discourse. These are elements every teacher will want to go over with his or her students well before venturing into the online writing space. Having those conversations in class helps set the tone and the expectations for students while providing them with safe limits.

However, the reality is that no matter how meticulously we seek to prepare our students for respectful online community participation, teachers are unable to police the digital world 24-7. While there are tech tools to help minimize risks (such as online community spaces that teachers control strictly), part of our job is to prepare students for life beyond the walled garden. Since the teacher can't be omnipresent or omniscient, we must teach students the importance of stepping up on behalf of themselves and others against the negative actions of their fellow students. It takes courage for students to cross those lines and not an insignificant amount of integrity to counter cultural norms ("I'm not a snitch"; "He was just joking") that promote silence instead of speaking out. That is why we consider stepping up to be the heart and soul of any digital citizenship effort. We seek to help students make connections—however remote they may seem at first—between the devastating silences that have enabled oppression and injustice throughout history and the silences that allow cyberbullying and the resulting loss of a sense of safety and community it engenders. We seek to use literature, history, contemporary world events, and powerful personal student narratives to provide students with effective models of speaking out, whether it is through poetry, in the court of law, or on the playground. Our Stepping Up page (http://digital-id.wikispaces.com/Focus+1+-+Stepping+Up) is a collection of voices—young, old, contemporary, and historic—that teachers can use to exemplify the personal responsibilities we all must accept as citizens if we are to reach our full potential as individuals and as a learning community.

If educators fail to step up to this challenge and neglect their responsibility, and if our students don't learn these vital qualities, students' digital writing communities will look more like *Grand Theft Auto* venues, where drivers carjack (and writers plagiarize) at will and muggings abound (in the form of derogatory posts, such as those found in just about any YouTube comment section), and our digital writing spaces will never be safe enough for the kinds of authentic student writing we aspire to and that led us to move to digital writing in our classrooms in the first place.

## Classroom Examples

In the following sections, we share a medley of real-life teaching vignettes that we have been collecting as co-curators of the Digital ID Project. These vignettes will serve as a window into K–12 teachers' praxis of developing digital citizens and writers. We hope this report from the trenches on teaching digital writing in the real world will provide a useful map for other teachers of writing who seek to guide their students safely into the online writing world.

These vignettes come from a fifth-grade science class, an eighth-grade homeroom, an eighth-grade humanities class, a twelfth-grade mathematics course, and a seventh-grade Advanced Placement Via Individual Determination (AVID) program, as well as from a districtwide student-led anti-bullying initiative. They represent best practices in teaching digital citizenship and online learning and writing. The relevant Common Core State Standards (CCSS) and International Society for Technology in Education (ISTE) Standards precede each example.

### The CCSS ELA/Literacy Standards: A Primer

Visit www.corestandards.org/the-standards to develop an awareness of the structure and general content of the CCSS. The Common Core State Standards for English language arts / literacy (NGA & CCSSO, 2010) consist of: (1) grades K–5 English language arts standards, (2) grades 6–12 English language arts standards, and (3) grades 6–12 standards for literacy in history / social studies, science, and technical subjects. The main document includes three appendices: Appendix A: Research Supporting Key Elements of the Standards and Glossary of Key Terms, Appendix B: Text Exemplars and Sample Performance Tasks, and Appendix C: Samples of Student Writing (NGA & CCSSO, 2010).

The following are key terms used in these standards:

#### Strands

The main divisions for grades K–5 and 6–12 are known as *strands*. The strands are Reading, Writing, Speaking and Listening, and Language. The Reading strand has two parts at these levels: Reading Standards for Literature (RL) and Reading Standards for Informational Text (RI). A third set of standards in the Reading strand for K–5 is called Foundational Skills (RF) (see NGA & CCSSO, 2010, pp. 15–17). For history and social studies, science, and technical subjects, the Literacy standards have two strands—Reading (RH and RST) and Writing (WH and WST; see NGA & CCSSO, 2010, pp. 60–66).

## Anchor Standards

Anchor standards define expectations for college and career readiness (CCRA). There are general, cross-disciplinary expectations for each strand—Reading, Writing, Speaking and Listening, and Language—as well as the two strands in the Literacy standards. Anchor standards are numbered consecutively in each strand. For example, CCSS ELA-Literacy.CCRA.R.1 signifies college and career readiness anchor standard (CCRA), Reading strand (R), and anchor standard one (1). In this book, we use a simplified version of the standard designation; in this example it would be CCRA.R.1. The Reading and Writing strands for literacy in history and social studies, science, and technical subjects have anchor standards. For example, Writing strand (W), history (H), science (S), technical subjects (T), grade band (9–10), anchor standard four (4) is written WHST.9–10.4.

## Domains

For each ELA/literacy strand, the categories of anchor standards are known as domains. Because domains are consistent across grades, they ensure continuity as the rigor and complexity of the standards increase. The four domains of the Writing strand are (1) Text Types and Purposes, (2) Production and Distribution of Writing, (3) Research to Build and Present Knowledge, and (4) Range of Writing (see NGA & CCSSO, 2010, p. 18).

## Grade-Specific Standards

Grade-specific standards describe what students should understand and be able to do at the end of the school year. Grade-specific standards correspond to anchor standards and use the same number designation. For example, RL.6.1 signifies Reading Standards for Literature (RL), grade six (6), and standard one (1) in the domain Key Ideas and Details. Similarly, SL.6.1 signifies Speaking and Listening (SL), grade six (6), and standard one (1) in the domain Comprehension and Collaboration.

## Grade Bands

Groupings of standards by grade levels are known as grade bands: K–2, 3–5, 6–8, 9–10, and 11–12.

### *Writing Emails*

**Production and Distribution of Writing:** Use technology, including the Internet, to produce and publish writing and to interact and collaborate with others. (CCRA.W.6; NGA & CCSSO, 2010)

**Communication and Collaboration:** Students use digital media and environments to communicate and work collaboratively, including at a distance, to support individual learning and contribute to the learning of others. (Standard 2; ISTE, 2007)

Erica Swift, an inspirational computer resource teacher at Herman Leimbach Elementary School (a Title I school), introduces fifth-grade teacher Kevin Ohama's students to the Common Sense Media (2013b) lesson on writing good emails and guides a conversation on how to communicate effectively by email, taking into account both the purpose and audience of a message. After Erica's lesson, Kevin introduces his students to a classroom blog he has created for their science, technology, engineering, and mathematics (STEM) projects. In explaining netiquette expectations for his students to post comments, Kevin also references the purpose and the audience of the messages. These fifth graders are already having opportunities—and guidance—to practice good digital citizenship, improve their digital writing and communication skills, and build on their college and career readiness skills, as outlined by the Common Core State Standards. Teachers collaborating help make this happen.

### *Cyberbullying and Intolerance*

**Key Ideas and Details:** Determine the central ideas or information of a primary or secondary source; provide an accurate summary of the source distinct from prior knowledge or opinions. (RH.6–8.2; NGA & CCSSO, 2010)

**Creativity and Innovation:** Students demonstrate creative thinking, construct knowledge, and develop innovative products and processes using technology. (Standard 1; ISTE, 2007)

At Elizabeth Pinkerton Middle School during homeroom/advisory period, eighth-grade students first learn the vocabulary of intolerance via Common Sense Media's (2013a) Crossing the Line lesson on cyberbullying. When these middle schoolers head to Jennifer Hammond's humanities class, they hear, see, and use the same vocabulary in a documentary about World War II. Students transfer and reinforce the concepts they learn during homeroom through discussions and a multimedia writing assignment. As students look at issues of citizenship across subject areas and historic timelines, they explore and reflect on how the past connects to the present—and how they, through their actions both online and offline, can bring about change.

## *Intellectual Property*

> **Research to Build and Present Knowledge:** Gather relevant information from multiple authoritative print and digital sources, using advanced searches effectively; assess the usefulness of each source in answering the research question; integrate information into the text selectively to maintain the flow of ideas, avoiding plagiarism and following a standard format for citation. (W.9–10.8; NGA & CCSSO, 2010)

> **Critical Thinking, Problem Solving, and Decision Making:** Students use critical thinking skills to plan and conduct research, manage projects, solve problems, and make informed decisions using appropriate digital tools and resources. (Standard 4; ISTE, 2007)

Todd Reiswig, a math teacher at Elk Grove High School, is one of the growing number of 21st century teachers who are experimenting with the concept of "flipping" their classrooms. Rather than adhere to the traditional model of providing direct instruction in class followed by individual practice for homework at night, Todd's student videographers record his lessons for his Advanced Placement Statistics students to view and study at home, which then frees up class time for them to practice applying what they have learned with his guidance and peer support. Todd provides the links to his lesson videos on his class blog, a venue that is open not only to his students 24-7 but also to a worldwide audience.

Through this practice, Todd extends the school librarian's lesson on copyright to make intellectual property issues memorable and real to his students. By licensing his work through Creative Commons, his students see that he has given permission to others to use his work with attribution and without modifications, an assertion of intellectual property rights. Additionally, Todd credits the students who help videotape and edit his lessons—including occasionally inserting screenshots with additional notations where they think his explanation calls for clarification—at the end of each lesson. Through a cross-curricular delivery model, these students build a positive digital footprint as well as create content for their e-portfolios.

## *Digital Citizenship*

> **Key Ideas and Details:** Cite the textual evidence that most strongly supports an analysis of what the text says explicitly as well as inferences drawn from the text. (RI.8.1; NGA & CCSSO, 2010)

> **Digital Citizenship:** Students understand human, cultural, and societal issues related to technology and practice legal and ethical behavior. (Standard 5; ISTE, 2007)

In Natalie Bernasconi's seventh-grade classroom at La Paz Middle School (a Title I school), she seamlessly integrates teachable moments for digital citizenship during the day, such as when preparing her class for a guest speaker—a former student who was now attending Georgetown University. To give the students some background on the former student's college-bound journey, Natalie googled her name. A quick search yielded her high school track-and-field scores; a Rotary Club post announcing her departure for her junior year abroad to Belgium; several quite insightful, if provocative, articles she wrote for her high school newspaper; and a public announcement of her $182,000 scholarship to attend Georgetown. This nineteen-year-old's digital footprint impressed the class and sparked a conversation about how it is never too early for students to start developing their own positive online identities. This is just one example of the many teachable moments of digital citizenship that teachers can weave, like golden threads, into the tapestry of their curriculum.

A remarkable example of a student-led digital citizenship–focused initiative that spanned an entire school district is the #UnfollowBullying project in the Elk Grove Unified School District. In figure 1.1, Aivi, a high school junior, demonstrates digital writing and digital citizenship at their finest in her blog post. Visit **go.solution-tree.com/technology** to access this and other materials related to this book.

Imagine the result if over the course of a student's academic career all of his or her teachers were to weave a rich variety of lessons in digital citizenship into their respective grade levels and subject areas, while the school site and district provided additional opportunities and support. It takes the combined efforts of the village to raise upstanding, outstanding digital citizens.

Meet Aivi Huynh, one of our #UnfollowBullying student guest bloggers. Aivi is a junior at Sheldon High School and serves as a member of Superintendent Ladd's student advisory committee. In this post, Aivi shares her reflections on the #UnfollowBullying campaign.

**Student Blogger:** Aivi Huynh

**School:** Sheldon High School

High school alone is tough. We, as teenagers, are consistently trying to adjust to the new workload, adjust to a new teacher, and adjust to the person we are growing to be. We are going through an awkward phase in our lives in which we are battling between who we really are and who everyone expects us to be. We are young, rebellious, and quite frankly, vulnerable. We pretend to be tough, but at the end of the day, words can hurt us just as much as any stick or stone; and more frequently than not, those hurtful words are exchanged behind the "safety" of a computer screen.

The #UnfollowBullying campaign puts a spotlight on the negative and aggressive transactions that often transpire online between teenagers today. This modern version of bullying is often overlooked or ignored if not brought to attention by the victims themselves. This campaign encourages those who see it to speak up and extend a helping hand to those who need it. It recognizes that not everyone needs a cape or power to be a hero. #UnfollowBullying is ultimately a group of everyday superheroes; by discouraging the negativity of one, they are encouraging the well-being of another. A lot of the time, people are hesitant to speak up, in fear that they will become the new target. #UnfollowBullying to me is sort of a support network. It reassures people that they ultimately are not in this alone and that standing up for someone else does not mean sacrificing your own well-being; it is allowing someone else the opportunity to enjoy theirs.

*Source: Aivi Huynh. Used with permission.*

Figure 1.1: Student blog post about antibullying.

## Your Turn

We firmly believe that just as teachers teaching teachers is the most powerful form of professional development, students teaching students is the most powerful form of learning. Students harness the power to deeply engage one another. A tour of our Student-Created Content page (http://digital-id.wikispaces.com/Student-Created+Content) shows the great breadth and depth of student contributions to the digital citizenship discourse. Ranging from simple classroom contributions to more complex, large-scale projects that move beyond the classroom—like districtwide initiatives—student-created work featured includes:

- Slides for the collaborative A–Z Glossary slideshow project and the Upstanders Together project

- Public service announcements (PSAs), in which students create ninety-second videos illustrating digital citizenship concepts

- Five-hundred-plus-word biographical research essays on a real person for the Gallery of Heroes project

- Multimedia for the California Writing Project's Digital Citizenship Month

- #UnfollowBullying (http://blogs.egusd.net/ub), the remarkable student-led initiative of Elk Grove Unified School District

- Recorded comments on the *Upstanders, Not Bystanders* VoiceThread (Desler, 2013a)

As this list shows, students are flexing their digital citizenship muscles and putting the concepts into practice. We created the four digital ID "I do" badges (figure 1.2) to honor students' growth as digital citizens. As students demonstrate evidence of their skills in each of the four foci, teachers confer these badges on them, which they then proudly display on their eportfolios, blogs, wikis, and so on.

*Source: Kathleen Watt. Used with permission.*

Figure 1.2: Digital "I do" badges students earn and display to document their growth as digital citizens.

We have a challenge for any teacher reading this chapter: now that you have seen the wide range of possibilities for your students to demonstrate digital citizenship skills, what can you envision for your own students to create and publish online—and that we could showcase on the Digital ID Project? Whether it is a project already listed, an idea you discover from some of the other chapters in this book, or a unique, innovative activity you and your students have designed, we encourage you to visualize it being published and inspiring students around the world to step up as digital writers and citizens.

**Gilda Martinez-Alba** is an associate professor in the Educational Technology and Literacy Department at Towson University in Maryland. Her research involves technology, motivation, and English learners. Her work has been published in the *Journal of Adolescent and Adult Literacy* and the *TESOL Journal*. Gilda is past president of the Maryland Teachers of English to Speakers of Other Languages.

**Sharon M. Pitcher** is a professor in the Educational Technology and Literacy Department at Towson University in Maryland. She is coauthor of *Collaborating for Real Literacy: Librarian, Teacher, and Principal* and the author of "The Great Poetry Race," which appeared in *The Reading Teacher*. Sharon teaches literacy courses and served as director of Towson University's reading clinic.

# CHAPTER 2

# The Language Experience Approach Goes Digital

By Gilda Martinez-Alba and Sharon M. Pitcher

During the language experience approach (LEA), students create and dictate stories to their teacher (Peregoy & Boyle, 2013), who acts as a scribe. This constructivist approach can help students learn to read and write by using their own experiences as the foundation for literacy learning. In this prewriting activity, the teacher models how to write a story using correct grammar and punctuation, prompts students for more information and in-depth descriptions, and asks about the sequence of events in the story. Because students generate the text and share something of interest— something they did or know about—they are motivated, and even reluctant readers are more likely to be engaged.

The language experience approach has been recommended for use with English learners (ELs; Herrell & Jordan, 2012). When creating a language experience approach with an EL, the teacher might want to focus on inserting vocabulary he or she would like students to learn. Intermediate-grade ELs are still developing their social language, so even though they may have sufficient vocabulary to get their message across, the teacher may want to add new words to their everyday language through this writing activity. Additionally, although advanced ELs can communicate socially, they may need help in the process of developing their academic vocabulary. Regardless of their language proficiency levels, the language experience approach can assist ELs in building their vocabulary.

With a digital language experience approach, students dictate stories about themselves or about some content of interest while adding digital pictures and illustrations to help them explain their stories. This is helpful for ELs because they need visuals to understand written texts, especially when they are at the beginning stages of learning English (Peregoy & Boyle, 2013). The goal is to motivate students to write (and read) while developing vocabulary.

## How Do I Do It?

To help students brainstorm and to get a sense of their interests to guide them in creating their texts, have them complete an interest survey. For example, the survey might ask what they like to do during their free time, what hobbies they have, or what they enjoy reading online.

As previously stated, in the LEA, the teacher usually writes what the students say word for word. However, when using a digital LEA with an EL, you might prefer to scaffold what the student says in a positive way, repeating and writing it in the correct form (without having to tell the student he or she is saying something incorrectly). This is very similar to repeating back to a young child learning a first language the correct form. For the EL, this could provide a model of how to pronounce English words, say words in the proper order (since syntax can be an area of difficulty for ELs), write words using correct spelling and grammar, and read in English (Martinez, 2007; Scarcella, 2003). You will need to choose what you want to focus on to correct. There are different views on correcting students' errors, so you need to find what works best for you and your students.

Done in a positive manner, this process can help create a nonthreatening environment where students can comfortably share their backgrounds. Digital LEAs not only provide an opportunity for students to share their culture, traditions, life experiences, or areas of interest but also provide the teacher with support to help students build their literacy skills. In this process, students use technology to develop their English skills while sharing their own stories.

Asking students to bring in their own digital pictures or to find pictures online about a topic of interest acknowledges the diversity that exists in the classroom and provides you with a lens into the values that students want to share. In turn, students realize that you want to learn more about them, which establishes rapport and helps ELs feel welcome in the classroom (Peregoy & Boyle, 2013).

For beginning ELs, you may choose to insert basic vocabulary words, such as adjectives, where they fit into the stories to describe objects or cognates (August & Shanahan, 2008). (Cognates are words that are similar in two or more languages.) For example, *English* is a cognate—it's similar to *inglés* in Spanish. If you can point out cognates between languages, students will understand that they already know many words in English.

For intermediate and advanced ELs, you may want to insert signal words into their stories. These include sequencing words (*after, before, finally, now, then, next,* and *while*), restatement words or phrases (*also, for example, just as,* and *too*), and comparing or contrasting words (*like, similar to, but, unlike,* and *yet*). Learning signal words helps ELs comprehend academic English or content-area readings. Other language strategies ELs can use to master academic language include using description (providing characteristics, locations, and dimensions) and asking and answering questions (using *who, what, when, where,* and *why*; Scarcella, 2003). Having a checklist like figure 2.1 containing these and other items can help intermediate and advanced ELs develop more comprehensive and sophisticated texts. Although you may initially ask intermediate and advanced ELs to dictate a text, you may invite them to write subsequent stories independently.

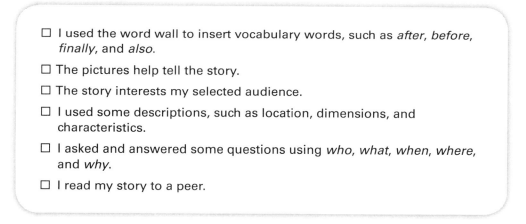

☐ I used the word wall to insert vocabulary words, such as *after, before, finally,* and *also*.

☐ The pictures help tell the story.

☐ The story interests my selected audience.

☐ I used some descriptions, such as location, dimensions, and characteristics.

☐ I asked and answered some questions using *who, what, when, where,* and *why*.

☐ I read my story to a peer.

Figure 2.1: Sample LEA checklist for intermediate or advanced EL students.

Visit **go.solution-tree.com/technology** to download a reproducible version of this figure.

Using a feedback form like figure 2.2 (page 24), students can provide one another with feedback that extends the activity and makes it more meaningful (Herrell & Jordan, 2012). This form can help students provide suggestions and positive, constructive feedback. It can also assist teachers in monitoring what students are saying to each other. The feedback form also provides them with time to reflect on the story and process the language; they can think about and carefully write out their explanations before having to say them. This is beneficial because ELs need extra time to process language.

One thing I learned was . . .

_____

_____

One thing I would add or change . . .

_____

_____

I liked . . .

_____

_____

Figure 2.2: Sample feedback form.

Visit **go.solution-tree.com/technology** to download a reproducible version of this figure.

Displaying new vocabulary on word walls is useful for future writing activities. Word walls are particularly beneficial in developing vocabulary words when teachers consistently refer to them, elaborate on their meaning, and add new and related words or terms regularly. For ELs, having a word wall with pictures and visuals is worthwhile, provides the extra support they need while learning a new language, and adds new words to their digital LEA stories (Harvey & Goudvis, 2007).

During the first days of school, you might want to allow ELs to dictate the story in their native language and provide the translation for them, creating a bilingual book. Clearly, this is possible only if you speak the students' native language—if you do, it is a wonderful opportunity.

## Classroom Example

Providing a model or an example of a digital LEA can help struggling ELs to understand the directions and questions you are asking, especially when there is a language barrier. Showing students a model of what is expected also clarifies the lesson's outcomes and, if you create the model, it shows that you value the activity enough to do it yourself. Bilingual models would further welcome students into the class and emphasize the importance of maintaining their native languages.

Figure 2.3 shows a sample digital LEA story for intermediate or advanced ELs. *What Did They Do on Mother's Day in This Home?* follows the format of a typical picture book, using a title page, dedication, and pictures to tell the story. Visit **go.solution -tree.com/technology** to access the complete story.

Title Page

What Did They Do on Mother's Day in This Home?

¿Qué Hicieron en el Día de las Madres en Este Hogar?

Page From the Story

Here is Lupita dancing to the "Mexican Hat Dance" song, which sounds like "Taran, taran, taran . . ." My mom always says she is doing it better than ever. (She's been doing it the same for the past ten years.)

Aquí esta Lupita bailando "La Raspa," que suena así "taran, taran, taran . . ." Mi mamá siempre dice que ella lo está haciendo mejor que nunca. (Ella lo ha estado haciendo igualito hace diez años.)

*Source: Gilda Martinez-Alba. Used with permission.*

Figure 2.3: Sample pages from a digital LEA story.

After reading a model digital LEA story, you can go over supportive features that help with comprehension and ask the class if the story included these features. Texts that support reading comprehension have five characteristics. They (1) are predictable, (2) represent cultural and similar experiences, (3) have visuals that support the text, (4) are interesting or imaginative, and (5) use natural language. Ask students to keep these characteristics in mind when sharing their stories, and ask them to expand in these areas as they dictate.

Students' English proficiency levels influence the model text's length. Start with a sentence per page or per picture for beginning ELs and have them create longer examples as their language skills emerge. Teachers can use this process in the content areas to explain concepts or areas of interest.

## Your Turn

To make a digital LEA, start by gathering pictures and images. Ask students to bring a flash drive to school with three to sixteen pictures and images to class about a particular topic or event. You can also take pictures of students in a sequence of activities, or you can have them locate pictures online that illustrate a content area topic, such as pictures about recycling. Use a published picture book as a model. For beginning EL students, you might want to start with fewer pictures.

Next, students dictate a story to go along with the pictures, as you capture their words and build their vocabulary in Microsoft Word, PowerPoint, or Movie Maker (you can download Movie Maker for free). You can also use free online resources such as Storify, ZooBurst, BoomWriter, Storybuilder, and Storybird. In time, students will write their own stories, and you can continue to build their vocabulary by discussing, suggesting, and elaborating on new words.

Finally, students read their published story to a peer, in small groups, or to their families or record it after practicing on their own. Reading their stories to the whole class is not recommended for ELs because they may feel uncomfortable speaking and possibly making English errors in front of a larger group (Herrell & Jordan, 2012).

Research suggests that classrooms do not sufficiently use technology even though many students find it motivating (Pitcher, Martinez, Dicembre, Fewster, & McCormick, 2010). Beginning with short, simple digital LEA texts using just a few pictures, you can scaffold students to longer and more sophisticated texts with richer vocabulary. This is a motivating activity that aligns with the following Common Core standards for writing.

> Use technology, including the Internet, to produce and publish writing and to interact and collaborate with others. (CCRA.W.6)

> Write narratives to develop real or imagined experiences or events using effective technique, well-chosen details, and well-structured event sequences. (W.9–10.3)

> Produce clear and coherent writing in which the development, organization, and style are appropriate to task, purpose, and audience. (W.9–10.4; NGA & CCSSO, 2010)

Getting students excited about writing, so that they practice often and improve their craft, is important and timely. Hopefully, the ideas presented in this chapter will motivate your students to write—and also to enjoy the process.

**Carol Wade Fetters, PhD,** is a researcher and independent consultant. Carol has served as a preK–12 teacher, administrator, university instructor, and supervisor. She earned a bachelor of science degree in elementary education from Lamar University in Beaumont, Texas; a master of education degree from McNeese State University in Lake Charles, Louisiana; an educational administration certification from Houston Baptist University in Houston, Texas; and a doctorate in curriculum and instruction with a specialization in reading education from Louisiana State University, in Baton Rouge. To learn more about Carol's work, visit her website, www.carolfetters.com.

# CHAPTER 3

# Integrating Expository Writing With Technology

By Carol Wade Fetters

We live in an expository world bursting with information. This information that surrounds us helps us make sense of the world. Like architects, educators must innovatively plan how to use instructional strategies integrated with technology to produce lifelong learners in an ever-changing society. Readers construct meaning from the online texts they read; therefore, literacy educators must adopt a broader definition of literacy that includes the utilization of technology in our expository world. To help students transfer information from multiple expository text resources—and apply that information in their daily lives—educators must integrate instruction with technology.

Research has consistently shown that the primary way we present new knowledge to students is through linguistics. Teachers either discuss the content or have students read about the content (Flanders, 1970). However, Robert Marzano, Debra Pickering, and Jane Pollock (2001) point out that explicitly engaging students in the creation of *nonlinguistic* representations stimulates and increases activity in the brain and therefore, enhances students' understanding of the content. By integrating new literacies (including global literacy, media literacy, and digital literacy) into writing instruction and connecting them with emerging forms of writing, expository writing will be meaningful and engaging for students of the digital era.

Students need access to multiple resources containing informational and non-fiction materials, commonly referred to as expository text. To expand students' conceptual knowledge, classrooms can provide expository texts and informational resource materials based on students' interests; basal readers for science or social studies areas; or particular district, state, or Common Core–required topics. Nell Duke (2000) acknowledges that classroom libraries have few informational texts, classroom walls or other surfaces display little informational text, and classroom activities on average spend only 3.6 minutes per day with informational texts involving written language. Findings from other studies have confirmed the underuse of informational texts in elementary school. The International Reading Association and the National Council of Teachers of English's Standards for the English Language Arts (IRA & NCTE, 1996) emphasize the importance of students reading a wide range of print and nonprint texts to build an understanding of texts, themselves, and world cultures. Nonfiction texts are among these print resources.

Additionally, the IRA and NCTE standards note that students must use a variety of technological and informational resources (for example, libraries, databases, computer networks, and videos) to gather and synthesize information and to create and communicate knowledge. The Common Core State Standards require students to have access to a wide array of informational texts.

With the arrival of the Common Core and other state and local school district standards comes the challenge of using research-based guidance when implementing them. To meet this challenge, we need to consider all aspects of implementation—including teacher preparation, professional development, assessment design, and integration of technology into curriculum and instruction.

As Jennifer Altieri (2014) emphasizes, to meet the ELA CCSS, K–3 students will need to be able to conduct research, analyze the information they find, collaborate with peers, and write for a variety of purposes.

This example of a Common Core State Standard shows that there are some major shifts toward integrating technology into all areas of the curriculum in order to prepare students for college and career:

> With some guidance and support from adults, use technology, including the Internet, to produce and publish writing as well as to interact and collaborate with others; demonstrate sufficient command of keyboarding skills to type a minimum of one page in a single sitting. (W.4.6; NGA & CCSSO, 2010, p. 21)

Reading and writing online changes what it means to read, write, and comprehend, since literacy practices involve both the creation as well as the use of multimodal texts. Creating multimodal texts requires knowing the properties and limitations of digital tools.

# What Is Expository Writing?

Expository writing is factual; its purpose is to convey information about the world (Duke & Bennett-Armistead, 2003). Since this genre usually explains something, presents information about a topic, or provides instruction and allows writers to use a variety of materials, students typically use expository writing to write reports in order to share information they have learned, write essays to describe a topic, compare two things, or specify how to do or make something.

Gail Tompkins (2010) states that expository writing exemplifies the following characteristics. It:

- Focuses on a single topic

- Applies expository text structures to organize writing and cue words to guide the reader

- Introduces the topic, stating the focus and grabbing readers' attention in the first paragraph

- Presents information using a topic sentence with supporting facts and specific details in the middle paragraphs

- Inserts smooth transitions between paragraphs and sections

- Summarizes ideas about the topic in the conclusion

- Uses nonfiction features and reader-friendly formatting to guide readers

As we explore integrating technology with expository writing, we need to consider the key stages of the writing process: prewriting, drafting (creating a rough draft), revising (sharing drafts and making changes), editing (proofreading to locate grammatical errors, misspellings, and areas in need of clarification and expansion), and publishing (sharing and publishing in an appropriate form). Classrooms can use this five-stage writing process with various expository text structures.

What are expository text structures? They are patterns used to organize nonfiction writing. Five common patterns are (1) description, (2) sequence, (3) comparison, (4) cause and effect, and (5) problem and solution (Harvey, 1998). Within each pattern, the writer organizes the information in a particular way. Expository text structures are prevalent in the content areas of science and social studies. Dolores Durkin (1981), Nell Duke (2000), and Carol Fetters (2010) point out that we are not spending enough time during the school day providing access to and using expository text and resources in these areas nor in mathematics.

As a pedagogical tool, technology lends itself well to the design and development of expository writing—for example, using graphic organizers to brainstorm ideas for prewriting and other prewriting activities to construct and produce expository writing products. If teachers integrate reading with both the content area and technology, they can integrate expository writing with technology in a variety of ways, beginning in the elementary grades.

Timothy Rasinski and Nancy Padak (2008) emphasize that many texts have multiple and embedded text structures, and guiding students through the complex task of discerning them can make meaning more transparent for students. Graphic organizers taught through in-depth, explicit explanation and authentic application (making and interpreting graphic organizers) using the gradual release of responsibility model of instruction empower students to organize their ideas and help them become successful writers. Graphic organizers are excellent for integrating expository writing (writing that describes, explains, informs, or summarizes ideas and content) with technology since they allow the teacher and students to examine the text structures that are prevalent in classroom expository text materials. Graphic organizers are also one of the most effective ways to assist students in generating nonlinguistic representations, since they combine both the linguistic (words and phrases) and nonlinguistic modes (symbols, arrows, bubbles, and so on) to represent relationships between the symbols and words. See table 3.1 for a list of interactive graphic organizers.

Table 3.1: Digital Graphic Organizers

| Graphic Organizer | Description |
|---|---|
| Inspiration, www.inspiration.com | Inspiration is a popular online graphics tool developed for grades 6–12 that helps students visualize (Silverman, 2005). There is a simpler version, Kidspiration, for K–5. Teachers can download either version for a free thirty-day trial, after which the software is available for purchase online. |
| Bubbl.us, http://bubbl.us | Bubbl.us is a free web 2.0 tool that enables students to create mind-mapping and brainstorming diagrams. To begin, students enter the main topic or concept into the parent bubble. Then, they record ideas and thoughts in colorful text bubbles linked to the parent bubble. Users continue to add text bubbles that are color coded according to hierarchy. |

| Graphic Organizer | Description |
|---|---|
| Socrative, www.socrative.com | This is a free website or app (for Android and Apple devices) that allows your device to be turned into a student response system. |
| Edmodo, www.edmodo.com | In Edmodo's secure environment, teachers and students can collaborate, share content, and use educational apps to augment classroom learning. These capabilities enable teachers to personalize learning for every student. Edmodo is correlated with the CCSS and equipped with tools to monitor student performance. |

Patricia Cunningham and Richard Allington (2007) point out that writing is a form of thinking, and that it is hard! Exposing students to and teaching them how to use digital graphic organizers will help them think through and organize complex expository information into ideas that they can transition into expository writing forms.

Teachers don't need advanced and sophisticated technology resources to use digital graphic organizers. They can use digital graphic organizers on a classroom computer with minimal resources to examine expository text. Since time is such an important factor during the instructional day, it is important to remember that integrating technology into content areas allows students to integrate the use of expository text resources with their other reading time throughout the day, and to therefore use their reading time more flexibly. Richard Allington (2001) encourages teachers to allocate about two hours a day to engage students in actual reading or writing (including reading and writing in content subjects). Technology can be integrated into those allocated instructional times for flexible use of the instructional time during the school day.

## How Do I Do It?

First, select an interactive graphic organizer (see table 3.1) and a nonfiction topic passage to:

- Organize students' thinking about a topic
- Help students remember their thinking processes
- Deepen students' understanding through connecting their thoughts and ideas

- Construct and explain the connections between the words and phrases they are reading

Second, introduce the information or topic of the lesson by making connections to background knowledge. Then, ask students to give examples of their knowledge about the topic, and list the students' ideas on the graphic organizer with the informational topic in the center, or hub, of the graphic organizer. This can be done in a large- or small-group setting using an interactive whiteboard.

Third, as students list their ideas about a topic by brainstorming during prewriting, help students organize what they know by reminding them of what they need to explain and assisting them in communicating with clarity, accuracy, and organization.

## Classroom Example

Nate Smith is teaching a lesson using a newspaper article from Tween Tribune (www .tweentribune.com) that he has projected onto the SMART Board, and the students are using a variety of wireless technology devices at their desks, including Kindle Fire, Nook, iPad, and other tablets; laptop computers; and smartphones. The students concentrate on critical thinking and vocabulary words in the article by responding to multiple-choice questions. Their answers are sent to their technology device (cell phone, tablet, or laptop) and are projected on a screen so that the whole class can see the answers and Nate can discuss the students' responses and why they are correct. Feedback for correct responses is immediate and provides information and expands background knowledge for the large group of students. In the subsequent expository writing assignment, students are the architects, or designers, of their own expository writing pieces as a result of the experience they are having with the integration of technology and informational text that uses pictures, advertisements, facts, and opinions. Nate can record the information and feedback from the class discussion on a large-group graphic organizer like Inspiration, or individual students can design their own graphic organizers and record their thinking.

## Your Turn

Integrating expository writing with technology, especially interactive graphic organizers, offers the following benefits:

- **Activates background knowledge**—Students are likely to have prior background knowledge about the introduced topic, and when they connect the topic to what they already know, they are more likely to construct meaning.

- **Employs questioning techniques**—Expository texts spark questions because the readers often lack *schema* (background knowledge) about the topic. Teachers can use questions to spark interest and inquiry about the topic.

- **Facilitates visualization**—Students can paint pictures with words and phrases to help them remember new information about the topic.

- **Provides access to a variety of expository resources**—The web offers a wide range of interesting, short text about the topic for the purpose of understanding the expository passages. Photographs, pictures, illustrations, diagrams, maps, and trade books often serve as resources for expository text topics.

Remember, students do not have to read nonfiction (expository) literature sequentially to derive valuable new information from it. Even reluctant readers can use a table of contents or index to locate topics or content that is interesting to them or that will serve the purpose for their writing.

To recap, in order to integrate expository writing with technology, consider the following three steps.

1.  Introduce the writing process (prewriting, drafting, revising, editing, and publishing) before you use the graphic organizer to brainstorm the topic.

2.  Select an expository text passage or topic of information.

3.  Choose an appropriate interactive graphic organizer (see table 3.1, page 32, for an example).

Figure 3.1 is a sample fifth-grade interactive graphic organizer using Inspiration Maps, a free-trial software for teachers.

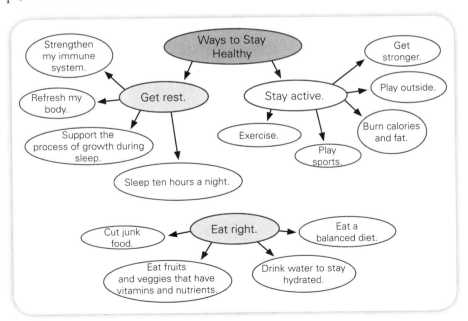

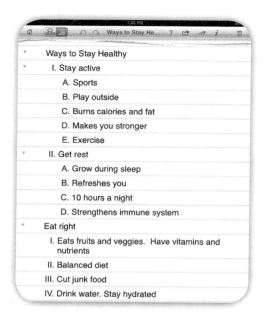

Source: Inspiration Maps and Carol Wade Fetters. Used with permission.

Figure 3.2: Outline of healthy-eating graphic organizer.

Figure 3.1: Sample interactive graphic organizer for ways to stay healthy.

After students brainstorm the topic, the teacher uses a feature of the Inspiration Maps software to change the graphic organizer into an outline that contains the same information (figure 3.2).

This outline provides a structure for students' first writing draft and helps them organize their ideas. Students can use a laptop, iPad, or any other appropriate and available technology to write. As Rasinski and Padak (2008) state, graphic organizers allow students to arrange their thoughts and ideas in a logical fashion and provide an effective map of how to go about doing an in-depth and multi-source investigation of an informational, or expository, topic. Additionally, graphic organizers allow for a gradual release of responsibility. Through teacher modeling during large-group instruction and collaborative writing, students build confidence with their own writing and organizing their thoughts as they become more accustomed to using the graphic organizers.

As students develop as architects, or creators, of expository writing pieces, make connections among multiple sources of information, integrate and utilize using interactive graphic organizers, and transfer their ideas into applications for lifelong learning, they become productive citizens in our expository world.

# PART II | The Reading and Writing Connection

Educators have long noted the complex relationship between reading and writing (Coker & Lewis, 2008; Pearson & Tierney, 1984). Obviously, there are differences: reading requires students to make "mental representations of words produced by others," while writing necessitates that they "formulate their own thoughts" and "transcribe those mental representations into words" (Coker & Lewis, 2008, p. 233). However, there is an important interplay between the two cognitive processes. Many educators are interested in how deepening this relationship helps students grow as both readers and writers.

Professional writers point to reading as critical to their growth as writers. The importance of reading has been found to be effective for instruction as well. Two research meta-analyses (Graham & Perin, 2007c; Hillocks, 1986) support the idea that through close readings of texts, students can develop effective writing techniques. Studying quality examples allows students to read and analyze what makes a piece of writing "good." Students can then emulate these elements in their own writing. Well-known practitioners such as Kelly Gallagher (2006) and Penny Kittle (2008) have examined the power of explicitly teaching students to deconstruct text to inform writing. They have noted that this not only teaches students about specific features of writing but allows them to create specific goals for their writing and empowers them to recognize the intentional decisions writers make.

In *Writing Next*, Steve Graham and Dolores Perin (2007c) report that writing is an effective instructional approach for learning content material. In this sense, writing becomes a tool for teachers to use with reading. Although the teacher might not explicitly teach students how to write, having students write in response to their reading can lead to closer reading of texts and deeper understanding of content. Writing, then, becomes a way to engage students in creating richer reading and learning experiences.

Technology supports the reading and writing connection in at least three key ways. First, technology presents an opportunity for students to access multiple genres and authors. Through technology, teachers can expand students' notion of what counts as reading—reading is no longer just lines of type on a printed page. Additionally, students get access to new models of writing. For example, they can not only read what others wrote but also see a variety of responses to those writings.

Secondly, technology creates an environment for students to share writing in and outside of class. Students read, students write, and then students read what their classmates have written. In this manner, students are engaged in a continual process of reading and writing.

The third connection revolves around new definitions of multimodal composition. Digital technologies provide new definitions of text. Students now read and respond to (write) videos, movies, animations, tweets, text messages, and so on. The constantly evolving technologies define what students read, what they write, and how they respond to others' writings.

All three strategies help blur the lines between reading and writing. Instead of two separate processes that have traditionally been unrelated to one another, reading and writing are seen as symbiotic and natural partners through the employment of technology (Pearson & Tierney, 1984).

Amber White and Paul Morsink describe in chapter 4 how the malleable genre approach to writing instruction can help foster engagement and deep learning with writing. In chapter 5, Timothy C. Pappageorge explores how using recordings during writing instruction can help students develop their writing voices. Sue Nash-Ditzel and Tammy B. H. Brown conclude this section by explaining how using digital reading logs can promote engaged learning.

**Amber White** is the language arts curriculum coordinator at Ruth Fox Elementary School in North Branch, Michigan. Her involvement with the Saginaw Bay Writing Project and the Michigan Reading Association and a collaborative learning partnership with Michigan State University have shaped much of her work with students, teachers, and parents. Her energy and time are spent exploring the thoughtful use of digital literacies and modeling content literacy strategies that assist teachers in balancing student choice and interest in an era of assessment and high-curricular demands. You can follow Amber on Twitter @AWhite100.

**Paul Morsink** is a doctoral candidate in the educational psychology and educational technology program at Michigan State University, with a specialization in literacy. He previously taught middle and high school English language arts for twelve years in Los Angeles, California. His research focuses on teachers' integration of instructional technology, eighth graders' strategies for finding health-related information on the Internet, college students' strategies for using the Internet to learn about controversial topics, and adolescents' knowledge of reading "routines"—not just reading strategies—for navigating diverse texts and contexts.

# CHAPTER 4

## Fostering Deep Engagement
## With Malleable Digital Genres

By Amber White and Paul Morsink

As far back as we can remember, teaching writing has put us on the horns of a dilemma. On the one hand, when students have choice and control over the topic and genre of their writing, their level of engagement invariably shoots up. As Barry Lane (1993) notes, "Writers don't need to be given formulas; they need to be shown possibilities" (p. 40). Research suggests that teacher-provided templates or rote memorization have big downsides for students: learners may only shallowly grasp new skills and may fail to develop the high-value strategic knowledge necessary for later transfer of what they've learned to new situations, tasks, and purposes (Graham & Perin, 2007a, 2007b; Purcell-Gates, Duke, & Martineau, 2007; Wiley, 2000).

On the other hand, we are also aware that before students can skip, they must learn to walk. The reality is that many students benefit from explicit, step-by-step instruction, extensive scaffolding, and the demystification and simplification of the complexities of writing (Delpit, 1988; Duke, Caughlan, Juzwik, & Martin, 2012; Fleischer & Andrew-Vaughan, 2009). We are also constantly aware of the many pressures on our time and the long list of topics, concepts, and skills we are responsible for teaching. Realistically, it's just not possible for us, on a regular basis, to devote large chunks of time to lesson plans that emphasize choice. Additionally, it is not feasible to allow a class to take an assignment in twenty or more different directions, with every student choosing a different topic, genre, or medium.

Further complicating this picture is that, with the proliferation of digital media and writing tools, writing and writing instruction have become even more complex. The students we see in our classrooms have diverse understandings about what can count as writing. They also bring to class a much wider range of skills for composing experiences—such as posting pictures and comments, instant messaging, video editing, remixing digital content to create original art, and more (Merchant, 2009). Therefore, when we talk about opening the door to student choice, we are aware that, for many of our students, what springs to mind may be, "Great—I'll finally get to make a video!" or "Great—I'll get to use Photoshop!" These are powerful and valuable energies, yet they present us with additional layers of work and worry—more to support, monitor, and manage. Can anyone blame the teacher who says, "To make tomorrow's writing lesson work, I've got to keep it simple. We're all going to follow the same guidelines so at least we all learn the basics of writing a halfway decent lab report [or five-paragraph essay, a haiku, or so on]"?

This chapter starts with this familiar teaching dilemma—a dilemma a large class size exacerbates, yet one that is just as pertinent to a class of ten as it is to a class of thirty: "Should I plan and prescribe and template as much as I can, or should I emphasize choice and favor exploratory learning as much as possible? Where is the right balance?"

Our message, in a nutshell, is that with students increasingly learning and composing in digital spaces with digital tools, we have new options for addressing this dilemma. If we play our cards right (and have the right cards—such as adequate access to technology—to play), we may actually be in a better position than ever before to turn a challenge into an exciting opportunity. We have the opportunity to support our students in doing a great deal of choice making, while at the same time keeping everyone focused on essential and universal concerns of composing, such as being as clear and informative as possible. Three key ingredients foster deep engagement and deep learning with writing. Assignments and instruction require: (1) a foundation of teacher-provided structure, (2) an invitation to students to augment or more radically reinvent this structure, and crucially, (3) an expectation that students will reflect on the pros and cons of different compositional choices and articulate what they gained (or lost) by augmenting or reinventing a text with digital elements.

It is this last ingredient—this imperative to reflect—that we see as a kind of breakthrough in our thinking about writing instruction and our students' learning trajectories. Previously, we saw digital composing as a *next step*—a step we might consider taking once our students had mastered the basics. For example, if we were doing a lesson on argumentative writing, the first step was always to compose traditional prose paragraphs combining claims and evidence. We typically postponed and separated the *digital moment* from the essential mental processes of composing. Having drafted their paragraphs, students might find a digital photo, map, or diagram to further support their argument. This separate digital moment added little to their learning about the essential underlying challenges of writing in this genre, such as how to show the connection between facts and claims, how to cite authoritative sources without allowing a source's voice to overwhelm yours, exactly when and how to take your intended audience into account and anticipate their thoughts and feelings, and so on. The new approach described here is about getting to that digital moment sooner and faster, with a view to dramatically increasing the amount of attention focused on these underlying and enduring challenges of writing. When students are given the option of digitally augmenting or more fundamentally altering their written texts—in order to make their writing clearer, more informative, more persuasive, and so on—and when they are expected to reflect on whether they have, in fact, succeeded in doing so, the outcomes are heightened engagement, deeper learning, and better writing.

Teachers can apply this approach (what we call the *malleable genre approach*) to writing instruction and to the design of writing assignments in many different ways, depending on grade level, content area, students' acquaintance with web-based technologies, and so on. Our main example is from a sixth-grade classroom in which the malleable genre approach was applied to the design of a multiweek inquiry project called the Wonder project. However, teachers can apply the same approach to shorter or longer-length assignments, to writing in other genres (such as lab reports, five-paragraph essays, and so on), and in classrooms with either more or limited access to technology.

## How Do I Do It?

Teachers can apply the malleable genre approach to a wide variety of units, lesson plans, or assignments. At its root are two elements: (1) a commitment to instilling in students a desire to make writing as clear, precise, informative, persuasive, and aesthetically compelling as possible and to follow that desire wherever it may lead them; and (2) the view that no medium, genre, style, convention of writing, or device is absolutely and universally superior to any other medium, genre, style, convention, or device. The result of combining these two notions (concern for making communication as effective as possible and a genuinely open-minded view of the available means of communication) is the core question we put to our students and that propels the malleable genre approach in our classrooms: "If I deviate from the suggested guidelines for writing this assignment, will it actually make the text I'm composing more effective?"

The beauty of the malleable genre approach is that teachers can ask this core question in a broad way every day or in narrower, targeted ways at just one or two moments in the writing process. The choice is yours. In the former scenario, students can be given free rein to digitally augment, alter, or replace any number of elements of the assignment. For example, with an assignment asking eleventh-grade students to compose an evidence-based persuasive essay advocating a specific action plan to address a local environmental problem, teachers could invite students to incorporate digital elements in whatever ways they wish, as long as the new elements increase the communicative effectiveness of their essay. In the latter scenario, students can augment, alter, or replace just one specific element. With an assignment asking sixth-grade students to explain how photosynthesizing plants make their own food, students could augment their explanation with a diagram (if they decide doing so would improve the clarity or precision of their text) and also decide (1) where exactly to place this diagram and (2) how much print information to embed in the diagram (in the form of labels and definitions, for example) based on their judgment of how to make their text as clear and readable as possible.

In both cases, the key activity of reflecting on how to optimize communication (in the context of weighing one's options and making reasoned choices) remains the same. Eleventh graders and sixth graders may be working at different levels of complexity, but the core thought processes are very much alike.

Whatever their current level of sophistication with words, digital content creation, and editing tools, all students are invited to ask themselves the same essential questions: "Given what I want to communicate, what is the best possible way for me to express myself or present my ideas and information?" and "Given alternative ways of communicating ideas or information, why is one better than the other?"

This last question is of particular interest and value when it comes to deepening students' thinking and learning about writing. It keeps everyone focused on those underlying goals of all good writing—clarity, precision, persuasiveness, conciseness, and so on—and how to achieve them. It also naturally leads students to think about *audience*. While working in pairs on an inquiry project about fast food, students discussed the pros and cons of including diverse elements. In the example in figure 4.1, both partners favored addressing the reader as *you* as well as including hyperlinks to give the reader easy access to additional information. One student wanted to open the report with a definition of fast food and an image of a specific example of fast food (draft image #2). Eventually, after further discussion and viewing examples of similar articles on the Internet, both agreed that the definition *and* image would be helpful to some readers without being distracting or burdensome to others.

Making decisions about compositional alternatives is often tricky. Students may have personal preferences (such as including a diagram with maximally detailed labels versus a much simpler diagram), but their initial preferences may lack a reasoned underpinning. It therefore makes perfect sense for them to turn to their intended audience in order to understand how a particular compositional choice is likely to shape a reader's comprehension and response. Younger students and less advanced writers will, in most cases, need more scaffolding at this juncture, but in our experience, the malleable genre approach reliably leads all students to engage with the issue of audience response, often without teacher prompting.

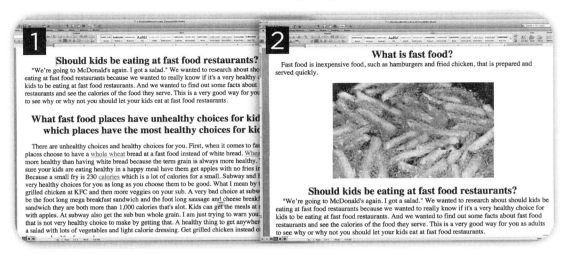

Source: Rachele Starking and Sarah Hogan. Used with permission.

Figure 4.1: Alternative drafts of a student inquiry project on fast food.

One final point about how the malleable genre approach works: it foregrounds digital tools, formats, and the many new compositional opportunities such tools and formats have created, but it does not prescribe or require the use of such tools. We see this as a crucial proviso. Before hitting on the malleable genres approach idea, we had certainly tried out all manner of digital writing lessons and assignments. The problem was that they had everyone doing the same thing—creating PowerPoint slides, embedding hyperlinks to online sources, designing digital posters, and so on. The crucial stage of reflecting, comparing options, and weighing the pros and cons of one design or textual element over another was missing. To be sure, students learned about creating PowerPoints (for example), but they were not prompted to engage in the deep thinking about composing and communicating we have described here. By contrast, the malleable genre approach recognizes that deep thinking and deep learning about writing stem from having choices and from needing to justify the choices one ends up making.

## Classroom Example

We now turn to a specific example of the malleable genre approach in action—a sixth-grade interdisciplinary inquiry project assignment implemented in the 2012 to 2013 school year. We found inspiration for this assignment on Wonderopolis (http://wonderopolis.org), in which every day, a new wonder is added to the Wonderopolis collection of daily Wonders. Wonders are short, multimodal informational texts organized around answering a question (such as, "Why do mosquito bites itch?" and "What is a Trojan horse?"). Wonders are multimodal in the sense that they typically incorporate at least one image and one video, and they span the content areas.

Drawing on the wonder genre, we designed a multipart inquiry assignment that involved students in five elements: (1) crafting researchable questions, (2) engaging in online research, (3) immersing themselves in subject matter, (4) studying text models and parsing their features, and (5) composing their own wonders (with the option of incorporating any number of digital features). For students, we framed the assignment from the start as an opportunity to research and answer a self-chosen question, become the school's resident expert on a particular topic, and finally publish the answer to their question online for the benefit of a global audience.

Given that our students were sixth graders, we spent a considerable amount of time brainstorming and narrowing questions, splitting big questions into subquestions, and moving back and forth between drafting questions and making initial forays into source materials. Much time was also spent scaffolding research activities, mostly online. This research phase immersed students in information; provided them with rich, hands-on opportunities for refining online research skills and strategies (for example, using advanced search engine features and evaluating the trustworthiness of websites); and exposed them to a wide variety of text genres and formats making varied use of multimodal elements (such as infographics, video, and reader comment features). This exposure to a variety of possible ways to present information was inherently interesting. It also fueled students' thinking when they started drafting their own wonders and started making decisions about the digital features they wanted to include.

The wonder-drafting phase of the assignment is always, for us, the most exciting to observe. Sixth-grade students still need a fair amount of scaffolding. However, we are always struck by the amount of spontaneous discussion—whether it is about how students are organizing their wonder, why they are thinking of deviating from the models on the Wonderopolis site, the pros and cons of including a multimodal element, or their reasons for placing an element in a particular location.

The final phase of the wonder writing project involved online publication. Students used the easy-to-learn, drag-and-drop Weebly platform. Given the high levels of student choice and student control, the emphasis of the experience fell squarely on the challenge of making the reader's experience as good as possible. Until the last day of the assignment, students remained motivated to rewrite text, revise layout, and add new elements for the sake of making their wonder clearer, more informative, and more compelling.

## Your Turn

Next, we look at practical tips that can inform your application of the malleable genre approach in your classroom. Keep in mind that there is no one right way to implement the malleable genre approach. Teachers can apply it in small or big ways, with short or longer writing assignments, and with younger and less advanced or with older and more advanced students. That said, we offer the following advice and suggestions.

- The deep-learning benefits of the malleable genre approach arise from combining student choice with the imperative to reflect; therefore, it is essential to lavish as much attention as possible on reflective activity. Such attention can take a variety of forms (for example, explicit modeling, ongoing scaffolding, or encouragement); it should start early and continue throughout the assignment.

- Consider having your students work in pairs. Paired students provide each other with a first interlocutor—right there beside them—to discuss their writing options, help them weigh the pros and cons, and provide audience feedback.

- Embrace the idea of experimentation, and play with new tools for digital content creation and multimodal composing. If you lack expertise in these areas, so much the better! Embrace the role of learning alongside your students—being the "guide on the side" who helps students explore and evaluate their options instead of the "sage on the stage" who ends up making choices for them.

We hope you find that the malleable genre approach can make *wonder*ful things happen—for student engagement, for deep thinking about audience and purpose, and for attention to key elements of the craft of writing. We think it provides a viable way out of the dilemma we described earlier—between our desire to honor student initiative and choice and our concern that unless we show our students exactly how to write a particular kind of paragraph, poem, or paper (with templates, if necessary), they'll never learn the basics. The malleable genre approach suggests that by giving students some amount of choice and digital creative license and by foregrounding the paramount importance of reasoned reflection to one's writerly choices, students can learn the basics *and* be engaged in deep learning about the craft of writing.

**Timothy C. Pappageorge, PhD,** has been teaching English for twenty-one years in the Chicago area. His research areas include argument writing and role-playing activities, as well as technology and writing. To learn more about Tim's work, visit his blog http://teachersofsignificance.blogspot.com, or follow him on Twitter @pappag.

# CHAPTER 5

# Reading for Tone and Writing With Expressive Voice

By Timothy C. Pappageorge

Whether playful or heartfelt, a vibrant writer's voice nets a student a range of benefits in his or her writing. This chapter explores writing methods for developing student voice in written composition, particularly through the unique leverage offered by technology.

By using recordings during writing, students learn greater precision and power in written expression and can gain better insights and appreciation of the texts that they read. Students learn to flex their vocal cords, and they enjoy the chance to do so. Also, in using recorded voice during drafting stages, students can harness the best of both the writer's *process* (craft and revision) and the actor's *performance* (spontaneity, relating to a real audience, and fully actualizing the texts that they have written). In this way, students develop the expert reader's skill of reading for authorial tone, often their own, while honing their writing to be more expressive.

Writing with a strong sense of purpose to address an authentic audience with a vital message remains at the forefront of the writer's task (Nystrand, 1987). In our information-saturated age, there is no shortage of fact and opinion buzzing around the Internet and available for our students, but it is a taste for shaping commentary, for interpretation and analysis, and for *perspective* that we have come to expect at a much-increased level from our students (Thomas, 2008). Layers of support—community, audience, performance, choice, and purpose—all help to make this process smooth and constructive, but the scope of our discussion here will focus on performance and choice.

## How Do I Do It?

Helping students read smoothly and fluently with emphasis, poise, appropriate volume, and so on can be a challenge, but it is one that we can overcome. Similarly, helping students to attend to the details of their own written work can also be challenging.

To meet these challenges, I am suggesting that we guide students to add vocal recording and playback at various points in their writing process. Formative feedback has been shown to be valuable for students across a range of contexts (Hattie, 2012b), and vocal recordings can give them the kind of valuable feedback that brings their words to life. As students hear their own feedback when they hear their own voices (literally), it is much more likely that they will hear their own voices (figuratively) emerging within their wordcrafting. I have seen such feedback assist students in meeting these challenges and crafting a distinctive writing voice.

Along the way, students begin to appreciate authorial tone in a way that analysis in class does not help them to do. This is because when we analyze a writer's tone in class—for example, guiding students to see that in his essay "A Modest Proposal," Jonathan Swift adopts an ironic tone through the rhetorical device of understatement—we are instructing students largely in a body of knowledge referred to as *declarative knowledge*. Through declarative knowledge, students can learn the *what* but not the *how* when it comes to authorial tone. When we ask students to read their own work or that of another author and to enhance the production of tone and voice through their performative choices, they then begin to understand tone on a deeper level. This happens because such an exercise guides students to develop procedural knowledge. Producing a stronger, richer, and more vibrant tone in one's writing is different from simply pointing it out in a class discussion. Of course, both processes complement each other and reinforce students' understanding of tone.

Thus, I propose reading for tone and voice at various points in the writer's process, and recording technology can offer an indispensable aid in making this count for students. If the typical writing process includes brainstorming, drafting, revising and editing, and publishing, I then suggest a modified process such as the following: drafting, drafting with director's notes, performing or recording, listening, reviewing peer work or other responses, revising, and publishing or performing.

Students may need some coaching on oral interpretation as well. With an analytical vocabulary that relates to oral interpretation (or *voice* from a literal standpoint), students rehearse their performance of their work and come to a stronger *authorial voice* in their writing—that is, voice from a *figurative* or qualitative feel. This quality or texture, however, is best articulated to students using literal terms like *volume level*, *pace*, and *tone*. Along the way, I introduce terms such as *performance*, *technical clarity*, *dramatic pauses*, and *oral interpretation*.

## Classroom Example

As students write their own essays, they prepare an annotated script, typically a seed paragraph for the longer paper. In some cases, they may have already written the longer paper, and this text for annotated scripting is an excerpt from the longer work. Students "score the text," much as they would create a musical document, adding adverbials and other descriptors to make their voices more explicit to the teacher and to themselves. Language arts practitioners with a background in drama and performance might call this a *director's notebook*.

In class, I show the students an example of a text that I or a student has scored and ask them to create their own. Students rehearse their enhanced oral interpretations to one another in supportive base groups and brainstorm for additional director's notes and ideas. In doing so, they are to include references to the oral interpretation vocabulary throughout. I also ask them to practice reading the script and judge for themselves whether their oral interpretation addresses their writer's purpose and carries their intended tone. Thus, we move back and forth between the oral rehearsal of a powerful reading and the written crafting of a powerfully written text, between responding as a fan at a recitation and responding as a book critic.

The student's annotations provide the teacher with diagnostic information about how the student is progressing. As a formative assessment, these insights provide valuable points of entry for the teacher to step in and coach the student, either by addressing word choice or vocalization.

Figure 5.1 (page 52) shows a director's notebook. Through the student's annotations, one can see the humor in the experience being recounted—in his stating *road trip* emphatically, aping Borat's voice at the end, and giving an excited, playful tone to his Teenage Mutant Ninja Turtles reference.

Make no mistake, however, he couples these efforts with the *stressed* six-hour ride to the tournament and the *cocky* delivery of their win at the end. In these attempts his purpose as a writer is an artful delivery. We see this in his annotations, some of which no doubt surfaced spontaneously as he recorded the various versions of his spoken script in the computer lab at school.

In making these performance choices, he is aware of his classroom audience as a community of writers (Wenger, 1998), an attitude that would value both the sports angle ("We wanted to win") and the human one ("We became a kind of family").

Were he creating this essay for his team or a group of soccer coaches, he no doubt would have scored the text differently and drawn out different voicing for the same material. Perhaps he also would have made subtle shifts in word choice or sentence patterns to accommodate this shift in purpose. As it was, the class found his work humorous and insightful, and the students smiled, laughed, and reacted at the appropriate moments, letting the writer know that his efforts were appreciated.

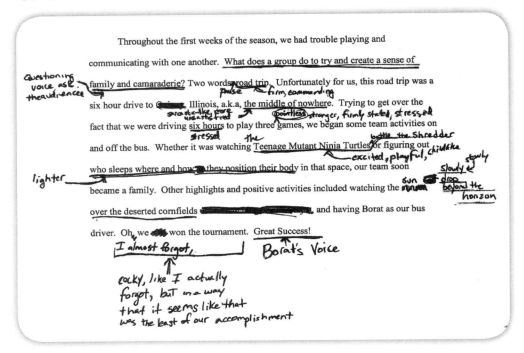

Source: Billy, eleventh-grade student. Used with permission.

Figure 5.1: A director's notebook.

It is worth noting that the student in the excerpt may have described himself at the time as often quiet in class, as would many students who have found their voice in a similar assignment. Students who may be more reticent in the classroom setting can often enjoy the precision of expression that comes with creating a recorded performance. In my own classroom, digital technology has given a wide range of my students a chance to sharpen their skills with fluency and interpretation.

Honing craft and addressing an audience can be highly motivating for students due to the presence of choice (Smith & Wilhelm, 2002)—of volume, pace, tone, and emphasis—that exists in so many aspects of performance. I have seen students become motivated to read famous or literary speeches with greater interpretive flair as a result of hearing, correcting, and honing their performed versions of these texts. I have also seen a reluctant reader discover the nascent dramatist within when challenged to make a recording of a text to go along with an analytical writing.

In these instances, the writing process is no longer geared only toward eventual written submission; it is a recorded performance in which craft and expression assist the student in fully actualizing a memorable voice.

## Your Turn

I suggest that from the first day of school, you begin thinking of reading and writing performance as mutual complements and thread experiences as the school year progresses in a fashion that increases choice, autonomy, and complexity (Tomlinson & Strickland, 2005). The first quarter might involve simple oral interpretation of existing texts such as a poetry slam or read-aloud of primary documents. The goal is for students to become familiar with recording their work and to begin to see it as a normal part of the experience. Second and third quarters might involve having students record their own original works, often as enhancements to the persuasive quality of what they are attempting to say or portray. For example, students can record a "This I Believe" essay for a class time capsule or write a public service announcement explaining difficult but important science content for publication on the school's website. Finally, in the fourth quarter, students can increase the complexity of their work when asked to create an original essay on an important topic and set it to music and visual accompaniment. In this way, a classroom teacher can weave complexity into performative student writing over the course of the year.

It's all about creating a writing community. Writing for an authentic audience in a meaningful context will foreground the presence of student voice and support its expression in the range of assignments and projects that you choose. Throughout, the ability of students to appropriate the vocabulary of performance and related techniques will emerge as keys to this process. Executing the project and crafting a polished work that sounds good will give the student a final rush of pride that comes with a job well done, whether you post the project on a private classroom website, which is likely, or online for an undefined audience.

Some students actually prefer to post their musings online on a site such as YouTube or SoundCloud, but I typically defer to student interest and comfort level when making these arrangements. I have also asked students to simply submit to me a digital recording of their work by uploading it to my district's private network server. For students who are new to audio blogging or recording themselves in any way, I prefer to keep the posting of their audio essays private and more secure. Of course, students can use their phones, iPads, or any number of devices with myriad apps such as Voice Recorder or Talk to Type, both on the Chrome browser, and free to use.

As for mixing music and offering students a range of choices in expression, you can use several innovative websites to stir their creativity. UJAM (www.ujam.com)

offers a free web-based program for creating music. WeVideo (http://wevideo.com) is an online Movie Maker–type program that allows students to collaborate across platforms and spaces on multimodal digital essays, which is especially valuable for a group project. Audacity provides a free cross-platform program for recording multiple tracks. Jamendo provides music available under Creative Commons licenses, and mobygratis offers free music for independent and nonprofit filmmakers.

Music selection can be a significant aspect of a digital story, but it is the aspect that has garnered the least research. As we consider the impact of this kind of composition on adolescents, it's important to remember how strongly one bonds with music during these years. With little lead from me, my students have selected interesting music clips from their collections, and some have used Freeplay Music (www .freeplaymusic.com) to select free instrumental clips. Still, others prefer to use their own instrumentation, adding something of even greater personal significance to the composition as a whole. They layer these clips in the background of their spoken words in order to more fully establish their selected tones. That is, for a dramatic moment in the essay, the student might select an emotionally powerful, loud, or intense moment in the music, or vice versa. We discuss the best fit of the song to a particular text, given the purpose, message, intended audience, and rhetorical choices in the writing itself.

In terms of assessment, shorter rubrics with fewer criteria are helpful for compositions on narrower topics, such as an oral interpretation of a poem, a brief podcast of a longer research paper, or the exploration of a character's viewpoint. For more complicated topics, I typically give students formative feedback along the way and give them the chance to apply the longer rubrics to a sample composition. Students explore most of the criteria throughout the year in lessons that ultimately serve as precursors, and I add descriptors, as these depend on the standard, year in school, and preassessed levels of mastery that students show throughout the year. However, giving students a chance to self-assess their work against these criteria both along the way and at the close of the assignment can help them to more fully appropriate the significance of the choices they have made.

At the end of the day, it does take time to adopt this sort of shift in the writing process, but it is one that almost always nets a positive result in terms of student effect. It often brings students' reading and writing to a level that may have seemed too polished or too expressive to achieve. Not only does this shift in writing elevate student product and process, but it also incorporates 21st century tools. By incorporating digital tools and sound pedagogy, students' writing becomes more connected and more personalized. In a time when student writing is often the product of a highly structured formula, a student's ability to incorporate 21st century tools, choice, and heart results in writing that validates the writer and intrigues the reader.

 **Sue Nash-Ditzel, EdD,** is the principal of Ledyard Center School in Ledyard, Connecticut. She has held positions as an elementary teacher, reading specialist, and college professor. Sue has a doctorate in literacy education from Rutgers University. She resides in Connecticut with her husband and two daughters.

 **Tammy B. H. Brown, PhD,** directs literacy education programs at Marywood University in Scranton, Pennsylvania. She has held positions as a reading specialist, developmental reading instructor, and university professor. She has a doctorate in literacy education from Rutgers University.

# CHAPTER 6

# Digital Reading Logs:
# A Third Space for Literacy Growth

By Sue Nash-Ditzel and Tammy B. H. Brown

Struggling adolescent readers typically not only lack a knowledge of successful reading strategies (Alvermann, 2003) but also engagement with text (Guthrie & Davis, 2003; Guthrie et al., 2007; Guthrie & Wigfield, 2000). Indeed, John Guthrie and Allan Wigfield (2000) suggest that engagement plays a greater role in students' reading achievement than instructional practices. What then does it take to engage the struggling reader? Struggling adolescent readers themselves report that having choices in reading material and using online resources improve their ability to comprehend (Pitcher et al., 2010), and research supports these students' perceptions of what they need. Gina Biancarosa and Catherine Snow (2004) indicate that diverse texts, motivation, self-directed learning, and technology are elements for effective literacy instruction for adolescents.

The integration of technology in literacy instruction is important for two reasons. First, although access to various types of technology can vary, the so-called *digital divide* is closing, and technology is an integral part of students' out-of-school literacy experiences (Lawless & Pellegrino, 2007). For example, Jeffrey Kluger (2012) reports that on average, each young adult sends eighty-eight text messages each day. Second, the literacies related to technologies are necessary to effectively function in our culture (IRA, 2009; Leu, O'Byrne, Zawilinski, McVerry, & Everett-Cacopardo, 2009).

Third Space Theory offers a useful lens through which to understand why integrating technologies into the literacy classroom, particularly for struggling adolescent learners, provides a crucial means of support for the development of literacy skills (Gutiérrez, 2008). Inherent in the concept of Third Space is the notion that the literacies used in school often differ from those used in the community, and such differences are often greater for students of non-dominant cultural groups.

The work of Elizabeth Moje et al. (2004) suggests that valuing students' out-of-school funds of knowledge facilitates learning in the classroom. These *funds of knowledge*—the knowledge and skills of a particular sociocultural group required to function as members of society—are a student's *first space* (Moll, Amanti, Neff, & Gonzalez, 1992). The academic demands of the classroom are the *second space*. The gap between these two spaces varies depending on the degree of match between the literacy practices of the student's sociocultural group and those valued in the academic community. When practices differ significantly, literacy learning can be complicated (Delpit, 2006; Heath, 1983; Purcell-Gates, 1997). According to Kris Gutiérrez (2008), by using Third Space Theory, teachers can create a "transformative space where the potential for an expanded form of learning and the development of new knowledge are heightened" (p. 152). As with Lev Vygotsky's (1978) zone of proximal development, in which teachers successfully use students' out-of-school funds of knowledge as a scaffold to help students succeed with academic tasks, Third Space Theory enables students to go beyond what they can do on their own and achieve at a higher level. In addition, a natural connection appears to exist between the collaborative nature of digital texts and the notion of Third Space Theory. Kris Gutiérrez, Patricia Baquedano-López, and Myrna Turner (1997) explain that when students are able to collaboratively engage in tasks "their knowledge and literacies became available to one another" (p. 370), creating a zone of proximal development, or third space.

## How Do I Do It?

The digital reading log activity we describe in this chapter (see pages 59–61) uses technology-based collaborative writing as a means of improving metacognitive strategy use and engagement with text in the academic setting. Sue developed the digital reading log activity as a means of using collaborative writing, as well as a way to recognize, value, and utilize students' out-of-school funds of knowledge for the purpose of improving their ability to comprehend at the level required in the academic setting. Specifically, she sought to help her students become self-aware, engaged readers who used metacognitive strategies effectively.

Sue had spent much time in the classroom modeling *think-alouds* (Davey, 1983). An activity in which the teacher verbalizes his or her thoughts as he or she engages with a piece of text, think-alouds are designed to help the struggling reader become more aware of the strategies that good readers use. However, as effective as the think-aloud strategy may be, getting students to verbalize their thinking as they read can be a challenge. Giving students a stopping point and asking them to share may elicit statements like, "I'm not thinking anything. I'm just reading." Likewise, providing students with sticky notes to affix to pages whenever they run into difficulty or use a particular strategy may result in a student going back to the text after reading to complete the task, implying that he or she came to the end of the reading and thought, "Now, what was I supposed to do with this?"

The digital reading log draws on students' facility with messaging and Microsoft Word as technology tools that support readers in using collaborative writing to become more metacognitively aware, use strategies, and engage with text. Students self-select an article from the Internet, copy and paste it into a Word document, and use the Comment function to record their thinking as they read. The document is then emailed to a partner, who reads the article and the comments and responds with thoughts of his or her own. (This activity can also present a "teachable moment" about avoiding plagiarism when writing for academic purposes. Cutting an article or a section of an article and pasting it into a paper is unacceptable, even when a citation is included. However, the cutting and pasting of the article required here is considered "fair use," for a noncommercial instructional purpose that is part of the school curriculum.) The following sections describe the process Sue uses to implement the digital reading log activity.

### *Metacognition*

Sue decided to use the track-changes feature of Word to create shared documents, as opposed to using Google Drive, because students who are not tech-savvy seem to have more difficulty with Google Drive than with Word. This is an important consideration when working with students who do not have adequate access to technology. The activity would be less effective if students were focusing on how to use a digital tool in addition to thinking about their reading.

Assisting students in becoming metacognitively aware is essential to the digital reading logs. To introduce students to the idea of metacognition, we have created hands-on activities for students. For example, a teacher could provide students with a small lump of modeling clay and direct them to make an animal. Next, the teacher asks them to make another animal, but this time to explain to a partner how to make the animal. Students compare their thinking processes during the two experiences. The student *was* thinking during both experiences—using both background knowledge and problem-solving abilities. However, the difference is in their own *awareness* of their thinking.

Once the students understand the concept of *thinking about thinking*, they need to understand what good readers think about. Research suggests that good readers engage in the following six strategies as they make sense of text: (1) making connections, (2) asking questions, (3) making inferences, (4) determining importance, (5) synthesizing, and (6) using fix-up strategies to repair comprehension when it breaks down (Harvey & Goudvis, 2007). The teacher needs to think aloud for students, modeling the use of these six strategies with many kinds of texts (Davey, 1983).

A think-aloud is an activity in which a teacher verbalizes his or her thoughts as he or she engages with a piece of text. Think-alouds are designed to help the struggling reader become more aware of the strategies that good readers use. Specifically, the think-aloud helps the student to see that good readers *do* wrestle with comprehension at times, but when the good reader's comprehension breaks down, they "fix up" their understanding. Examples of fix-up strategies include re-reading or stopping to differentiate between main ideas and details.

### Text Selection and Readability

Teachers should not assume that students know how to conduct an efficient search or evaluate the suitability of an article. Therefore, teachers should model how to locate texts that will be a match for the reader not only in terms of interest but also of readability. For example, the teacher might go to two different articles about aquatic animals and do a think-aloud showing how one would determine whether or not each article is a good match (in this case for the teacher as a reader). The teacher would first look at the title, headings, and graphics to see if the article looks interesting and if he or she has relevant background knowledge about the focus of the article. Next, he or she could start to read; if five unfamiliar words are encountered on the first page, it is probably too difficult. If the font, print size, and vocabulary suggest that the article is for young children, the article may be too easy. However, teachers should be cautious in assuming that a student is "trying to take the easy way out," and allow a student to try an article. If it's truly too easy, there will be little for him or her to comment on. In this case, the teacher might suggest that the student look for an article with more complex ideas.

### Text Selection and Students' Interests

Students often select texts that are not sanctioned as "real reading" in the classroom. For example, they may select celebrity or sports-related articles or texts that are considered edgy and perhaps not fully aligned with the standards of the community. This requires careful discrimination. Under certain circumstances, if used carefully, such texts may be valuable on several levels. First, for a struggling reader, it may be one of the few times he or she engages with an in-school reading task. Second, by allowing for choice, the teacher affirms the student's out-of-school literacy practices as valuable. And third, while working with the material, the student will nevertheless be learning to use the strategies of an established successful reader.

### *Use of Language*

It is important for teachers to allow students to use language in their own ways, because language is a cultural tool that can be part of creating a successful third space. "I'm friends with Tia so we both kinda talked like we would normally talk," explained Vicky, another of Sue's students, when asked about the comments she had written to her partner. Students bring their own ways of using language, including slang, abbreviations, and references to popular culture and shared experiences. When "no single language or register is privileged, the larger linguistic repertoires of participants become tools for meaning making" (Gutiérrez, Baquedano-López, Alvarez, & Chui, 1999, p. 89). The digital reading log validates these ways of using language by bringing them into the "sanctioned" space of the curriculum.

### *Creation of New Texts*

After students select the text, they add their own comments to the document. In this way, they transform the text, resulting in a coconstruction by the original author, first reader, reader's partner, and in some cases, the teacher. Donna Alvermann (2008) argues that the creation and alteration of texts is enjoyable to adolescent learners, and they are skills students will need in the future. In addition, the sharing and collaborative construction of documents is a means of engaging students and is a crucial aspect of the new literacies—global literacy, media literacy, and digital literacy—that are emerging in our technology-rich culture (Leu, Kinzer, Coiro, & Cammack, 2004).

### *Strategy Use*

The goal of the digital reading log activity is to promote engaged reading and metacognitive strategy use, which result when teachers meet the following four criteria: (1) teachers adequately introduce and model the metacognitive strategy, (2) the readability of the article is appropriate for the student—that is, it is neither too hard nor too easy, (3) the student is interested in the article, and (4) students have a forum for sharing their thinking with peers, using their own language as a tool for the construction of meaning (Nash-Ditzel & Brown, 2012).

## Classroom Example

The students in Sue's developmental reading course are adolescent readers with a history of failure. They have had few positive experiences with literacy by the time they enter Sue's class. Selecting reading material based solely on their own interests and writing responses using their own ways with language are new experiences for them—but have the potential to empower them as literacy learners. Figure 6.1 (page 62) can model for students how proficient readers might respond to an article about working moms.

October 14, 2010

**The Kids Are All Right: Few Negative Associations With Moms' Return to Work Soon After Having Children**

*Children from lower-income households benefit more when mother enters work force*

WASHINGTON – Children whose mothers return to work before their offspring turn 3 are no more likely to have academic or behavioral problems than kids whose mothers stay at home, according to a review of 50 years of research. "Overall, I think this shows women who go back to work soon after they have their children should not be too concerned about the effects their employment has on their children's long-term well-being," said psychologist Rachel Lucas-Thompson, PhD, lead author of the study conducted with Drs. JoAnn Prause and Wendy Goldberg at the University of California, Irvine".

For some families, having a mom on the job is better for children, according to the meta-analysis of 69 studies conducted between 1960 and 2010. For example, children from single-parent or low-income families whose mothers worked had better academic and intelligence scores and fewer behavioral problems than children whose mothers did not work, the authors found. This was probably due in part to increased resources that the income afforded, they said. The findings appear in the November issue of *Psychological Bulletin*, published by the American Psychological Association.

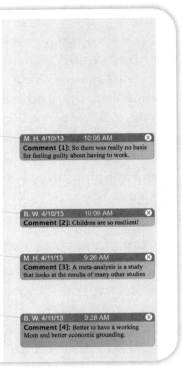

M. H. 4/10/13          10:06 AM
**Comment [1]:** So there was really no basis for feeling guilty about having to work.

B. W. 4/10/13          10:06 AM
**Comment [2]:** Children are so resilient!

M. H. 4/11/13          9:26 AM
**Comment [3]:** A meta-analysis is a study that looks at the results of many other studies

B. W. 4/11/13          9:28 AM
**Comment [4]:** Better to have a working Mom and better economic grounding.

*Source: http://www.apa.org/news/press/releases/2010/10/working-mothers.aspx.*

Figure 6.1: Modeling how to comment on a newspaper article.

The comments suggest that the readers are engaging in the following strategies and behaviors of proficient readers (Harvey & Goudvis, 2007).

- **Engagement with text:** The readers seem to care about the issue of working mothers and child care because it affects them firsthand.

- **Connections:** A connection is made between the article and personal experience with daycare centers that are only open until 6:00 p.m.

- **Questions:** The readers ask thoughtful and important questions, utilizing their background knowledge about working mothers and child care.

- **Inferences:** The reader infers that stay-at-home mothers can devote more attention to a child. This requires the use of background knowledge along with an understanding of the information in the text.

- **Opinions:** The readers have clear opinions about the benefits of working. This seems to be rooted in an understanding and evaluation of the information presented in the text, combined with their background of experience.

# Your Turn

To implement a digital reading log activity in your classroom, follow these six steps.

1. **Search for articles:** Students begin by searching the Internet for articles of interest. Student choice is a key factor in engagement. While the academic setting will dictate some parameters for appropriate readings, give students as much latitude as possible in selecting the article. The teacher may want to suggest websites that link to current themes students are studying in class, but students should not be required to use them.

2. **Convert to a Word document:** When an article of interest has been selected, the student copies and pastes the article, including all reference information, pictures, graphics, and links, into a Microsoft Word document. The students should save the document before proceeding.

3. **Read the article:** Students read the article carefully, thinking about their thinking as they read. Students highlight items that are confusing, questions that arise, ideas with which they strongly agree or disagree, passages that they reread, strategies they use to clarify, words they don't understand, and so on.

4. **Use the Comment function:** Students click on the Comment function of Word to record their thinking as they read. In addition, students can record any thoughts or strategies they used before or after reading, such as looking at the title or headings. To do this, students highlight the key part of the text, click the Review tab and then New Comment. A dialogue box will emerge on the right-hand side of the page. Students are encouraged to write as much as they want; the box will expand accordingly. The student then saves the document with comments.

5. **Collaborate:** The student emails the document with comments to his or her partner. Using the Comment function once again, the partner reads the article and comments and responds to both the article and the first reader's comments. The student resaves the document and emails it back to the original reader.

6. **Perform a teacher review:** The teacher reviews the article with both readers' comments, noting the metacognitive thought processes and levels of comprehension that occurred during the readings. The teacher may respond with comments of his or her own.

Research has shown that incorporating technology into literacy tasks increases engagement, interactivity, and motivation (LeLoup & Ponterio, 2003; Leu et al., 2004; Meskill & Mossop, 2000; Warschauer, 2006). Mark Warschauer (2006) notes that integrating technology into the classroom improves literacy engagement in struggling readers. The interactive nature of digital texts may explain why students' engagement and comprehension increase when reading such materials (Labbo, 2006; Warschauer, 2006). Warschauer (2006) proposes that by supplying students with the opportunity to "actively participate in text-mediated intermental dialogue around issues of importance to their lives and communities" (p. 8), positive literacy outcomes will indeed follow.

In conclusion, the digital reading log instructional technique has been shown to be a powerful means of helping struggling adolescent readers engage with text and use metacognitive strategies during reading. This technique also uses collaboration and enhances connected learning. These pedagogically sound components all mesh together to create an opportunity for students to reach new heights with their literacy skills and writing products.

Not only can this technique assist students, but it can also be enlightening to the teachers who use it. Using a digital tool in conjunction with personally motivating writing affords teachers a small window in which to see their students' thought processes. This glimpse can help them to better assist their students and, in turn, help students reach their fullest literacy potential.

# PART III | The Process Approach

The process approach to writing instruction is a broad concept. Most educators define it as a means of providing students with extended opportunities to plan, write, edit, and revise their work. Student ownership, inquiry, and conferences with teachers and classmates are also critical elements of process writing.

The process approach is based on the work of Linda Flower and John Hayes (1980), who find writing to be a recursive practice rather than a linear event. Writers do not simply move linearly through stages of prewriting, writing, and rewriting, but rather they are engaged in a complex and continuous process. Research supports the process approach to writing instruction as an effective pedagogical practice (Graham & Perin, 2007c). Outstanding researchers and practitioners, including Janet Emig (1971), Peter Elbow (1973), Donald Graves (Graves & Sunstein, 1992), Donald Murray (1999), and Nancie Atwell (1998), have been proponents of this approach to writing instruction. The National Writing Project also cited the process approach as foundational (Graham & Perin, 2007c; Pritchard & Honeycutt, 2006).

Because writing occurs over time, students need the opportunity to produce multiple drafts and revise. The writing process approach emphasizes the need for students to have ample time dedicated to writing daily. When students are engaged in effective and authentic writing activities and instruction, with time to write every day, they gain confidence and grow in their ability (Graham et al., 2012). One way to keep students engaged in their writing is to provide a choice of topics, so students can write about what they know or want to learn more about. The key is flexibility and recognizing that a holistic and authentic approach to writing instruction is necessary for cultivating and developing writers.

Time and space are two of the most important components of process writing. Using technology, of course, students have the opportunity to write anytime and anyplace. Instead of being an activity that happens in a specific time frame and classroom, students' writing moves with them through multiple storage locations and technologies. They might start writing in Microsoft Word on a school computer, continue their writing on paper or on their smartphone or tablet on the way home from school or while waiting for an appointment, and complete it on a laptop at home. New technologies have made writing—both as a process and as a product—ubiquitous. Teachers need to find ways to capitalize on this anywhere-and-anytime aspect of process writing.

In chapter 7, Monica T. Billen and Renee M. R. Moran explore how to use screencasts to engage students in the writing process. Julia Kara-Soteriou and Ashley Callan share in chapter 8 how to engage students in digital storytelling during a writer's workshop. Sally Valentino Drew concludes the section in chapter 9 with a demonstration of how digital writing workshops can help teachers and students meet the Common Core State Standards.

 **Monica T. Billen** supervises preservice teachers and teaches reading education courses at the University of Tennessee. A former elementary education teacher, she is now a doctoral candidate in the Theory and Practice in Teacher Education Department of the University of Tennessee.

 **Renee M. R. Moran, PhD,** is an assistant professor of reading education at East Tennessee State University. Previously, she worked as a primary-grade teacher in North Carolina and California for eight years. She received her doctorate at the University of Tennessee in teacher education with a focus on literacy studies.

# CHAPTER 7

# Screencasts: The Integration of Reading, Writing, and Technology

By Monica T. Billen and Renee M. R. Moran

Janet Emig's (1971) landmark study on the composing process of twelfth-grade students posited that student writers use methods similar to those of professional authors as they work through a series of stages. Emig also noted that many writing teachers oversimplify the time-consuming hard work of creating a written piece. Her work, and that of others (Elbow, 1973; Macrorie, 1970), pioneered a departure from traditional methods of teaching writing to instead emphasize writing as a process (Graves, 1983). The *writing process* focuses on the stages that writers go through when producing a written piece. These stages are commonly known as *prewriting, drafting, revising and editing,* and *publishing* and involve recurring cycles rather than linear activity (Tompkins, 2010). Although professional authors routinely engage in revision, Emig (1971) noted that in the 1970s, schools did not teach revision, pointing out that "there is no time for major reformulation or reconceptualizations" (p. 99). Yet, revising and editing are vital aspects of writing that should not be overlooked.

In this chapter, we introduce ways to use screencasts to encourage students to engage in all stages of the writing process.

Many readers will be familiar with the term *podcast*, which refers to downloadable audio recordings. *Screencast*, a less familiar term, is similar to a podcast in that it includes audio recordings. A screencast is a short demonstration video file with audio commentary (Notess, 2005). While college librarians have been using screencasts to help students understand how to use databases, webpages, and the Dewey Decimal System for quite some time (Oud, 2009), screencasts may be new to teachers. Screencasts can be created on iPad applications (apps) that begin with a blank slate and drawing tools with a variety of colors and allow individuals to record audio information to explain their own drawings, written comments, concept maps, and imported photos (Castek & Beach, 2013). In addition, one can add words, arrows, lines, and other elements to the document during the recording as the teacher explains the concept. After recording, the user can embed the presentation in a blog, send it through an email, or share it on Facebook. A teacher or student can play back the recording to teach another individual a concept or to present information. A screencast app is, in a sense, a recordable whiteboard. Screencast apps include:

- ReplayNote
- Explain Everything
- ScreenChomp
- ShowMe
- Educreations

## How Do I Do It?

You can use a screencast app in a variety of ways. For example, if you wanted to explain how to complete a mathematical equation, you could record an explanation while completing the equation on the screen. One can discuss events that led to a world crisis while displaying the relevant maps or reveal the scientific explanation for a chemical reaction with relevant photos.

We have used screencast apps to engage students in an authentic writing task that encourages process writing and peer collaboration. Following are the nine steps we took to engage both first- and fifth-grade students in a writing activity in which we asked them to create an alternative ending to a story.

1.    In the weeks leading up to the unit, we introduced students to a variety of picture books.

2.    Each student or group of students reread a book of interest, perhaps one with a problem or conflict that the students could adapt in some way.

3.    We explained that the purpose of the writing activity was to create an alternate ending to a story. We modeled our own alternate ending using a book we were particularly interested in.

4.  Once students could see the end goal and understood what they were going to be creating, we allowed them to explore the screencasting app on their own. We asked them to practice inserting an image, using the writing utensil, typing on the document, and recording their own voice. After exploration, we explicitly modeled how to use various aspects of the app. The students figured out a lot by themselves while exploring but still paid attention when we modeled specific steps.

5.  Next, we had students begin the process of using a screencast app to brainstorm an alternate ending to a story. Some students inserted pictures or photographs that corresponded to their ideas. Some relied heavily on verbal explanations.

6.  Students recorded their thoughts and explained their brainstorm on the screencast app. They were careful to provide clear descriptions, as they knew their peers would be viewing their creations.

7.  Students shared their recorded brainstorms with fellow students. They were able to push play and present their creation to their neighbor. In this way, student feedback was offered before the rough-draft writing process even began.

8.  The students then took their creation, along with feedback they received from others, and wrote their alternate ending to a specific literature piece. In this manner, the process of brainstorming moved from being an individual tedious act to one that integrates technology and social interaction as a scaffold to the writing process.

9.  Finally, the students used the same screencast app to publish their work. They created illustrations and typed their final draft directly on the app and recorded themselves reading the finished product.

## Classroom Example

Ruth Michaels, a fourth-grade teacher, uses the iPad to increase engagement in writing and reading as well as to emphasize the writing process. After attending a professional development workshop, Ruth was prompted to try a new technology strategy. Her fourth graders seemed uninterested in writing. They were especially uninterested in planning and revising their ideas before writing a final piece. While many of Ruth's students described writing as tedious, they viewed technology in a much more positive light. She felt that bridging current technology and writing would enhance student motivation and create a social classroom environment that prepares students for the future.

Ruth read *The Great Kapok Tree* (Cherry, 2000) to her students during a previous unit study of the rainforest. In the story, a man has come to cut down the great kapok tree, but before he does so, he falls asleep underneath it. As he slumbers, a variety of rainforest animals whisper in his ear reasons why he shouldn't cut the tree down. They explain that animal homes will be lost, natural resources will be unavailable, and the beauty of the tree will be destroyed. When the man awakes, his perspective is changed. He picks up his ax and walks away.

Ruth's fourth graders reacted strongly to the story, with many expressing feelings of distress or empathy. For this reason, she believed the story would interest students and be a good candidate for creating an interesting alternate ending. She began by rereading the story to her class. Afterward, the students brainstormed possible alternate endings together. Students discussed what might have occurred if the man had decided to cut down the tree despite the warnings of the animals. What would have happened to the sloth, toucan, or jaguar? Would only one tree be cut down, or would that have been just the beginning? There were many possibilities. Ruth modeled a final draft that she created on a screencast app. She also showed them a brainstorm she created on the app that helped her organize her ideas. Students saw the final product and the plan that helped her organize her thoughts.

Ruth then gave her students the opportunity to explore a set of iPads that the school purchased. After some time exploring, students began brainstorming their ideas. Because there were not enough iPads for every student, students planned a rough sketch of ideas on paper before it was their turn to use the iPad. Ruth called this a *brain dump* and the iPad brainstorm a *prewrite*. Some students created graphic organizers, some uploaded images to express their thoughts, and all talked through their strategy on the recordable device. Figure 7.1 shows an example of a student's brainstorm. During the brainstorming process, Ruth circulated through the room and provided feedback and assistance and made time to individually confer with students. She noticed that students who often struggled with encoding felt empowered as they verbalized ideas using the audio recorder.

After completing their brainstorms, each student met with a partner and presented his or her prewrite presentation. The partner then provided feedback and gave suggestions. Some students changed their idea for the alternate ending based on their partner's suggestions, while others simply tweaked and clarified different aspects of their prewriting. Each student then had a clear brainstorm. This served as a guide as students began to draft their story in prose.

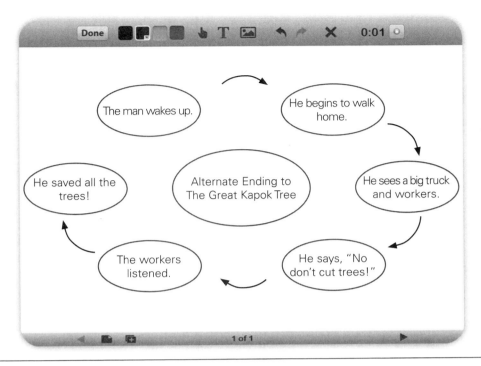

Figure 7.1 Sample student brainstorm using an iPad.

After revising and editing, students completed their final version of an alternate ending. Each student illustrated the pages of the story on paper, took a picture of his or her illustration, and uploaded it to the screencast app. The students then typed the text that accompanied each illustration and recorded themselves reading their final story on the app. They saved the final project as a video file. The students then posted their files to a class blog so that fellow students and parents could enjoy their work. The students also posted their brainstorms so that readers could see the development of the idea and their progress along the way.

Please visit **go.solution-tree.com/technology** to download more examples, as well as suggestions of how to integrate this strategy.

## Your Turn

Now that you've seen how Ruth implemented technology with her literacy instruction, consider how you can adapt this strategy for your own classroom. The following sections present several important elements to consider before, during, and after instruction.

### Before Instruction

Long before beginning this activity, it is important to encourage the growth of a literate community (Allington, 2001), one in which students are interested and engaged in books. It is also important that students have experience engaging in creative thinking—and have been given opportunities to create, design, and imagine. In addition, to participate in such a community, students must have had experiences discussing concepts with peers. We recommend teaching and modeling for students what a peer conversation looks and sounds like. Also, consider teaching students how to give appropriate feedback in this community.

Before engaging students in a new technology application, it is also important to explore the technology yourself. Find time before implementing this activity to create your own presentation using a screencast app. In fact, create a couple of presentations using different elements of the application. Then, choose one to present to the students so that they have an example to guide them.

Finally, you will need to address with your students both the content and the skills required to engage with the technology. In the case of our example, the students will need instruction on:

- Comprehending text
- Engaging in creative thinking as they create an alternate ending
- Creating a prewrite brainstorm
- Using a brainstorm to guide writing
- Turning on an iPad
- Opening up the app
- Drawing in the app
- Typing in the app
- Recording one's voice on the app
- Saving and sending a presentation

Think through each of the elements we have presented here before planning your unit.

### During Instruction

When you have worked with the concepts presented in the previous section, engage your students in the activity. We recommend following steps similar to those Ruth took. Every classroom of students is different, however, and should be treated as such. Make the needed adjustments based on the individual needs of your students. If you already have literature circles, this activity would be great for groups to work on together. Books presented as class read-alouds are good choices for the activity. After you have chosen a book, introduce both the content and the new literacy.

We also suggest spending some time each class period presenting creations that you and your students have previously developed. For example, before implementing this technology activity in your classroom, create a presentation and show it to the students. Thereafter, encourage student sharing, as students may provide ideas that you hadn't considered.

Before we ask students to learn to read, we hope that they have had many opportunities exploring, perusing, and investigating books in their home or in their early education. We believe the same should be done for technology. Of course, teachers should set some guidelines and expectations for appropriate behavior during this exploration time. You might want to talk about how to hold and touch the equipment and the kinds of things one can say and write on the whiteboard.

Throughout this process, students may need guidance. It is daunting for some to comprehend a text, create a new ending, and brainstorm their ideas on paper, let alone learn a new technology application. However, with proper guidance and mentoring, all students can be successful. Spend the time needed at the beginning of each class period to teach and review skills that you notice students may be struggling with. Allow yourself time to circulate the room to assist them with questions they may have. Also, use this time to create a list of things that you notice and address them later in a small- or whole-group minilesson. Minilessons are short, usually ten-minute-long lessons that provide explicit, targeted instruction about a particular concept. Remember that students are practicing myriad skills in this single activity.

In addition to your own teacher guidance, allow students to help guide peers. Consider putting students in working groups or with partners, but be thoughtful of whom you put together. For example, if one student struggles with the content (that is, creative thinking and writing) and another is strong in the content but weak in technology, they might form a great partnership. Sometimes peers can offer more guidance to one another than the teacher.

### *After Instruction*

In our experience, engaging students in prewriting, drafting, revising and editing, and publishing (Tompkins, 2010) can feel like pulling teeth. We have found that using technology encourages students to engage in these important steps. After instruction, it is important to continue to encourage students to engage in reading, writing, and technology. Consider having iPads available for students to watch more of their classmates' creations during their free time. Additionally, consider having the books that students responded to available so that they may reread them and imagine the alternate endings that their classmates suggested. You may want to consider engaging in this process throughout different units and with different genres of writing.

As you consider using students' creations as a form of assessment, you may want to create a rubric with which to score their work. This rubric can also be given to students to give one another academic feedback. The rubric should also help you, as their teacher, understand what instruction is needed at this point. For instance, if you noticed that one student's final screencast creation was identical to his or her prewrite, then that student may need additional help understanding revision. Or you may notice that a group of students struggled with organizing their thoughts, while another group struggled with the conventions of writing. Using your rubric and anecdotal records, you can create small groups for further instruction.

We hope that this activity can be a springboard to many more technology-teaching ideas. Although incorporating technology into the curriculum can be challenging and time consuming, we believe it is important to do so as often as possible. In our experience, students are interested in technology and are quite engaged with it. Including the strategies in this book in your repertoire will help prepare students to contribute to a technologically advanced society (Kress, 2003).

 **Julia Kara-Soteriou** is an associate professor of reading and language arts at Central Connecticut State University. Her research focuses on the integration of literacy and technology and the preparation of teachers to apply new literacies in their classrooms. Julia coedited the book *Innovative Approaches to Literacy Education: Using the Internet to Support New Literacies.*

 **Ashley Callan** is a reading specialist for West Hartford Public Schools in Connecticut. Her research interests include the use of technology, such as blogging and digital storytelling, to better prepare students for the future. She holds a master of science degree in reading and language arts from Central Connecticut State University.

# CHAPTER 8

# Digital Storytelling

By Julia Kara-Soteriou and Ashley Callan

As a modern version of the ancient art and practice of storytelling (Rule, as cited in Barrett, 2011), digital storytelling is the process of telling a story with the use of multimedia tools, such as digital pictures, audio, video, graphics, and music. Although still in its infancy in the educational arena, digital storytelling is gradually gaining more popularity as its supporters argue for the learning benefits it can have for students of all ages. Students who immerse themselves in the creation of digital stories have the chance to practice digital information and visual literacies and develop a variety of skills, including research, writing, organization, and presentation. Further, researchers have reported the educational benefits of digital storytelling, such as motivating reluctant readers and writers and helping struggling writers compose more strategically (Figg & McCartney, 2010; Kajder & Swenson, 2004; Sylvester & Greenidge, 2009).

Digital storytelling is a great use of technology when applying the process approach to writing instruction. While it helps students develop familiarity with new technologies, digital story development requires several drafts and revisions of a script in preparation for recording it and supporting it with pictures and audio. When classrooms apply it correctly, especially during writing workshops, digital storytelling encourages the development of an environment in which ownership, time to write, and response to one's writing can flourish.

Educators have access to an increased number of resources for integrating the writing process with digital storytelling (Miller, 2010), employing specific technologies to turn a story into a digital story (Standley & Ormiston, 2010; Thesen & Kara-Soteriou, 2011), and finding samples of completed digital storytelling projects and ideas to use in instruction (Barrett, 2011). Changes in technological advancements and access, along with a change in how teachers and students use multimedia (Brown, Bryan, & Brown, 2005), will make digital storytelling a popular venue to aid reading and writing instruction in the near future. Teachers can use digital storytelling to introduce or reinforce a topic of instruction, and students can use it to show new knowledge and skills. In this chapter, we provide information on how teachers can use digital stories to support the process approach to writing instruction, and we share an example of integrating writing and digital storytelling in a second-grade classroom.

## How Do I Do It?

Regardless of who creates the digital story, teachers or students, the process can be recursive, depending on how comfortable one feels with writing in a particular genre and with technology use. The following sections describe what we do when we work with our students on digital storytelling.

### Step One: Choose the Type of Story

We begin by choosing the type of digital story students will create, keeping in mind that our selection will influence our students' choice of topic. While there are many types of digital stories, the most common are personal narratives, historical documentaries, and stories that inform or instruct in content areas, such as mathematics, science, and literature (University of Houston, 2014).

### Step Two: Brainstorm

Students start the brainstorming phase of the writing process by jotting down the story's purpose and audience. They also make notes on how their script will address the seven elements of digital storytelling (University of Houston, 2014). Prior to this step, you can introduce the seven elements of digital storytelling in several minilessons.

1.  **Point of view:** As the author of the story, what will your perspective be?

2.  **A dramatic question:** What is one key question you can ask that will keep your audience's attention and that you will answer by the end of the story?

3.  **Emotional content:** What are some serious issues that can speak to the audience in a personal and powerful way?

4.  **The gift of your voice:** Can you personalize the story to help your audience understand the context?

5. **The power of the soundtrack:** What music do you think can support your storyline?

6. **Economy:** Can you tell the story with just enough information and without overloading the audience?

7. **Pacing:** How fast or how slow do you anticipate the story will progress? Think of its rhythm.

### Step Three: Write the Script

Drawing from the information they gathered during the brainstorming phase, our students write their script's first draft. Writing the script can take several days and involves making changes to sentences and paragraphs that do not seem to fit the story's purpose or to address elements such as the dramatic question or emotional content. We then give our students time to share their draft with classmates and receive feedback, especially regarding the purpose and the elements of storytelling. The feedback leads to revisions of the script. When the script is done, students proofread it in preparation for using selected parts on the digital story's slides (see step five). Even though it is unlikely that students will use all written text on the slides (most will be audio), we advise them to proofread all the text in case they use excerpts they were not initially planning to use.

### Step Four: Collect Images and Audio

With a good sense of how the final script looks, we ask students to consider images (that is, photographs, pictures, drawings, maps, and graphic organizers) and audio (music, interviews, and environmental sounds) they would like to use. Students begin to collect and organize what they already have available, electronic or not. As they collect images and audio, we remind them of copyright issues and plagiarism. We also remind them to make a note of additional images and audio they might need to create themselves. This is a good time to revisit step two in order to consider the impact of voice and soundtrack on the story and to consider the storytelling element of economy.

### Step Five: Develop a Storyboard

Teaching students to develop a storyboard is another important step in the digital storytelling process. A storyboard is a graphic organizer in the form of images and text that are displayed in sequence for the purpose of helping us visualize the unfolding of the story. An easy-to-use storyboard consists of several frames, which represent the slides of the digital story, and contains information about each slide's content (for example, a digital photo, scanned drawing, slide title, or piece of text copied from the script). This information also describes the audio, if any, that will accompany each image and includes comments about the parts of the script our students will record. Creating a storyboard earlier in the process, after students gain some experience in developing digital stories, is also an option.

### Step Six: Create, Scan, and Import Original Drawings

If the students' collection of images and audio resources does not adequately help them complete their storyboard, we ask them to create, scan, and import drawings into their computer. Students can also scan photos and pictures that are not in electronic format. If needed, we also ask students to record additional music and sounds and save them on the computer.

### Step Seven: Practice and Record the Script

Before our students begin to record their script using a computer microphone, we require that they practice reading the script several times, experimenting with intonation, pitch, stress, and pauses. After they complete the recording, they listen to the narrated script, keeping the elements of storytelling in mind, and if needed, they rerecord parts that they think need improvement.

### Step Eight: Use the Software to Assemble the Script

As a final step, we help our students put together their digital story using the application we have chosen. We like user-friendly applications that are free or inexpensive and compatible with the computers at our schools. Following our modeling, students import the digital images, audio files, scanned drawings and pictures, and recorded script into the application. They then use their storyboard to guide them in the sequencing of the images and rearrange them, if needed. Students add the audio files to the appropriate images on the application, finalize the digital story by saving it in a compatible version for everyone to view, and present it to their target audience.

## Classroom Example

Ashley developed a two-week unit for her second graders on transforming personal narratives into digital stories. Ashley had introduced her students to the elements of personal narrative earlier in the year; therefore, this unit focused only on the development of short digital stories. What follows is a description of the lesson activities that led her second graders to develop digital stories. You can modify these activities, of course, to address the needs of students who have different experiences with technology, writing, and storytelling.

During the first two days of the unit, Ashley introduced students to digital storytelling with the viewing of online digital stories and a discussion with students of what they thought was required to create them. Students' suggestions revolved around voice inflection, strong images, and audio. Next, the students began a short narrative about a small but important moment in their lives. Allowing students to choose their own topic is a significant aspect of Ashley's writing instruction, because she knows that students are more invested that way. Students used these two days for brainstorming and drafting the narrative that would represent their script. During drafting, Ashley discussed in small groups the importance of using a dramatic question and of including content that would appeal to an audience.

Students devoted half of each day over the next three days to sharing their stories in small groups and revising independently. In preparation for the script's recording, Ashley allocated the rest of these three days for storytelling exercises that taught students how to read with more expression. Ashley modeled, and the students practiced from the script. They practiced reading with different emotions (sad, happy, surprised, and so on), placing emphasis on different words in the same phrase, and using different tempos and silences. Every day, after they completed the oral activities, students revised their scripts to include words and phrases that would give their recording more expression. At the end of the week, they also proofread their scripts.

On the first day of the second week, Ashley explained the use of storyboard and shared examples of storyboards from online sources, such as Storyboard and Digital Storytelling (http://digitalstorytelling.coe.uh.edu/index.cfm). She next asked the students to create their storyboard on paper. Then she asked them to break their story into only eight sections because, as expected in second grade, their personal narratives were short. Also, the students did not have any visual or audio files of their own saved on the school's computers and were not familiar enough with the computer's software or the Internet to gather more images and audio for their story. Instead, Ashley asked them to create their own pictures and showed them how to find music and sound effects in Microsoft Photo Story 3, the software application she chose for this project. Students then created eight quick pencil drawings inside the eight frames of the storyboard and added short notes about the audio and script they wanted to use in each frame. As they completed the storyboard, students moved on to develop their illustrations using colored pencils and crayons.

The following day, Ashley modeled how to scan an illustration and use a USB microphone to record the narrative. She also showed the students how to organize the images on the computer desktop and import them and the recorded narrative into Photo Story 3. She even showed the students how to use sound effects from the application. Some students began to scan their color illustrations, while the rest began recording their narratives until the single scanner in the computer lab became available. Most students continued to scan illustrations and record their narratives for one more day. Then, for two days, students worked to put the story together by first importing audio and images in Photo Story 3. They sequenced their images the way they did on the storyboard, added the recorded narration, customized motion to the story, and inserted music that matched the tone of their story directly from Photo Story 3. While in the computer lab, students were free to interact and comment on each other's work in progress, and this led to revisions of the digital story before they completed and saved their final version.

The publishing phase of the narrative writing was completed a few days later with a formal presentation of the students' digital stories in front of the whole class. Ashley also prepared a CD of the students' digital stories and sent it home for parents to watch.

## Your Turn

Before you introduce digital storytelling in your classroom, familiarize yourself with websites that deal with the technology. Two great sites to get started with are the University of Houston's Educational Uses of Digital Storytelling (http://digital storytelling.coe.uh.edu) and Helen Barrett's Digital Storytelling (http://electronic portfolios.com/digistory). Watch several videos posted on these and other websites.

Next, create a digital story yourself. The process will help you internalize the steps and prepare you for questions your students might have. We recommend creating your digital story in the same category you ask your students to use. First, of course, you must choose a software application. Microsoft Photo Story 3 (for use only with Windows XP), Windows Movie Maker (free with Windows), and Apple iMovie (free with Apple OS X) are three options that are available at school, relatively easy to use, and free and come with online tutorials.

Learn how to use the scanner at your school, since it is very likely you and your students will need to scan materials that you do not have in electronic format, such as drawings and photographs. Also, learn how to use audio recording software on the computer, as you and the students will need to record your script and import it in the software application. In anticipation of your students looking for images and audio online, prepare to discuss copyright issues and share websites that host public domain material, such as Flickr, PDSounds, and SoundBible.

Develop a unit on a topic that invites integration of writing and digital storytelling. Set clear objectives not only for the subject-area knowledge but also for storytelling and technology use to encourage student development of a wide range of skills, including speaking, using technology, organizing, and researching.

Merging 21st century technology and literacy can open a wide range of possibilities for students of all ages and ability levels. The implementation of digital storytelling provides them with an opportunity to not only acquire necessary literacy skills but also demonstrate creativity and build confidence. Additionally, the implementation of digital storytelling provides teachers with an outlet for meeting instructional objectives and increasing student motivation. Although digital storytelling is a relatively new technique, it is certainly an exciting and promising option for educators who want to bridge the gap between an ancient practice and a modern medium.

 **Sally Valentino Drew, PhD,** is an assistant professor of elementary teacher education at Central Connecticut State University. Her research examines the intersection of clinical practice and teacher education related to disciplinary literacy, writing instruction, and struggling learners. She supports teachers in their development and implementation of literacy-rich experiences within the STEM disciplines. Sally earned her MA degree in education from Syracuse University and PhD in educational psychology from the University of Connecticut.

# CHAPTER 9

# Digital Writing Workshop

By Sally Valentino Drew

The nature of writing itself has changed to include forms and functions beyond the traditional. One result of this shift is that students spend a great deal of time "writing" online (Kaiser Family Foundation, 2010). Teachers are now asked to prepare students to communicate in a globally networked, multimodal, digital age of information and communication (Organisation for Economic Co-operation and Development [OECD], 1996)—a world that many teachers themselves are unfamiliar with. This shift requires a whole new rhetoric, with different writing audiences, purposes, products, and contexts (Writing in Digital Environments [WIDE] Research Center Collective, n.d.). The Common Core State Standards (NGA & CCSSO, 2010) provide us with some insight for this shift but may not do enough to prioritize online writing instruction.

Writing is an essential gateway skill for success in school and beyond. Students are expected to write for a variety of purposes in and out of school, and many of those purposes involve communicating digitally. Students' grades, graduation, access to college, and success in the workforce are dependent on their writing skills (Graham & Perin, 2007c). More than ever, digital technologies such as text messaging, email, and shared documents stress additional and novel skills for success and full participation in a global economy (Leu et al., 2011). Technology is changing not only the mode of communicating in writing but also the process. Online technologies shape the form, function, and process of writing in online environments (NCTE, 2008b). Writing offers a unique invitation to integrate information, communication, and technology (Lacina & Griffith, 2012; Partnership for 21st Century Skills, 2009).

Yet, students may not have developed adequate writing competencies in traditional or digital writing environments. Nor is improving writing instruction a quick fix, because students' instructional writing needs are as diverse and complex as each individual student's background (Graham & Perin, 2007c). Unfortunately, efforts to improve writing instruction are virtually nonexistent in school-reform initiatives (Kiuhara, Graham, & Hawken, 2009). To prepare students for 21st century writing demands, schools need to shift toward an attention on improving writing instruction, especially in digital environments.

The WIDE Research Center Collective (n.d.) proposes a pedagogical vision that will help to prepare students for 21st century writing demands (National Writing Project, 2010). In this vision, students are first provided with spaces and assignments that allow for digital writing, along with the pedagogies to support them in these tasks. Second, teachers consider traditional as well as new audiences, contexts, and purposes that digital writing offers. Third, teachers lead students in thinking critically about the purposes, benefits, and limitations of specific technologies. Also, because technologies are changing so quickly, teachers and students adopt a learning-how-to-learn approach. They must develop the habits of mind to figure out new technologies since they will never be able to contain and understand all the possible technologies out there. Finally, teachers and students acknowledge that digital writing is not one-dimensional; multimodal aspects such as text, images, audio, video, and hyperlinks contribute to online "text" in interactive ways. As a pedagogical structure for this shift, the 21st century writing workshop offers much promise.

## How Do I Do It?

A 21st century writing workshop allows teachers to address the vision of the WIDE Research Center Collective (n.d.) while meeting the requirements of the CCSS. It creates a space for students to participate in an online writing community that considers 21st century audiences, contexts, and purposes for writing. Additionally, it teaches students to match emerging technologies appropriately to those audiences, contexts, and purposes by adopting a learning-how-to-learn mentality.

In a 21st century workshop, or digital writing workshop, the grounding principles of supporting and growing writers remain (Atwell, 1998; Calkins, 1994; Fletcher, 1993; Hicks, 2009). Yet, certain principles emerge as critical to success. Choice and inquiry, the writing process, timely feedback, and author or designer craft serve as foundational themes, borrowing from effective practices of the traditional writing workshop but moving the writing tasks online or in other digital forms. The structure of the workshop remains the same, with a teacher-directed minilesson followed by a student work session in which teachers and students write, confer, and collaborate. The workshop ends with a sharing session in which students share their writing products and processes with the intention of building an extended community of writers (Atwell, 1998; Fletcher, 1993). However, teachers can bring each component of the workshop online or digitize it. For example, teachers can replace the teacher-directed minilesson with an online clip of an authentic author describing her craft.

### Setting Up the Workshop

To set up your 21st century writing workshop, you need to create a space in which students can write. Ideally, you will have a one-to-one device ratio using either tablets or laptops with a wireless Internet connection. In the absence of a one-to-one ratio, you may take your students to the computer lab, have them bring in approved devices, or allow them to share devices. The goal is for each student to be able to compose digitally, rather than having students compose with pencil and paper and then transfer to a digital space. You will want to share some overarching principles of the writing workshop with students, as well as allow them an opportunity to contribute to the working norms. Share guidelines for acceptable-use policies, on-task requirements, directions for meeting deadlines and turning in work, grading policies for work in progress and completed work, student or peer conferencing, and so on. It is best to work within the digital structure your school or district has set up and that families and students are familiar with. Ultimately, for accountability purposes, students and families should sign acceptable-use contracts.

### Establishing Digital Writing Routines

Once you've created the space, students will need to establish digital routines that fit within the workshop. Students can use the technologies available to them to plan, draft, revise, edit, and publish writing. They can use Google Docs or other document-sharing programs, classroom blogs such as Blogger, Kidblog, or Edublogs, as well as classroom wikis such as Wikispaces. Students can create their own websites on Weebly or post their work on district-owned classroom webpages. As teachers, you will want to consider using interactive learning management systems such as Blackboard, Schoology, Moodle, or Edmodo, among others. You will want to teach these routines until students can independently use the system to produce and even publish their writing. Another routine you need to consider is keyboarding. If your school does not offer keyboarding instruction, provide students with the opportunity to develop their keyboarding skills in class or at home. There are many online keyboarding programs and apps—for example, Typing Agent (www.typingagent.com) and Type to Learn (www.typetolearn.org)—for students to practice at home, during unscheduled class time, or in study halls. Some are free, and some require district subscriptions.

The following five steps outline a typical digital workshop lesson:

1. **Determine the purpose of the day's workshop as a teaching point or minilesson**—Writing projects for students are typically ongoing in the digital writing workshop, yet each day you will select a focus area from a variety of online or hybrid writing objectives (skills, strategies, features, or processes). Objectives, or teaching points, can emerge from the CCSS, district writing curriculum, or students' particular needs to address specific online audiences, purposes, and tasks.

2. **Gather examples of the feature**—Ahead of time, collect both good (and poor) digital writing samples reflecting the objective you wish to present to students in a minilesson. Consider the purpose and effect of the modeled writing technique on the overall online composition and design while planning the minilesson. If you cannot find appropriate writing samples, you can create them yourself.

3. **Teach the minilesson**—This is where you explicitly teach the online technique (skill, strategy, feature, or process). For example, you can explain the differences between traditional and online informational text, while exploring the purposes for those differences. With ample modeling, you help students understand the purpose and function of online writing so they can improve their skill. Remember to use the gradual release of responsibility model of instruction through explanation, modeling, discussion, and feedback. You will build toward independent mastery during the work session that follows the minilesson. Draw from numerous online resources to support your directed instruction. Keep it brief and focused.

4. **Provide feedback to students as they try it out**—Following the minilesson, while students are working independently or collaboratively, confer with them to assess their understanding of the objective. Once you give and receive feedback from students, you will be able to determine if they met your objective or if they need an additional day or days of focus. The majority of the class may be ready to move on, but some students may require additional supports to reach the objective. This can be accomplished by providing differentiated instruction (conferencing, small-group instruction, graphic organizers, annotated rubrics, and so on) in upcoming workshops.

5. **Have students share their writing**—Following the work session, students can share their applications of the objective, even if it is a

work in progress. Encourage dialogue and constructive conversation as students receive feedback from one another and explain the effect that technology had on the communication of ideas.

## Classroom Example

For the first couple months of school, Jan Rose's sixth-period sophomore English class has been working on growing as a community of writers through using the blog feature on Schoology. The blog ties into an integrated topic from their history course—the poetry of the civil rights movement. Jan has determined that the project aligns to several Common Core State Standards for writing (W.9–10.4, W.9–10.5, W.9–10.6, W.9–10.9, and W.9–10.10; NGA & CCSSO, 2010). On the blog, students share poems about civil rights topics, analyze the poet's life and purpose, and write their own poetry about the civil rights movement. In their postings, they are free to combine text, images, hyperlinks, and videos. Each week, Jan expects students to post one entry to the blog and provide at least one meaningful comment on a classmate's posting. Lately, she has noticed that students are struggling to post meaningful and contributory comments—so, she has taken this as the focus of the minilesson today in her digital writing workshop.

Jan gains the attention of her students. "I can see that you are already taking out your laptops—great. Today, we are going to learn about providing *quality* feedback to other students on our course blog. I am noticing that many of your comments to peers are superficial or unrelated and not helping your classmates to improve their writing. Today, we will examine examples of high-quality comments and talk about certain elements that your feedback should include."

During the minilesson that follows, some students look up to the interactive whiteboard as Jan outlines the elements of high-quality feedback and gives some examples. Other students follow along on their laptops and tablets. Jan displays an interactive digital checklist that students can use to rate their peers' writing. She reminds students that they can also use the checklist to critically examine their own writing.

This vignette shows the 21st century writing workshop in action. In this particular case, the teacher is using blog technology to create an interactive online writing environment connected to content-area learning. It is clear that Jan has established working norms for her workshop and established routines, such as blogging and commenting on peers' blogs. She is lucky that she has a separate writing block four days a week in addition to her literature block; yet, her literature and writing blocks are intertwined. Students are typically reading about their writing and writing about their reading. Often, one block spills over into the other, with students clearly seeing the connection between their reading and writing. She designs her digital writing tasks for specific online audiences, purposes, and contexts. All of her assignments require students to compose extended text combined with images, audio, visual, or hyperlinks. Most assignments are taken through the writing process (planning, drafting, revising, editing, publishing), with students interacting with each other and with her to improve their communication for the intended audience and purpose. Students often share their writing with a broader writing community.

Jan's typical schedule for a forty-eight-minute writing block is as follows.

- **Welcome and announcements (up to five minutes):** Setting the tone for the day; the goal is to attend to the needs of the community and communicate important information related to routine and schedule; students set daily writing goals aligned to long-term writing goals.

- **Digital minilesson (ten to fifteen minutes):** Sharing the teaching point objectives related to online or hybrid writing techniques (skills, strategies, features, and processes aligned to the CCSS and district writing outcomes); comparing and contrasting digital writing to traditional writing

- **Digital work session (up to thirty minutes):** Student planning, composition, design, revision, editing, publishing, and collaborating on a specific online writing task; teacher feedback, facilitation, and formative assessment

- **Sharing (five to ten minutes):** Student interaction and reflection; solidifying understanding of the objective

Visit the Writers Workshop section of the Digital Sandbox (http://digisandbox .wordpress.com) for more information about setting up a digital writing workshop. See also *The Digital Writing Workshop* (Hicks, 2009) and visit Troy Hicks's blog (http://hickstro.org) for more about digital writing instruction. Visit **go.solution -tree.com/technology** to access live links to the websites in this book.

## Your Turn

Now it's your turn to use the writing workshop to prepare students for 21st century writing demands. The CCSS provide us with some guidance on this matter but leave us unprepared in many ways. Using a 21st century writing workshop, you can better match your classroom writing purposes and scope to the writing students are already doing outside of school and to the skills they'll need for the global marketplace of ideas. Most importantly, a 21st century digital writing workshop offers innovative ways to engage reluctant writers, which could perhaps be the first step in narrowing the achievement gap between successful and struggling writers (NCES,

2012). Finally, with the next, computer-based wave of assessments (Smarter Balanced Assessment Consortium [SBAC] and Partnership for Assessment of Readiness for College and Careers [PARCC] assessments), a 21st century writing workshop will help you prepare students for digital writing environments.

Engaging students in a 21st century writing workshop cannot be optional in this digital world. We must collaborate, create, and refine instructional techniques that assist students in becoming learners who are prepared for success in a global environment. Implementing a digital writing workshop is just one piece of this pedagogical shift; however, it is a piece that begins molding students into the next generation of great writers.

# PART IV | Awareness of Audience and Purpose

Purpose, context, and audience are intricately related. In order for writing to be meaningful and relevant, students need to know why they are writing and who is the intended audience for their work. Too often, however, students view writing as an assignment for the teacher to read and determine a grade. When this happens, students are likely to become detached from their writing and view it as less than authentic.

Flower (1979) distinguishes between writer-based and reader-based prose. In *writer-based prose*, a student does not conceptualize someone reading his or her work but writes as if he or she will be the reader. Flower (1981) explains that "writer-based prose reflects the interior monologue of a writer thinking and talking to himself" (p. 63). Novice writers trying to articulate their thoughts often write from this stance. As teachers, however, we strive for our students to write with their audience and purpose in mind, or *reader-based prose* (Flower, 1979). When students write from a reader-based stance, they must consider their readers when composing, which can be difficult and challenging for student writers. Yet, researchers have linked this concept to writing achievement (Graham et al., 2012; Graham, Harris, & Mason, 2005; Graham & Perin, 2007c). When students can identify the purpose for writing (that is, establishing an argument) and recognize who might be the reader, they can write with specific goals in mind, which has a positive effect on students' writing quality (Graham & Perin, 2007c).

Teachers can help students develop their ability to write from a reader-based stance by providing authentic purposes for writing. Teachers and students can together explore genres that students might see in their daily lives and can have discussions about why these genres are important. This type of inquiry-based writing instruction allows students to consider the purpose of a specific genre. Students can ask questions about why and how authors compose in specific genres, and this leads to conversations about audience. They begin to recognize that authors craft with a specific audience in mind. Teachers should also consider creating opportunities for students to have multiple readers, not just the teacher, for their writing. When students are writing for an authentic purpose, with an authentic audience, they are more likely to be engaged and motivated in their writing.

Technology can significantly support this strategy by providing access to authentic audiences. This could be done in a very simple way. For instance, a teacher could set up online, password-protected portals so that students can share their work with parents and others outside of the classroom (a feature that is often inherent in a learning or content management system). This could also be done in a more complex manner; for example, teachers have often created online magazines and newspapers for students to manage.

It is worth noting that access to external, authentic audiences is a function of the choice of the technology. For instance, a tweet or blog comment is automatically open to the world. Many students have been surprised to find that others have commented on or followed their online presence. Obviously, classrooms must consider safety issues; however, the point is that technology quickly becomes the intentional or unintentional means by which students write for authentic audiences.

In chapter 10, Victoria Seeger and Robin D. Johnson describe how family messaging journals create authentic writing experiences and connect families to classroom instructional practices. Ewa McGrail and J. Patrick McGrail document their learning from a yearlong research project on blogging in chapter 11. Concluding this section in chapter 12, Lynda Williams shares her experiences producing the *Reality Skimming* blog and offers suggestions for how teachers can use this resource in the classroom.

 **Victoria Seeger** is an education program consultant at the Kansas State Department of Education. She was formerly an assistant professor at Northwest Missouri State University and Stephen F. Austin State University, teaching coursework in literacy, math, and social studies and was a literacy coach and elementary teacher in Topeka, Kansas, for fifteen years. Victoria is the coauthor of *Building Classroom Reading Communities*. You can follow her on Twitter @vseeger.

 **Robin D. Johnson** is an assistant professor at Stephen F. Austin State University in Nacogdoches, Texas. She is also a literacy trainer for Abydos Learning International and is author of the teacher practitioner book *Time to Write*. She and her husband, David, have two children, Caleb and Sophie.

# CHAPTER 10

# Electronic Family Message Journals

By Victoria Seeger and Robin D. Johnson

A family message journal is a communication tool for students to write letters to their families about what they are learning in school. A parent or other family member responds in writing to the student, asking questions and building on the child's writing. Family message journals are based on Julie Wollman-Bonilla's (2000) *Family Message Journals: Teaching Writing through Family Involvement*. This chapter focuses on electronic family message journals. The premise behind an electronic versus a paper-and-pencil-generated journal is about honoring the digital natives in our classrooms and reinforcing the integration of 21st century learning skills into the elementary classroom setting. In this chapter, you will learn about electronic journal entries from two first-grade classrooms and a second-grade classroom. The classrooms reside in a suburban school district in a midsized midwestern city, a small rural town in the South, and a rural elementary school in a very small midwestern town, respectively.

Authentic writing experiences are important to support students' writing development (Fletcher & Portalupi, 2001; Hansen, 2007; Olshansky, 2006; Wollman-Bonilla, 2000). When students *know* who they are writing to and feel that their writing is for a purpose, they are more likely to remain engaged in the task and increase their stamina for the writing itself. Writing is one of the keys to communication and achievement (Britton, 1970; Gere, 1985; Vygotsky, 1978).

Bridging the gap between home and school has long been a concern for teachers (Baumann & Thomas, 1997; Moore, 2004). We typically ask students' families to participate in their child's education in supplementary ways—practicing spelling words, using flash cards to assist students in mastering mathematics facts, and listening to their children read for a certain amount of time each evening. We communicate with families in routine ways through newsletters (electronic or traditional text), teacher-authored websites sharing information about what students are learning at school, and messages sent home with students each day. However, involving families in transformative ways (that is, relationship-altering practices that welcome families into the classroom as partners in the education of students) values what families can contribute to what a student is learning (Moore, 2004). The family message journal serves to invite families to participate in their child's world at school, to honor what a child is learning at home, and to become a partner with the teacher in a writing process between home and school (Wollman-Bonilla, 2000). The quality of parent responses to questions and topics is vital to students when they are writing in the classroom (Fletcher & Portalupi, 2001; Hansen, 2007; Moore & Seeger, 2009; Olshansky, 2006). A parent or caregiver knows better than anyone how a child wants to be responded to, and these responses transfer into the written communication between adult and child in the family message journal entries.

Thomas Friedman (2005) notes that in order to be a successful and functioning member of the global society, students must have the knowledge and skills necessary for communicating through the written word. However, it does not matter what form we use for that written word; we can handwrite and mail our messages to one another, type them on a computer screen, or present them with media to an audience-filled room. As teachers shift to instruction that is seamlessly infused with technology, they need to consider the following themes (National Writing Project, 2010):

- Proficiency with digital tools
- Construction of collaborative relationships locally *and* globally
- Fluency with a constant stream of information in diverse formats
- Our responsibility to students, in an ethical sense, for understanding the complicated electronic environment we are a part of

Even our youngest students need multiple experiences in the classroom to help them "use technology to research, organize, evaluate, and communicate information" (Larson & Miller, 2011, p. 122). We also know that in order to be 21st century ready, our students are going to need to learn to keyboard. Keyboarding alleviates the physical difficulty that often comes with handwritten work. Ralph Fletcher (2006) refers to the keyboard as the *great equalizer* and notes, "Letters and words always look the same, no matter who happens to type them" (p. 76). Digital family message journals take the handwriting struggle away from the task and allow our students to focus on the content.

## How Do I Do It?

Electronic family message journals mirror Wollman-Bonilla's (2000) processes and procedures and honor the assumption that *all* parents want to be involved in their child's learning at school. Four critical steps for implementation include: (1) discussing the process with families and students, (2) modeling the writing of journal entries for students (so families know how to write entries and what to write), (3) using students' writing as opportunities for further instruction about writing in the classroom, and (4) assessing student writing through the journal entries.

Implementing electronic family message journals in the classroom differs from implementing the pencil-and-paper version. In the examples we cite, acquiring the technology took some time. The idea of an electronic journaling process was embraced in one school setting and met with skepticism by another. One principal did not want a teacher to move to electronic journals, because he felt it would not be fair to the students who were not given that opportunity. But, through negotiation and problem solving by the classroom teacher (which included professional learning about family message journals for other teachers in the building), the project met with approval of all involved.

## Classroom Example

From the beginning, in Jessica Miller's school and district, her grade-level partner, administrator, and technology coordinator met the idea of an electronic family message journal with complete trust; the board of education even embraced it. Initially, the district allowed students to use the school's iPads at school and home. Later, the school set up Google Docs accounts to send the messages home through parents' emails. This would prevent any loss of or damage to the iPads.

On the night Jessica met with families of the combined second-grade classrooms, twenty-five of twenty-nine families were represented, with many students attending with their parents. The technology coordinator assisted parents in setting up email accounts in the computer lab. Afterward, three fathers stayed behind to ask specific questions. One father said, "Our kids need to learn how to write electronically. When I work from home, that is what I do, and they *have* to know how to do this. It's important that they learn how to write without using text messaging conventions." Extensive discussions like this beforehand with parents and caregivers resulted in families who were knowledgeable about the process before the students wrote their first messages.

Grace Jones's school was not as open to the idea of electronic family message journals. In a series of negotiations with the principal and the instructional coach, they decided that electronic family message journals would work for some students, while others would begin to write through a traditional paper-and-pencil journaling process. Grace had the opportunity to talk with families at the school's open house. She knew which students had iPads at home and discussed the journaling process with their parents. The result was that thirteen students participated through electronic processes, keyboarding their messages on school computers that were sent to home email accounts. In both Jessica's and Grace's settings, students set the bar for the messages, modeling for parents what was expected in the exchanges between home and school.

Tanya Franklin began electronic family message journals in her classroom by sending home a letter asking parents if they were interested in writing to their child electronically and if they had access to the Internet or an email address. All parents wanted to participate and provided email addresses for this purpose. As a result of journaling, Tanya's students' parents reported they had more information than ever before about what was occurring in the classroom. Even if students were writing only a sentence or two, parents received more information than when they asked their children how their day went. Tanya's enthusiasm for the journaling spread to other colleagues as students talked about how excited they were anticipating an electronic message from a family member. And parents from other classrooms have asked why Tanya's students tell their parents so much about their days at school. Writing in a journal provides students with a safe, uncensored writing environment, creating a positive experience for students—and their parents.

Figure 10.1 is an electronic exchange between Ellie (all names are pseudonyms) and her mother. The messages are exactly as they appeared in the Google Doc the two of them share through a special email account for journaling.

Reading and writing are reciprocal learning processes; one influences the other. Students often write about their reading in reflective and important ways in their family message journals. Ellie wrote in a sophisticated and knowledgeable way about the books in the series, she knew the author's name, and she was dedicated to the notion of collecting all of the titles for her new bookshelf. Her mother also made a text-to-media connection in a very natural way by telling Ellie that she watched the television series when she was younger. The amount of literacy learning for Ellie that took place around these three family message journal entries goes far beyond what would likely have occurred in a "forced" assignment to write about what she was reading in the classroom setting. Moreover, Ellie's mother demonstrated that she was also a writer perfectly capable of modeling for and communicating with her child.

1–22–13

Dear Mom,

Yes I am ready for the weekend. I think Chase will eat his cake. I am almost finished with Little House In The Big Woods. I am also reading Little House On The Prairie to the class. When you are done eating with Izzie on Thursday will you give me a hug? I am going to try to read all of the Laura Ingalls books. I hope you have a good day.

Love Ellie

___

1–24–13

Dear Ellie,

I love how you have such a love for reading. I remember reading some of the Little House on the Prairie books when I was younger. I also watched it on TV after school! They are good books with a great message. I won't be able to eat with Izzie on Thursday since I had to stay home from work on Wednesday with him. It will be a couple weeks before I can eat with him because I have a meeting at work on my next day off. Have a good time at piano lessons after school. You sound great, keep up the hard work! I had a wonderful evening with you and the rest of the family. It was nice not having to be anywhere but home :) I love you.

Hugs and Kisses,

Mom

___

1–24–13

Dear Mom,

I think I will have a good time at piano with Kat. I am Exited to get my new piano books. When I get my bookshelf I want to get all of the Little House On The Prairie books! what time will you get home on Thursday? In Science we are making an Experiment about Matter and Mass. When can Maddie come over? I hope she can come over soon!

Love Ellie

Figure 10.1: Sample electronic family message journal entries.

## Your Turn

Just as a classroom teacher has to decide what kinds of paper journals to use, you will need to decide what technology to use for your electronic family message journals—just like Grace, Jessica, and Tanya. The logistics for technology choices were not simple for our classroom teachers, but with the assistance of others in the school setting, teachers implemented the journals successfully with few problems. Each had to decide what time of day would work best for writing (usually the end of the day, because students tend to be more reflective then about what they have learned) and how often the students would participate. In Jessica's school, a classroom set of iPads was available, meaning that she and her grade-level partner shared them. They worked out a schedule so that students write electronically every other day. Tanya had two iPads and five computers in her classroom that students could rotate and use during their writing workshop time each day. Fortunately, all sixteen of her students' parents had email accounts their children could use.

It is important for you to begin with the premise and mindset that all families want to participate and communicate with their child and that there are ways to problem solve for those families who are unable to write through family message journals. In Jessica's classroom, a board of education member attended the parent meeting. Afterward, she approached us asking if any parents had not written back to their child. Jessica said she was worried about two families, and the board member, demonstrating the value the community places on learning, said she wanted to be involved in writing to any student whose parents were unable to write. Grace responded, "I have had a couple of teachers volunteer to write to any students whose parents don't write back." The librarian at Tanya's school also volunteered to write students.

In Tanya's classroom, three of the families spoke Spanish in the home. She was concerned about translating the electronic messages, because she knew those students were not fluent in reading Spanish. An easy solution came in the form of Google Translate (http://translate.google.com). By working with those three students in a small group, she was able to teach them how to translate their parents' text before reading and responding, providing another opportunity for the young students to cultivate self-sufficiency in the use of technology devices.

Electronic family message journals are an example of how classrooms can use technology to build stronger family-school partnerships; increase parent-child interactions; strengthen reading and writing skills through enjoyable, novel, and non-threatening experiences; and provide multiple opportunities to interact with new technology and develop the skills necessary to communicate in our digital world.

 **Ewa McGrail** is an associate professor of language and literacy at Georgia State University. She is the winner (with Anne Davis) of the *Journal of Research in Childhood Education* Distinguished Education Research Article Award for 2011 and the recipient of the National Leadership Fellowship Award Program from the Conference on English Education, National Council of Teachers of English, and the Society for Information Technology and Teacher Education. In her research, she examines digital writing and new media composition; copyright and media literacy; and multimodal assessment. She also explores innovation and newer technology applications for research.

 **J. Patrick McGrail** is an associate professor of communication at Jacksonville State University in Alabama. He teaches the theoretics of production in television. Previously, he was assistant professor of communications at Susquehanna University, where he taught a broad range of courses in news and entertainment. His research interests include copyright law and policy, objectivity and narratives in journalism, and international broadcasting, especially in Great Britain. Prior to his career in academia, Patrick worked in television as an actor, announcer, and anchor. He also has a keen interest in music production and holds a number of musical copyrights.

# CHAPTER 11

# Blogging and the Tool of Storytelling

By Ewa McGrail and J. Patrick McGrail

Both research and practice have shown that storytelling can be a powerful way of getting young writers to notice their audience, care about it, and structure their message so that someone else can understand and appreciate it (Miller & Pennycuff, 2008). Story writing is (or should be) an essential part of the elementary school writing curriculum. Moreover, storytelling, a mainstay of all effective writing (Wallace, 2000), is an excellent method for mastering the concept of audience. Without a good story, prose would be no more interesting than reading a phone book. The Common Core State Standards (NGA & CCSSO, 2010) emphasize storytelling (narrative writing) in elementary school (see W.1.3, W.2.3, W.3.3, W.4.3, W.5.3, and W.5.6).

## How Do I Do It?

Blogging, as a technology writing application, facilitates and augments student story writing development in several ways. First, as a technology writing application, the instantiation of text on the page speeds up the process of creation and review (NGA & CCSSO, 2010).

Second, since stories are meant to be told to others, the blogging application provides an immediate audience, one that can extend beyond classroom teacher and peers to the world at large. This enhances the communicative purpose of story writing and storytelling (McGrail & Davis, 2011). Third, interaction with candid readers helps young writers become aware of their readers and their readers' cognitive needs, and as a result, increases their awareness of both the audience and the reader's role in the writing process. This is an important consideration, since young writers often find the concept of audience difficult to grasp and apply to their writing. This is because in traditional classroom writing, students are asked to write for an abstract or imaginary audience (Barbeiro, 2011). In sum, blogging is a strategy that can connect young writers and readers and thus develop in students a powerful ability to whet an audience's interest with the use of material that more than just one person might find intriguing and provocative.

In our yearlong research project on blogging, we accomplished this by exposing our fifth-grade bloggers to a special audience member and storyteller—Harley, a dog with whom our student bloggers "corresponded." Harley's owner assumed the identity of her dog, created a blog for him, and wrote posts attributed to him. In the course of doing so, she imbued him with a personality, likes and desires, predilections, and, most importantly for us, the desire to communicate with other bloggers.

Research has shown that, in order to enter a conversation with an audience, writers need to get to know their audience well (Barbeiro, 2011). More to the point, young writers need to have "a tangible experience with audience" (Miller & Pennycuff, 2008, p. 40). Harley thus allowed the young bloggers to really get to know him and therefore provided an important first foray into a blogging conversation—and through that, an experience of him as a member of their audience. Getting to know Harley also provided the fuel for our student blog writers' fire—the fuel of information. Skillful writers use pertinent information to help them with invoking and addressing an audience (Ede & Lunsford, 1984). An *addressed audience* "refers to those actual or real-life people who read a discourse" while an *invoked audience* refers to an audience "called up or imagined by the writer" (Ede & Lunsford, 1984, p. 156). The newly gained knowledge about Harley as audience helped our bloggers shrink the distance between the invoked and addressed audience by addressing Harley in their blog correspondence with him. Still, even if young writers know *what* their readers want to read, they don't always know *how* to present it to them. How can we help blog writers learn to do that?

Our recommendation is to use the tool of storytelling. The tool of storytelling takes bare and unorganized facts and weaves them into the skein of narrative, sense-making pieces that together form a whole experience. For this to occur, two elements are necessary: *causality* and *resultancy* (Prince, 1982). These terms mean that one event is said to cause another event by having occurred before it (causality), which creates the event that we think of as the result (resultancy). "I went to class, and there I learned a new word." Going to class caused the result of knowledge of a new word. This contains the essence of what is called *syntagmatic* storytelling (Prince, 1982); one thing happened, then another, and the second was the result of the first. Together, they form what are called *narrative syntagms*—that is, the sequence or order of events in a story.

When teaching syntagmatic storytelling, it is also important to introduce students to the concept of the *narrative arc*. A way to do this is to ask students to think of fireworks that rise into the sky—arcing up—and then explode in a climax. A story has to start well but get even more interesting over time. There is an introduction that launches the characters and situations. Then, a *rising action* follows, where the main characters respond to the first events. (Gesturing when you describe this can be helpful.) Then, like the expansion and burst of fireworks, there is a climax—a conflict or *complication*—with which the main character struggles. Following the struggle, there is a *falling action*, in which more minor struggles and resolutions occur. Finally, there is a *conclusion*, or grand finale to the story. All of the strands come together here, and the nature of the ending tells us whether we are witnessing a tragedy, comedy, or drama.

However, for a story to be interesting and attention getting, it must have a *paradigmatic* nature (Todorov, 1981). Paradigmatic storytelling involves relating a narrative using elements that recall the powerful peaks and valleys of all human experience, such as struggle, conflict, love, loss, and yearning. For example, many ancient cultures use the paradigm of the deluge myth, in which the world is submersed in water and everyone dies, except for some small number of "good" people. Think of Noah's Ark.

Harley's experience is a superb example of paradigmatic storytelling, involving classic elements of human experience such as abuse, loss, and the desire to belong and be loved. A former shelter dog, he is rescued just prior to being euthanized. His blog relates a simple tale of a terrible beginning of abuse and neglect followed by a very happy ending with a loving owner.

## Classroom Example

Figure 11.1 (page 110) is a screen capture of Harley, a dog who blogs. The screenshot is followed by a post in which Harley introduces himself to our student bloggers, after which appears our analysis of the Harley story. Lani Ritter Hall is Harley's "ghostwriter." The bracketed words illustrate the use of the paradigmatic and syntagmatic storytelling framework. Visit http://harleyspaws.blogspot.com to read more about Harley.

The story begins with "I have lived with my mom and dad for about three and a half years." This leads to the *once upon a time* story element. Next, we have the technique of foreshadowing, with "I am so glad that they found me." The next sentence, "I had been neglected and abused," is the essence of the introduction—Cinderella before her metamorphosis. "A nice lady came and got me . . . the day they were going to euthanize me" is perhaps the most important sentence, because it contains the elements of the victim hero, Harley, whom a noble lady saves just prior to his execution for crimes he did not commit. This is the complication, with which the protagonist contends. This tale segment is one of the most common—the cruel early circumstances that Harley endures endear him to us and bond him to us emotionally.

## From the paws of --

I give them my absolute all. They are the center of my universe. They are the focus of my love and faith and trust. My mom and dad!

**Sunday, February 4, 2007**
### About Me--
Hi Blogicians,

I'm glad to hear that you liked my picture; I didn't know that my mom had posted my picture until she told me that you had seen it.

My mom said you wanted to know a bit about me, so here goes. I have lived with my mom and dad for about 3 and 1/2 years. I am so glad that they found me. I had been neglected and abused. A nice lady came and got me from the dog warden the day they were going to euthanize me. She took me to her house because she ran a "rescue" for German Shepherds and posted a picture of me on the Internet. That's how my mom found me through Petfinder.com. It's wonderful website that helps with adoptions of dogs all over the U.S. Mom ended up at Dogs Hope and saw my picture and the rest is history!

So Dr. Culek (my veterinarian) thinks I'm 8 years old now. That's getting old for a big dog; do you know how old that is in people years? I weigh 95 pounds now with the good food I get at home (I weighed only 69 pounds when I came to live here). My favorite treats are my homemade dog biscuits, peanut butter, carrots, and pumpernickel bagels.

I love walking in the park with my mom and dad! Usually mom and I go twice every day. When my dad comes we have so much fun; I watch out for him. I like walking in the snow if it isn't too cold. I won't wear my boots and sometimes the snow and ice are too cold. But boy it tastes really good!

I just had a good meal and a big dog biscuit so it's time for a nap-- One quick question, do you have anybody like me at your house?

Til next time,

Posted by Harley at Sunday, February 04, 2007

**4 comments:**

Anonymous said...

> I have a dog in the house and she is a black lab mix and her name is sparky. We found her with a broken leg. she respects me and loves me. she likes ribs, beef bones, and peas. I think of drawing a picture of her on my blog. my blog is at this URL: http://itc.blogs.com/mind13.
>
> from, Michael
>
> February 9, 2007 at 9:42 AM

*Source: L. R. Hall, 2007. Used with permission.*

Figure 11.1: Harley's About Me blog post.

The student bloggers were not only moved by the tale told by Harley, but more importantly, they learned important information about Harley as an audience member himself, which helped them to close some of the gap that had existed between their initial conception of an audience (the invoked audience) and the audience that was actually out there (the addressed audience). They gleaned from Harley's story how to structure and present a compelling story that uses the paradigmatic and syntagmatic storytelling framework. As such, Harley's narrative served as an exemplar of such writing.

The story we share here we wrote for teachers to use in the classroom in response to Harley's introductory story. We follow with an analysis of this story that indicates the elements of a paradigmatic and syntagmatic storytelling within the narrative.

### The Mystery of the Missing Ham

One day, my mother prepared a holiday ham of quite considerable size for our large family and proudly placed it on the centerpiece of the formal dining room table. She left the room for a minute or two to retrieve other "fixins" for the Thanksgiving holiday meal. When she returned, she looked around and didn't see the ham. The plate was there, the centerpiece was there, everything was where it belonged—but no ham. She assumed she had brought it back into the kitchen with her, but it wasn't there, either. She looked everywhere. There had been no noise, no commotion to indicate that someone had removed it, so it became the Mystery of the Missing Ham.

However, not long after, my mother noticed our dog Ashley licking his chops and not touching his kibbles and bits. We have no proof, and we never accused him, but we always suspected that it was Ashley who was the culprit who had secretly and quietly made off with the ham. He had always preferred human food to his dog food. In fact, when our car broke down and we couldn't get to the grocery store, we ordered in a submarine sandwich for Ashley.* Perhaps he thought the ham was just for him. Perhaps he ate it somewhere out of sight of everyone or buried it. We loved him too much to accuse him without proof, though. What do you think happened to the ham?

### Analysis of the story

In our story, the introduction is the appearance of the ham on the holiday table. The complication is, of course, the fact that the ham went missing. The resolution is unknown; although it may be likely that the dog Ashley took the ham, we might expect that he would make noises while retrieving it or eating it, but none were heard. We are therefore unsure. The resolution remains a mystery.

*And what kind of sub was it? Steak and cheese, with extra cheese!

## Your Turn

Storytelling has the ability to help young writers notice and connect to an audience. We list here some suggestions on implementing this strategy in your classroom.

In doing this, we hope that you will find ways to bring storytelling into writing with an audience *beyond* the classroom, utilizing blogging or similar spaces for interactive online communication. You might want to begin by having students "blog" to each other in the classroom only. Then, explain that they will have the exciting opportunity to write to people that they don't necessarily know. This will introduce students to an authentic audience, the audience beyond the student's classroom teacher and his or her peers.

Before you begin blogging with the world at large, review the concepts of an invoked and addressed audience but use language and examples of student correspondence with commenters from student blogs. Walk students through the framework for developing a paradigmatic and syntagmatic story. Mention that it should start out at the chronological beginning and gradually move toward a crescendo (a challenge, issue, or complication of sorts). Complete the task with an explanation of what happens to the main character or characters as they attempt to resolve the issue. Scaffold the understanding of new terminology and the new elements (for example, *rising action* and *falling action*).

It may occur to you at this point that there needs to be a starting point of information, a *jumping-off point* to give your students something to blog about with people around the world before they get to know them. Google and Wikipedia are excellent ways to find out things about almost any country and let students inquire with their newfound audience about something that intrigues them, such as typical foods, dress, language, or fun things that kids in that country do. Ask students to incorporate into their stories what they learned about their readers.

There are alternatives to print-based storytelling, and story development can take many different genres and forms (for example, folktale, personal narrative, essay, or poem). Have your students post photographs or videos they have recorded or audio clips that will enhance their stories. Write Me a Story (www.kidscom.com/create /write/write_howitworks.html), MakeBeliefsComix.com, and the Comic Book Project are just a few examples of the websites that offer writing prompts, storyboards, comic strip printables, and other resources to help students write their own creative stories. Finally, ask your students to publish their stories to their own blogs, and ask them to welcome responses from their readers. Storytelling may be the oldest writing form, and yet it works remarkably well with the latest technology.

Finally, ask them to publish their stories to their own blogs, and ask them to welcome responses from their readers. Storytelling may be the oldest writing form, and yet it works remarkably well with the latest technology.

 **Lynda Williams** teaches introductory web development at the British Columbia Institute of Technology and is learning technology analyst and manager for learning technology with the Teaching and Learning Centre at Simon Fraser University. She is the author of the ten-novel *Okal Rel Saga* and produces the *Reality Skimming* blog. She formerly managed the online literary journal *Reflections on Water*. Lynda holds two postgraduate degrees and has received three awards for community-based innovations in applied technology. To learn more about Lynda's work, visit www.okalrel.org, or follow her on Twitter @okalrelsrv.

# CHAPTER 12

# Engaging the Okal Rel Universe

By Lynda Williams

Fantasy and science fiction can be safe and stimulating places for young adults to experiment with self-expression through writing (Rish, 2011). As a science fiction author, I know this through personal experience and have created the *Reality Skimming* blog (http://okalrel.org/reality-skimming) so that students can share that experience with others. *Reality Skimming* is a WordPress blog maintained by a group who supports and participates creatively in extending the reach of the fictional setting established in the ten-novel series the *Okal Rel Saga* (Okal Rel Universe, 2013).

Because having an audience is important to writers, publication of student work on the *Reality Skimming* blog motivates students to tackle writing objectives like (Aguilar, 2011; Ormrod, 2008):

- Brainstorming to generate ideas
- Demonstrating critical thinking through developing differing opinions
- Working collaboratively to develop material
- Following an editorial process
- Gaining experience with writing for an audience

The lesson described here invites teachers to work up blog entries with their students for publication. WordPress blogs allow for categories of posts. The target category for blog entries for this lesson is Dialogues and features two contributors' side-by-side discussion of a controversial science fiction or fantasy topic.

Students contributing to Dialogues on *Reality Skimming* will be working first with their classmates and teacher as their audience, but they are ultimately writing for a wider audience of science fiction readers and creators interested in the Okal Rel Universe, students in other classes who are working on dialogues, and web users who chance upon the articles when searching for key terms.

# How Do I Do It?

Student publication on *Reality Skimming* follows a four-step process.

### Step One: Decide Content Suitability

Teachers should check for suitability before engaging students with *Okal Rel* content and images. *CM Magazine* recommends it for students in grades 8 and up (Hore, 2007). However, originally written for adults, the dialogue contains sexual politics, invented religions, portrayals of bioengineered variations on human nature, and explorations of culture clash that may offend some readers. The books may be most suitable for upper-division high school classes where popular culture is an acceptable subject domain. (For more on the Okal Rel Universe, see Canada Writes, 2012; Lott, 2009; OkalRelsDaughter, 2013.)

### Step Two: Contact the Blog Administrator

To negotiate submission details, including dates and deliverables, teachers should contact the blog administrator, David Lott (david@okalrel.org), in advance to avoid scheduling disappointment. Classrooms can contact the author, Lynda Williams (lynda@okalrel.org or via http://facebook.com/relskim), for variations on basic article ideas. For example, subject to availability, classes that submit publishable articles could be sent one copy of an *Okal Rel Saga* book and an *Okal Rel Legacies* title (for example, as a donation to the library, as a gift to key student volunteers for the project, for use as classroom books, as awards given out, and so on). Digital copies of passages for debate and "interviews" with characters are also available.

### Step Three: Satisfy Local Requirements for Permission

School policy may require consent forms for the publication of student work. *Reality Skimming* does not require copies of any consent forms but relies on the teacher taking care of local requirements. Teachers are welcome to use a lesson even if publication on *Reality Skimming* isn't possible due to local regulations. For material that is published, where a teacher believes it's meaningful the blog can use pseudonyms or first names only. With regard to copyright, authors of dialogues are welcome to re-use their own compositions in other venues.

### *Step Four: Decide Lesson Emphasis and Focus*

Consider the following lesson prompts for use with the *Okal Rel Saga* or other science fiction or fantasy class writings.

- Identify questions with more than one plausible answer in the tensions and stresses reflected in popular culture portrayals of fantasy or science fiction.

- Write questions with more than one plausible answer.

- Complete a writing exercise after examples that follow the pattern.

- Articulate an original opinion in response to a topic.

- Identify similarities and differences in two different responses to the same topic.

- Express differences of opinion within a respectful framework.

- Review a peer's short essay and make critical suggestions.

- Copyedit a peer's short essay and give constructive feedback.

- Prepare work to meet teacher-set standards for publication on the Internet.

## Classroom Example

The Dialogue category of the *Reality Skimming* blog gives science fiction and fantasy authors a forum to compare their positions on a topic of possible controversy.

Figure 12.1 (page 118) is a dialogue between authors Krista D. Ball (http://kristadball.com) and Lynda Williams. Krista, whose latest book is *The Shadow Guards*, has written more than a dozen novels, four novellas, and a collection of short stories and is the creator of the Irish Devil and Texas vampire series.

To execute the lesson, students take the place of the authors. Students may develop the topics through brainstorming, or the teacher might select suitable questions.

## Your Turn

To help you decide whether the exercise described would be a high-interest means of achieving your learning objectives for brainstorming, critical thinking, working through editorial processes, and sharing work, visit the *Reality Skimming* blog to examine some previous dialogues.

## Dialogues: Perspectives from two authors of SF on Dark & Light.

**Topic:** Dark & Light in SF

**Krista D. Ball** tells lies for a living, according to her mother. She is the author of several short stories, novellas, and novels. Krista incorporates as much historical information into her fiction as possible, mostly to justify her B.A. in British History. Krista enjoys all aspects of the writing and publishing world, and has been a magazine intern, co-edited four RPG books, self-published several short stories and a novella series, and has been a slush reader for a small Canadian press. Whenever she gets annoyed, she blows something up in her fiction. Regular readers of her work have commented that she is annoyed a lot.

**Lynda Williams** is the author of the Okal Rel Saga originally published by Edge Science Fiction and Fantasy and the publisher behind Reality Skimming Press. *Part 10: Unholy Science* will conclude the series in 2014. Lynda's work features larger than life characters contending with radically different attitudes to sex and social control surrounding space warfare and bio-science. Drop into the scene at Reality Skimming Press at http://facebook.com/relskim. Lynda works in learning technology and teaches applied computing.

### 1) What's your position on dark and light in human nature?

**Krista:** Many people like to think of humans as inherently good creatures. We have the capabilities for such kindness and compassion that, underneath our dark natures, there must be something that makes us want to be good. I do not believe this. I look at the world and see a struggle between good and evil, what is right and what is selfish, and the disregard for humanity. Unless raised to be compassionate, caring, and an upstanding member of the global community, people need to be taught how to be such individuals. It's no wonder that fiction reflects that darkness.

**Lynda:** I discovered the depths of man's inhumanity to man as a previously innocent teenager by joining Amnesty International and volunteering with a crisis centre. I've been working on coming to terms with it ever since, because my gut reaction to darkness is to fight it. How to be sure it's really darkness and to what extent one personally can or should fight back are details I'm still working on. Theoretically, at least, I finally found the math to support my instincts in a biography of the statistician who uncovered the mechanics of why a sense of ethics is the only non-genetic trait that can be selected for on the basis of group dynamics -- provided the ethical group is in competition with unethical ones. Which is fascinating when one looks at the way bad guys are so essential to a good story in SF. The book is The Price of Altruism by Oren Harman.

*Source: Krista D. Ball and Lynda Williams. Used with permission.*

Figure 12.1: Perspectives of two science fiction authors on dark and light.

Consider the following steps, and do some or all depending on your lesson outcomes. For example, if generating ideas in collaboration with a peer is the most important objective, you might dispense with the editorial processes beyond the initial draft. But if working on getting from concept to publishable work is the goal that attracted you to this lesson, you might want to prepare prompts like the following in advance and assign them to students.

- Ask students to name well-known science fiction or fantasy stories and identify controversial ideas in them. For example:

- Should people use science to make human beings smarter?

- Should artificial intelligences (AIs) have human rights?

- What if AIs don't respect our rights? (This question is as old as Frankenstein's Monster!)

- Are there universal ethics all cultures should abide by or should right and wrong always be judged in cultural context?

- Pair students up to brainstorm a question. Encourage them to pick something they have differing opinions about. For example, one student thinks we should change our genetic makeup to improve intelligence, but the other student thinks this would be hazardous.

- Encourage students to share their ideas in a larger group or with the whole class to refine their arguments. If desirable, allow students to switch partners or revise their topics based on feedback. (This is the substantive editing phase of the editorial process.)

- Assign pairs of students to write:

  - A bio each of about a hundred words, which can be real or fictional, if students are using a made-up name or adopting a persona

  - An opinion each of one to two hundred words addressing the controversial question

- Have students peer review their work to make improvements. (This is the copyediting stage of the process.)

- Collect and share finished work in whichever way you've decided. For example, have them:

  - Make a booklet of the finished dialogues and distribute to each student as a PDF by email

  - Put the finished work on the school's intranet for internal sharing beyond the classroom

  - Send all submissions that meet the lesson's standards for publication to the *Reality Skimming* blog for publication

  - Decide what to submit for publication on the *Reality Skimming* blog

For writing to be meaningful and relevant, students need authentic reasons for writing and an authentic writing audience. In many instances, teachers are the only readers of students' writing; however, this does little to help students develop an awareness of audience and purpose for their writing. By engaging in blogs like *Reality Skimming*, students can plan, organize, and write for an authentic audience.

# PART V | Collaborative Writing

Writing is usually perceived as a solitary activity. However, more and more teachers are recognizing that writing is often a collaborative venture that contains significant benefits for students. Kenneth Bruffee (1973, 1984) is credited with developing collaborative writing instruction as a pedagogical practice. From a theoretical perspective, this adheres to a sociocultural view of literacy in which reading and writing are social and cultural practices (Schultz, 1997).

*Collaborative writing* can encompass a range of formats. Usually, it means students are composing and crafting a piece of writing in pairs or groups. Students work together from the initial brainstorming to submitting a final piece of writing (Kittle & Hicks, 2009). Research finds that collaborative writing can be very beneficial for students (Rish & Caton, 2011; Schultz, 1997). Collaborative peer groups can serve as scaffolds for students when learning specific writing strategies or when providing constructive responses (Graham et al., 2012). The National Council of Teachers of English (2008b) recommends collaboration as a means for students to develop an "understanding of voice in writing" (p. 5).

While there are many benefits to collaboration, educators have also highlighted some of the concerns and tensions surrounding collaborative writing. Students must learn how to work as a group and manage responsibilities in terms of authorship, roles, responsibilities, and deadlines. Despite these concerns, the advantages of collaborative writing are important enough that teachers should consider how to use this pedagogical practice.

Technology continues to change the ways in which we write collaboratively. Much of this book, for instance, was written with Google Docs. At any one point in time, all three editors could be online and editing the same document, regardless of our physical location in the world. In classes we teach, we also often use wikis. We give students a topic and ask them to define that topic. However, they must all negotiate the same document using the wiki.

Such tools are useful in shaping and enabling our pedagogical strategies of collaboration in writing. More importantly, these technologies have value because they are helping to shape how writing is changing and becoming more collaborative. Educators using collaborative writing strategies with technology are not only informing the writing process but are also giving students access to 21st century skills they will later need in the workforce.

Laurie O. Campbell introduces this section by offering insights into how technology can provide collaborative writing opportunities. Michael S. Mills follows in chapter 14 with a demonstration of how students become engaged in multiple forms of media through digital content curation—the process of collecting, customizing, and sharing digital information. Jenifer Salter Thornton concludes the section in chapter 15 with a description of a specific instructional approach—the 4E Wiki Writing Model—to help students have a deeper level of understanding of writing and content.

 **Laurie O. Campbell** is a visiting lecturer of instructional design and educational technology for the Department of Educational and Human Sciences at the University of Central Florida. Her interests include graphic organizers, the use of emerging technologies in instruction, and The One Minute Video Project, a video teaching strategy. Her research focus seeks to answer how visuals impact and effect learning.

# CHAPTER 13

# Using Technology for Collaborative Writing

By Laurie O. Campbell

Twenty-first century skills and college-readiness standards are replete with references to collaboration and communication (Partnership for 21st Century Skills, 2013). Educators at every level are expected to integrate collaboration and communication in all subject areas. Collaborative writing mediated through a variety of technologies is one way to teach students these skills. While collaboration may not be a tested outcome, the skills they practice in a collaborative writing assignment can benefit students later in college and in the workplace.

As defined in this chapter, collaborative writing is writing between collaborators for the purpose of creating a new work, such as a report, manuscript, poem, rap, song, or even graphic organizer. For the sake of this chapter, collaborative writing is *not* a situation in which a teacher assigns each student a section or portion of the writing. It is not the type of writing in which one person has more editorial responsibility than another. Rather, it is one piece of writing to which all the writers contribute their thoughts, words, and research at every stage of the writing process. It is the type of writing in which the authorship of the work is difficult to ascertain, because each collaborator contributed to the final product all along the way. The collaborative writing discussed throughout the chapter is mediated through the use of web-based cloud applications or programs. These include:

- **Cacoo** (http://cacoo.com), a collaborative diagramming and drawing tool that allows users to chat together while developing word or writing maps, Venn diagrams, and common text

- **Etherpad** (http://etherpad.org), an open-source, online editor that facilitates collaborative writing

- **Florida Institute for Human and Machine Cognition CmapTools** (www.ihmc.us/cmaptools.php and http://cmap.ihmc.us), digital tools used to create concept maps and to collaboratively develop ideas

- **Google Drive** (http://drive.google.com), a robust, online collaborative and synchronous suite of office tools

- **Google Maps** (http://maps.google.com), a web-mapping application that can be annotated and synchronized collaboratively

- **Google Sites** (http://sites.google.com), a website development program on which multiple people can collaborate synchronously

- **Lucidchart** (www.lucidchart.com), an effective tool when you are trying to have students explain or diagram a process

- **MeetingWords** (http://meetingwords.com), a simple but highly functional online text editor that highlights each person's written contribution in a different color

- **MindMeister** (www.mindmeister.com), a collaborative brainstorming tool that allows users in different locations to brainstorm with each other

- **Pirate Pad** (http://piratepad.ca), an online text editor similar to MeetingWords, in which a user shares the URL with other potential collaborators

- **Popplet** (http://popplet.com), an online concept-mapping service and visual brainstorming tool that works on both the web and on an iPad

- **Prezi** (www.prezi.com), a nonlinear web-based presentation software that fosters collaboration in creating and presenting information

- **PrimaryPad** (http://primarypad.com), an online text editor that even young students can use collaboratively

- **PrimaryWall** (http://primarywall.com), a digital bulletin board for contributors to post "sticky notes" for each other

- **TitanPad** (http://titanpad.com), a collaborative pad, like Meeting-Words and Pirate Pad, that can be started immediately and uses eight author highlighting colors

Visit **go.solution-tree.com/technology** for live links to these resources.

Before technological advancements, geographical location limited most collaborative writing, and participants' contributions occurred in parallel rather than simultaneous time. However, with the continual iteration of cloud computing and mobile multimedia devices like the iPad, iPod touch, Microsoft Surface Tablet, touchscreen laptops, and Kindle Fire HD (along with the ever-growing assortment of free online collaborative writing tools), collaborative writing methods, models, and strategies are expanding. The simultaneous nature of these growing technologies has the potential to change what we formally understood as collaborative writing.

Serial writing, compiled writing, and co-authored writing are types of collaborative writing (Haring-Smith, 1994). Serial writing includes various collaborators contributing to the same writing with little regard for continuity. For instance, three writers may each complete one section or paragraph of writing. A fourth person gathers the individual's contributions and distributes the completed writing. Individuals are only concerned about their own contributions. In a compiled writing, like a book with authored chapters, contributors are identified and revisions are completed by the contributor. Each compilation adds to the whole. An editor may weave the chapter together for the purpose of continuity. Co-authored writing is writing in which it is difficult to ascertain each collaborator's contributions. Each person contributes at the word, sentence, paragraph, and section level. The ownership of the writing may or may not be equal.

Collaborative writing is grounded in Vygotsky's (1978) sociocultural theory and in the computer-supported collaborative learning approach (Koschmann, 1996). Vygotsky suggests that to make meaning of content, students need to be a part of a community. Further, he purports that to learn, students need to be active in their own learning. In a computer-supported collaborative-learning approach, teachers mediate the community's social interactions through technology (for example, using chat screens, digital whiteboards, Skype, Twitter, or text), and the technology itself is the common means to construct knowledge (for example, creating a Google map and presentation to identify where the branches of the U.S. government physically reside in Washington, DC, and then using a Prezi to explain how the branches function together) (Stahl, Koschmann, & Suthers, 2006).

Research continues to grow regarding collaborative learning and writing using technological advances.

## How Do I Do It?

Because geographical location no longer limits collaboration, collaborative writing can be a global activity. It can occur among students in another classroom in the same school, across town, or on the other side of the world. Teachers can pair or group students and then assign them a document or virtual space to use (such as Google Drive, Etherpad, PrimaryPad, or Microsoft SkyDrive).

The students are then given the writing assignment and begin writing. Writing can take place synchronously or asynchronously, as the document automatically saves each user's contribution to the final product. As writers read the emerging work, they can make modifications that other collaborative writers are able to view at the same time. When pairs or groups have questions for each other during the process, they can use the comments and notes feature within the document, or they can convey them in an instant message, or call from computer to computer. All of these functionalities are free when using an online virtual space like Google Drive. The student writers then complete the assignment and turn in a shared link or PDF of the file that they worked on together. If they are using Google Docs or Google Presentations, which makes their work easy to access for review and assessment purposes, students can effortlessly share the document with the teacher. Conversely, the teacher can review and offer feedback for the students to note and use as a basis for revisions.

Collaborative writing is not limited to completing a manuscript, book, or paper to be read for a grade or for publication purposes. Students can create or complete presentations, create rubrics, conduct book chats, facilitate conversations, and develop graphic organizers. The options are almost endless. Graphic organizers are a practical collaborative writing assignment that provide a framework for students to connect known knowledge to unknown knowledge (Ausubel, 1960). Graphic organizers can vary as a preinstruction activity, an activity during instruction to classify information, or a postinstruction activity or assessment. Using a graphic organizer as a collaborative writing assignment could mean providing students with a template or asking students to create their own organizer.

## Classroom Example

The types of assignments that teachers can assign as a collaborative writing exercise are vast and typically content related. For instance, a high school geometry teacher may post a graphic of a problem and then ask the students in two separate locations to solve it collaboratively and write a rationale for their answer and perhaps also write out the steps they used to solve the problem. Fourth-grade teachers in the same locale could assign "citizen scientists" to write a field study of their observations of the same type of area in each of their locales. An English language arts teacher might ask students to create a presentation about a text the students had read. By creating a presentation together, the students can collaboratively give vision to their writing. Fourth-grade teachers could have their students become citizen scientists by, for example, observing bird migrations, calculating rain totals, or examining pollen. The citizen scientists would then record their field observations and share with each other through a collaborative program or website.

Students in two different geographical locations might watch a video about hammerhead sharks and create a brick summary frame. A brick summary frame is a graphic organizer that looks like a brick wall. Users answer questions in each brick to build the wall and create understanding. The students then access their digital workspace and open the assigned brick summary frame (figure 13.1) and complete it together. When they do not agree on their rationale for choosing their selection, they discuss the issue until they reach a consensus. Each person in the collaboration has an equal voice in and responsibility to the words committed to the digital paper.

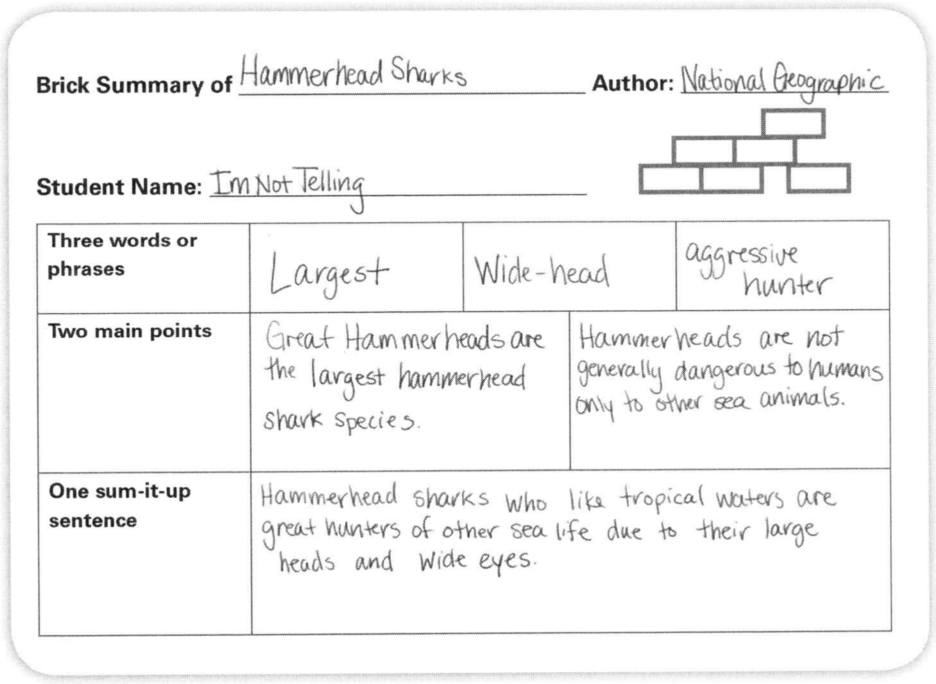

**Brick Summary of** Hammerhead Sharks **Author:** National Geographic

**Student Name:** I'm Not Telling

| | | | |
|---|---|---|---|
| **Three words or phrases** | Largest | Wide-head | aggressive hunter |
| **Two main points** | Great Hammerheads are the largest hammerhead shark species. | Hammerheads are not generally dangerous to humans only to other sea animals. | |
| **One sum-it-up sentence** | Hammerhead sharks who like tropical waters are great hunters of other sea life due to their large heads and wide eyes. | | |

*Source: Laurie O. Campbell. Used with permission.*

Figure 13.1: Sample brick summary frame.

Collaborative writing can broaden global awareness, as was the case in the Cultural Crossovers Project. Its aim was to create a new virtual community between schools from different countries. During the 2012–2013 school year, eighth-grade students from Malaysia and the United States engaged in a collaborative writing adventure and created the website Cultural Crossovers. Students from both nations collaborated locally (within their school) and virtually (with the school in the other country) to write about cultural aspects of each country that they considered important. Together, the students from both countries wrote about topics like holidays, slang words, school tuition, social networking, and field trips. They enriched the writings on their collaborative website with images and video. The teachers involved in this successful project developed the collaborative writing assignment out of a desire to provide students with a global learning experience and to foster global communication and understanding (Nexus International School, 2013).

Another example of technology-mediated collaborative writing includes graduate teachers in a technology teacher certification program who used Google Docs as a means to facilitate a book chat. The teachers interacted in groups of three or four and answered a series of questions related to the book. The teachers found that they were able to develop their own thoughts more fully as they read other responses and left questions for other collaborators. One aspect of their book chat was to create a collaborative conclusion statement in thirty words or less for each chapter. Students worked both synchronously and asynchronously to craft these statements. The collaborators attributed the benefits they derived from the assignment to the method of collaborative writing. These included feeling support from others during their book chat project, establishing long-term collegial relationships, and finding a means to broaden their professional development. One teacher from this project went on to adapt the activity with her own professional learning network.

## Your Turn

Creating a collaborative writing assignment begins with looking at the expected outcome of your lesson. Once you have determined that outcome, you can choose the type of collaborative writing and the appropriate application. Next, you assign collaborators, whether they are in your class, your school, or in other schools. The teacher then develops directions, expectations, and rubrics for the collaborative assignment.

Collaborative writing is beneficial when there is understanding between contributors (Cerratto Pargman, 2003). Communicating guidelines prior to writing is important—whether through instant messaging, in-application comments, or a shared space with voice or video capabilities. The collaborators should meet each other, either face to face or virtually, to establish parameters and expectations.

One suggested practice for creating a collaborative document is for each user to use his or her own designated font color. For instance, if Henry, Krista, Brianna, and Jake are authoring a research paper, Henry's font color could be green, Krista's purple, Brianna's orange, and Jake's blue. Assigning font colors enables collaborators to recognize areas in which they need to edit and contribute. Using one's own font color is another layer to tracking changes, which 50 percent of collaborative writers found to be a beneficial feature of collaborative writing software (Noel & Robert,

2004). When students complete their collaborative writing, they can turn the entire text back to the standard font color of black.

When revising in a collaborative fashion, it may be a good idea to not delete unwanted words and phrases from a document. Instead, cut the words from the current location and paste them at the end of the document under the subheading "Deleted Words." Keeping the currently non-needed words until all students complete their revisions avoids rewriting content. By following this protocol, words are not totally lost; they are still available to use in another portion of the document, if appropriate. Other suggestions include making sure collaborators know how to use the collaborative application prior to launching the collaborative writing activity and ensuring that students know the assignment expectations (Marjanovic, 1999). These suggestions may seem self-evident, but they are foundational to the writers being able to effectively communicate with other collaborators and ultimately provide a successful collaborative learning experience.

Once the teacher establishes and defines guidelines, expectations, and assessments, the collaborative writing assignment can begin. I recommend that the writing groups share their collaborative writing with the teacher from the beginning of the assignment. Teachers are then able to pop in on the writing to encourage, challenge, or contribute guidance and support to the students throughout the writing process. Engaging in a collaborative writing assignment mediated through technology provides all students with equal opportunities to interact with other learners in an authentic manner despite geography and time zones while giving them practice in improving their 21st century skills.

**Michael S. Mills** is an assistant professor of teaching and learning at the University of Central Arkansas. He has served nineteen years as a public high school teacher, literacy specialist, and university professor. His research focus is literacy development and the practical uses of educational technology, particularly on the use of collaborative tools to better engage students and design strategies for effectively integrating mobile devices in the classroom. He is an SXSWedu, International Society for Technology in Education, and Society for Information Technology and Teacher Education presenter and has been recognized as an Apple Distinguished Educator. To learn more about Michael's work, visit www.AquiAmigo.com, or follow him on Twitter @AquiAmigo.

# CHAPTER 14

# Digital Content Curation

By Michael S. Mills

Digital content curation—the process of collecting, customizing, and sharing digital information—gives students an opportunity to become engaged learners literate in multiple forms of media. Digital content curation incorporates several aspects of effective literacy instruction, allowing students to expand their understanding of multimodal texts as they consume, create, and collaborate.

The Internet's vast, dynamic resources have prompted many to consider the importance of increasing the focus on multiple literacies in preparing students for success in contemporary society (Lankshear & Knobel, 2003; Leander, 2008). In the Internet information culture, literacy spans multimodality not only in the form of text, images, and audiovisual elements but also in the form of dynamic features that redefine themselves based on a user's input and interaction with others through social media. The drawback of the Internet is the enormous volume of information and the general lack of focused resource platforms that are flexible, student-centered, and socially interactive and that facilitate appropriate levels of multimodal literacy instruction (Rosenbaum, 2011).

Digital curation helps frame an inquiry-based process geared toward student engagement, collaboration, and multimodal literacy comprehension (Barton & Hamilton, 1998; Lewis & Fabos, 2005). Digital curation is the sifting and aggregating of Internet and other digital resources into a manageable collection of what teachers and students find relevant, personalized, and dynamic. It retains the constantly updated components of the Internet while providing a repository that is easily accessible and usable. As teachers, we can develop dynamic, inter-active, social resources that supplant mundane textbooks containing outdated information. Additionally, students can develop their own customized resources, drawing from all aspects of the Internet to build their own anthology of videos, news feeds, tweets, and whatever else is pertinent and engaging and supporting their inquiry-based projects while allowing personalization of the curriculum.

## How Do I Do It?

Teachers must provide authentic digital content projects and assessments so that students are fully engaged and collaborate on material that matters to them. The process of curating digital content offers students the chance for engagement and collaboration as well as the chance to personalize, customize, and share news and information. There are six steps to thoughtful digital curation.

### Step One: Consume and Comprehend

The first step in selecting and customizing digital content to curate is to consume it. Consuming digital content means to find content on the web and attempt to understand the content's central and underlying messages. The intent here is not only to find and collect specific content but also to gain as much information as one can in multiple formats on a variety of related subjects, so that a reader can form a broad understanding of a topic. This facilitates the contextualization of the topic later in the process. It is critical that teachers prioritize multimodal comprehension strategies throughout the curation process. Examples of efficient media consumption resources include mobile apps like Flipboard and Zite and multiplatform resources like Twitter, Feedly, Pocket, Instapaper, and YouTube.

### Step Two: Aggregate

To aggregate content, teachers and students must first define the purpose for the curated site—the purpose serves as a filter for sifting through discovered content—and then select a web resource that allows for the collection of salient examples of multimedia news and information. A variety of web resources and mobile applications can facilitate the aggregation process; select the ones that best accommodate efficient mining and collection of information to be curated and the stockpiling of this information in a format that will lend itself to easy filtering and customization. Examples of aggregation resources include Padlet, Pocket, Evernote, Pinterest, edu-Clipper, Learnist, LiveBinders, and Blendspace.

### Step Three: Evaluate

To effectively filter what your class will publish and share, the curator first antic-ipates the needs of the audience and selects materials that are useful, timely, and credible. Being selective goes to the heart of minimizing information overload, filtering only that which is remarkable and useful. Curators must also meet the needs of a diverse audience by ensuring users can easily access and comprehend collected resources within the context of the topic and that the material is relevant and timely.

### Step Four: Contextualize and Repurpose

During contextualization, the curator customizes the content for the intended audience, since curated content is meant to be shared and is meant to engage. This customization requires the curator to prioritize, reformat, and edit the aggregated content. To achieve accessibility, readability, and engagement, the curator must also sometimes rewrite the titles of articles to make them more accurate or appealing. Every element (visual, print, and so on) must complement every other component in the digital content to maintain a coherent flow. Users of some aggregation and curation sites (most notably Padlet) can supplement individual posts and resources with additional multimedia and text. For example, if a teacher posts a web clip highlighting a particular author, students could add audio and video files, as well as other document-based files to that one resource to better contextualize and repurpose the material.

### Step Five: Prioritize and Reformat

Prioritization gives the curator the opportunity to rank content based on the criteria for the assignment and within the limitations of the particular curation site. Prioritization of digital content frequently involves reordering it in an object-based environment. This means curators and users interact with each artifact, each nugget of information, as an object that they can manipulate and move. To maximize reader engagement, curators should prioritize and reorder content by juxtaposing high-priority images toward the top and center and then place subsequent content below in a hierarchical fashion (Nielsen & Pernice, 2010).

### Step Six: Share and Collaborate

Users can share curated content through emails, Facebook likes, tweets, or posts on a variety of other social networking sites, blogs, and wikis. Digital curation is an effective exercise in dynamic collaboration, because the nature of the literacy shifts with each collaboration, and meaning can alter dramatically as more users add text, multimedia, or interactive content. Because of this, shifting content may make it difficult or even impossible for the teacher to evaluate student understanding. The impetus for the teacher, then, is to define mastery of the instructional objective in terms of the process as well as the content, rather than in terms of the content alone.

The digital curation process takes many weeks to implement and should be ongoing throughout the entire term of the course, so students will be able to see how dynamic and varied the media we consume every day are. After students begin to embrace the process of collecting, repurposing, and sharing multimodal resources to facilitate their learning, they may even begin to wonder why that bound textbook is even on their desk.

## Classroom Example

My students curate their own collection of web-based class resources. Even though students are still required to purchase a textbook for the course, the collection of class resources supplements the textbook as a repository of theories, articles on current events, and practical strategies that the curator and his or her classmates continually update throughout the semester. This collaboration increases the value of the resources, as students constantly consume, scrutinize, and tailor them to meet the needs of the class.

Although curation can be done within a wiki or a blog, my students prefer two curation resources: Padlet and Blendspace. Both of these services have a simple method for adding multimedia (that is, images, video, and audio) and customizing layout, unlike wikis and blogs, which students feel are too entrenched in a text-based style. Blendspace, in particular, has been very popular because it allows users to create lessons centered on a certain topic and then fill the lesson with text-based notes, images, documents, audio recordings, video, and web clippings (see figure 14.1).

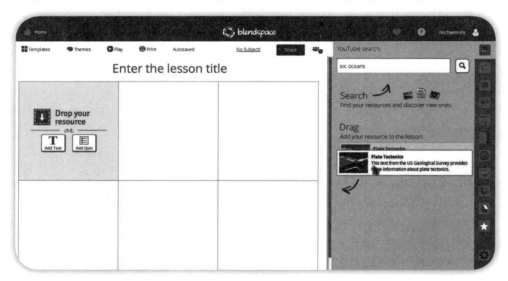

*Source: Blendspace (https://blendspace.com). Used with permission.*

Figure 14.1: Blendspace's add content options.

Here's how the process unfolds in a typical curation project. First, have students research and read as much as they can. In addition to the web resources you suggest, consider letting students explore sites outside the mainstream. Typically, I ask them to sign up for Google News Alerts, mark relevant and engaging YouTube videos as favorites, and browse news and information sites through Feedly and Flipboard (on a smartphone, tablet, or any computer), as well as through their own web browsing.

The next step is the aggregation (collection) of resources. Notably, teachers should encourage student curators to collect a variety of dynamic multimedia, like text notes, web clips, audio files, videos, and images. So far, the one aggregation resource that allows for all levels of the curation process is Blendspace. However, there are a number of other options for adding limited content, including email and browser extensions.

Blendspace allows users to reorder content (resources) by priority and allows for sequential or selective viewing. Selective viewings give the user complete flexibility in the placement of individual resources.

Students should have the opportunity throughout the entire term to evaluate the collected resources for usefulness, timeliness, and credibility. Rather than allowing students themselves to remove resources that they feel do not meet the criteria the teacher set, students should post comments to the resources within the lesson. The rest of the class, as well as the instructor, will then have multiple perspectives regarding the value of the resources within the lesson and can decide later if the content needs to be repurposed, contextualized, or deleted.

Students next share their suggestions for modifying or reclassifying springs in a number of ways, ranging from traditional face-to-face classroom discussions to tweets, emails, or comments within the lessons. The critical aspect of this step is to have a collaborative effort toward making sure the collected resources are relevant, accurate, and engaging. In addition to allowing written comments for lessons, Blendspace allows users to post audio resources.

Besides being able to share lessons by email, Twitter, and Facebook, teachers can also embed lessons in Edmodo, a popular learning management system; Facebook; or any other website that accepts embedded codes. Instructors can also share a QR image that links directly to lessons, which allows instructors to post the image in a variety of ways.

## Your Turn

If permissible, have students create their own Blendspace student accounts. A student account allows students to both follow teacher-created lessons and also create their own lessons. Accounts are free but require students to either log in with an email address or link to a Facebook, Twitter, Google, or Yahoo! account. Check with school officials to make sure students can use a school email address for this or if other methods of linking social media accounts are acceptable.

There are two options for having students curate their resources through a Blendspace account.

1.  If students are permitted to create their own Blendspace accounts, add students as *contributors* to a class-managed lesson. Although you will be the primary owner of this lesson, student contributors will be able to add, modify, and delete resources within the lesson. Students will be able to access this shared lesson through their own Blendspace account.

2.  If students are not able to create their own Blendspace accounts, their access to the curated lesson will be limited to viewing content and adding comments. So, the alternative is to share the teacher-managed account login information with students. Notably, this could be troublesome, as there is no tracking feature enabled to ensure the integrity of the lesson.

As the focus of this assignment is to determine understanding of digital curation and multimodal resource evaluation, the assessment of this project should focus on the process of curation rather than mastery of the content. This is best facilitated by an open approach to curation—allowing students much latitude, providing them with clear guidelines for resource evaluation and strategies for repurposing text and other media, and assessing them with a rubric that focuses on the process rather than the content of the curated sites.

 **Jenifer Salter Thornton** is an independent consultant and instructor at Texas A&M University–San Antonio. Previously, she worked as an assistant professor in early childhood and elementary education at the University of Texas at San Antonio, where she developed and taught a broad range of courses that focused on differentiated instruction. Jenifer is a former classroom teacher with experience in both general education and inclusive classroom settings. Her current research and instructional focus center on differentiated instructional practices for in-service and preservice teachers.

# CHAPTER 15

# The 4E Wiki Writing Model

By Jenifer Salter Thornton

For many of the digital natives sitting in our classrooms, technology is a relevant and meaningful way to explore and make sense of the world around them. Not every lesson calls for the inclusion and use of technology, but there are times when it makes sense and can facilitate learning, enhance skill sets, and promote deeper understanding. When combined with a specific writing model known as the 4E Wiki Writing Model (Thornton, 2013), wiki applications can help students reach deeper levels of understanding about the writing process and develop content knowledge.

So what exactly is a wiki? A *wiki* is a web application that allows people to collaboratively add, modify, or delete content in real time. One of the largest and most well-known wikis is of course Wikipedia. Thousands of people all over the world have contributed to the content found there. Originally adapted from the Hawaiian phrase *wiki wiki*, meaning to hurry, wikis are included as part of the web 2.0 technologies that incorporate other applications, such as blogs and podcasts (Wheeler & Wheeler, 2009).

Wikis incorporate a familiar Microsoft Word–based, user-friendly interface that allows different writers to insert written content as well as formatting and design features like images and graphics, audiovisual components, and hyperlinks on the page. Students who are familiar with Microsoft Word can quickly become familiar with the wiki format, and once they have some practice and experience with the wiki space, they will be ready to begin using the wiki to house their writing. Users can save and immediately update changes, so wiki pages reflect the most up-to-date user edits.

Mary Engstrom and Dusty Jewett (2005) argue that wikis by nature function as collaborative environments. Furthermore, they have the capacity to promote a cooperative or collective intelligence, in which the sum of what users produce collectively brings more conceptual understanding than what they could produce independently—potentially creating what Mark Seaman (2008) refers to as *communities of practice*. Seaman (2008) explains that a "community of practice not only shares knowledge but also creates, organizes, revises, and passes on knowledge among the members of the community" (pp. 271–272). It could be argued that communities of practice may well emerge as students collaborate and work with one another throughout the writing process.

Integrating wikis into course content can also add a layer of rigor to writing assignments. Aaron Doering, Richard Beach, and David O'Brien (2007) suggest that the utilization of these tools requires writers to think both "*multimodally* and *semiotically*" (p. 43) throughout the process as they consider not only the actual text that they will include in their final product but also the media, audio, visual, and graphic components to include to help them share the information they have learned. In addition, if students use wikis to house their writing, they must also consider how to format their digital pages in ways that most effectively communicate their information.

Wikis also have the capacity to effectively engage students in the learning process by supporting differentiated instructional practices. Carol Ann Tomlinson (1999) refers to differentiation as ways in which educators vary the content they teach, the processes they use to teach and have students investigate course content, and the products that students generate that reflect their knowledge and understanding of the content. When integrated into course content in purposeful ways and combined with a specific writing model like the 4E Wiki Writing Model, wikis have the potential to facilitate differentiated instruction—especially when combined with opportunities for choice.

Consider a fifth-grade teacher who is beginning an integrated unit on the Civil War. She decides to incorporate the use of a wiki throughout the unit as a means by which students synthesize and present information that they gather about different facets of the Civil War. She provides students with an extensive list of different people and events associated with the Civil War and asks them to select one of the topics (or propose a related topic) on which to concentrate their research. Each student contributes to the class wiki by developing his or her own wiki page, which will include a written synthesis of their topic. The completed class wiki includes each student's page and provides a multidimensional overview of topics associated with war.

In this way, the teacher is able to differentiate the content students will focus on, and as students begin to investigate their selected topics, she can further differentiate by varying the processes or activities that students engage in to help them to make sense of the content. The incorporation of a wiki into this unit allows for differentiation in the types of products students produce. As they develop their wiki pages, they make choices regarding the written and visual information that they incorporate, selecting from among various fonts, pictures, videos, hyperlinks, colors, and audio tracks.

# How Do I Do It?

One way for students to better structure their writing experience is through the use of the 4E Wiki Writing Model. This model, which is also useful for facilitating collaboration, takes students through four distinct writing steps.

### Step One: Establish a Topic

In the first step, students work on establishing or creating a topic that correlates to the overarching subject area selected by the teacher. I typically give students a choice of topics to choose from, but they can also be assigned. Once the topic has been chosen, students begin to research and write about it. They find and review current and relevant resources including books, journals, webpages, and newspaper and magazine articles. They then synthesize this information and begin writing on the actual wiki page. The goal for this step is for students to create two or three well-developed paragraphs, citing all of the resources they used. (Of course this can be modified to better fit the needs of your particular group of students.)

### Step Two: Extend and Expand Another Student's Wiki Page

In the second step, students temporarily switch from working on their individual writing topic to extending and expanding on another student's writing topic from step one. This enables students to become familiar with a topic established by one of their peers and to further that student's initial research by adding information to the wiki page entry and continuing the writing their classmate began.

### Step Three: Elaborate and Embellish a Third Wiki Page

In the third step, students elaborate on and embellish on the writings contained on a third, different wiki page. During this step, students read through the writing the previous two authors of this page established and extend and elaborate on it further by adding embellishments that provide additional perspective and context. These embellishments might include Internet-based videos, websites, blogs, or journal articles that students either embed within the wiki page or provide hyperlinks to. Students are also encouraged to add graphics, images, pictures, music, tables, or charts to the page. The choices and selections students make regarding the inclusion of these wiki components and even the decisions they make in terms of text formatting, color, and font tie into a differentiated learning model and allow educators ways to vary the instructional process and provide choices to students.

### *Step Four: Edit and Complete the Original Page*

In the fourth step, students return to the page they originally established and complete their final edits. Students read through all of the information contained on the wiki page and make any edits they feel are necessary to further clarify and strengthen the page. This could include making sure peers have appropriately cited sources; correcting spelling, sentence structure, and grammar usage; deleting or adding words; and making other additions or changes to the text. Students should also consider the effectiveness and readability of the page, including the formatting, layout, font size, and font type. They should ensure that embedded hyperlinks work, videos are accessible, and all of the elements on the page are relevant to the topic. Ultimately, the student who established the topic in the first step has final editorial say regarding the appearance of (and content contained on) the final wiki page.

Unlike traditional writing activities in which the scale of the assignment can overwhelm students, the 4E Wiki Writing Model allows students to work on discrete tasks throughout each of the steps, resulting in a completed paper at the end of the process. The 4E Wiki Writing Model also offers students several benefits that might not otherwise be offered through the use of traditional writing assignments. Throughout the process, students have opportunities to write and collaborate with one another. For many students, this collaboration makes the writing process much more engaging and appealing. Furthermore, collaborative writing promotes an environment in which students may feel more comfortable taking creative risks.

Throughout this process, students are also exposed to multiple facets of the overarching topic as they review and add to the pages of other students. This allows them to consider other information and perspectives that ultimately provide them with a more comprehensive view of the topic. Additionally, as students work through each of the writing steps, we as teachers have opportunities to check over their wiki pages and oversee their writing. This allows opportunities to monitor students' progress and address issues early on and in real time.

## Classroom Example

The 4E Wiki Writing Model is extremely flexible and can be incorporated across grade levels, content areas, and instructional settings. It also provides a nice way for instructors to differentiate for students' strengths, readiness, and interest areas. In my university-level classes, I have replaced most of my traditional written research assignments with wikis used in conjunction with the 4E Wiki Writing Model. At the beginning of each semester, I compile a list of topics and subtopics related to course content. Students are presented with the list and encouraged to choose a topic of interest to them that then serves as the focus of their research and writing. I next introduce students to how the wiki site works and allow them the opportunity to investigate the space before any formal writing takes place. After they are comfortable using the wiki, I present the 4E Wiki Writing Model.

Although I have experimented with different time frames in the past, I generally allow one to two weeks for students to work through each of the steps. I also dedicate a portion of each class to talking through any big issues that I see or hear about and troubleshooting with students. Throughout each of the writing steps, I review the work on each student's wiki page and provide feedback in the form of a rubric or written comments left on their wiki page (figure 15.1; most wiki sites have a comment tool that allows users to communicate with one another on the page). In addition, other students who are working on the wiki page can leave comments recommending additional areas of research or make suggestions they think might be helpful to the page's original author. This allows students the time and the opportunity to correct mistakes, extend understandings, and address any issues they might have throughout the writing process.

| Grading Criteria | Progress | | |
|---|---|---|---|
| **Comprehensiveness** | **Needs Attention** | **On Target** | **Exceeds Target** |
| Entries thoroughly cover necessary information. Entries contribute to a comprehensive wiki page. | Content contributions exclude essential or basic information or several factual errors exist. | Includes essential knowledge about the topic. Subject knowledge appears to be good. | Covers topic in depth with details and examples. Subject knowledge is excellent, and significant contributions are made. |
| **Organization** | **Needs Attention** | **On Target** | **Exceeds Target** |
| Entries are well organized and clear. Ideas are clear, coherent, and reader friendly. Headings and subheadings are used. | No continuity exists between one topic and the next, or entries are difficult to follow. | Most entries are clear and easy to follow. | Content is logically and clearly organized. Entries flow seamlessly with previously written segments, and include headings or subheadings that enhance clarity. |

Continued on next page →

| Grading Criteria | Progress | | |
|---|---|---|---|
| **Grammar and Style** | **Needs Attention** | **On Target** | **Exceeds Target** |
| Good attention paid to APA style.<br><br>Accurate grammar, spelling, and punctuation<br><br>Sources appropriately cited and support wiki content. | Most wiki entries do not follow APA style, or major issues exist with spelling, grammar, or punctuation. | The majority of wiki entries follow APA style. Overall, attention has been paid to the spelling, grammar, and punctuation. | All wiki entries follow APA style. Grammar, spelling, and punctuation are accurate and contribute to the overall understanding of the page. |
| **Hyperlinks and Graphics (3rd Phase Only)** | **Needs Attention** | **On Target** | **Exceeds Target** |
| Images, videos, hyperlinks, and graphics included.<br><br>Colors of font and font style enhance the appearance of the page.<br><br>Hyperlinks and graphics enhance wiki content and assist with understanding. | Fewer than two hyperlinks and graphics have been included on the wiki page, or hyperlinks or graphics do not add to the overall content of the wiki page. | More than two hyperlinks, and graphics have been included on the wiki page. Each adds to the overall content of the wiki page. | Excellent use of font and color on page. There are substantial contributions of graphics, effects, and videos which enhance the content of the wiki page. |
| **Comments for ALL sections (required):** | | | |
| **Comprehensiveness** | | | |
| **Organization** | | | |
| **Grammar and Style** | | | |
| **Hyperlinks and Graphics** | | | |

Your Name: _____ Peer Evaluated: _____

Date: _____Wiki Phase: _____

Figure 15.1: 4E Wiki Writing Model peer-editing rubric.

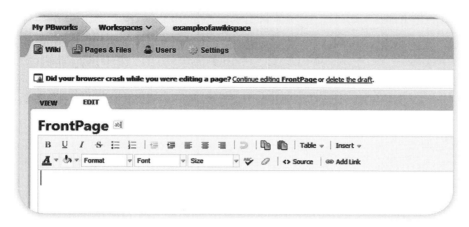

*Source: PBWorks. Used with permission.*

Figure 15.2: A wiki dashboard in Edit mode.

## Your Turn

After you are confident in your abilities, you will need to establish a class wiki and add your students as writers to the site (typically, students should not be administrators or editors of the site). Be sure that the site is private (through the Settings function) and that individuals not affiliated with your class cannot access your wiki. Next, you will need to introduce the wiki to your students. *Wikis in Plain English* (www.commoncraft.com/video/wikis) is a great video resource on wikis. It provides a brief, creative, and informative overview of wikis.

Students will need opportunities to investigate and explore the wiki space before they are expected to create their own pages. You can introduce wiki pages through small-group and whole-group instruction. After your introduction, give students plenty of time to familiarize themselves with the space before introducing the writing component. Before my class writing assignment begins, I usually assign small tasks in which I encourage students to play with our wiki space and explore its different functions. One fun way to do this is by having students add their favorites to the class page—such as books, songs, people, or quotes. Once they upload their favorites, I usually have them practice changing fonts and font colors and include additions such as graphics, music, or other elements. Students could also be allowed to access the wiki space outside of school, which permits additional time in which to explore how the site works.

Before introducing the 4E Wiki Writing Model, you will need to select a course-related topic that provides a range of interrelated subjects for students to research and explore. You will also need to devote some time to thinking through how students will work on their wiki pages. Will students have access to a computer lab where they can work on their pages all at once, or do they have access to laptops at your school? Are there computers in the room that students can use to upload their writing throughout the week? Will students upload writing to their wiki pages as part of their daily homework assignments? There are multiple ways in which to facilitate this type of collaborative assignment, and you will need to select a way that best meets your needs and the needs of your particular group of students.

After students are comfortable with the wiki space and know the topic they are writing about, you can introduce them to the 4E Wiki Writing Model. Be sure to communicate your expectations about the assignment to students and provide them with assignment guidelines and rubrics. It has been my experience that some students will need additional information pertaining to how to edit and evaluate others' work. You will also need to think through peer-editing groups and decide what wiki pages students will add to or edit and the timelines for doing this. Make sure that there is a dedicated writing time each day, and check in with your students as they progress through the steps. Remember, there are many ways to integrate this writing model into your course content. Be flexible, make it your own, and encourage your students to add their own personal touches.

# PART VI | Grammar Instruction

Many teachers struggle with how to teach grammar. Often, teachers teach it in isolation by exposing students to lists of rules that they are expected to learn and apply in their writing. Peter Smagorinsky (2008) claims that "the teaching of grammar apart from speaking and writing is among the most widely employed, yet least effective, practices in the English teacher's repertoire" (p. 159). Additionally, the National Council of Teachers of English (1985) states that repetitive grammar drilling "hinders development of students' oral and written language" (¶1). Furthermore, research confirms the idea that this type of instruction is not only ineffective but also has a negative effect on students' writing (Graham & Perin, 2007c). It becomes difficult for students to understand when and how to use grammar when it is not embedded within writing instruction. However, knowledge of grammar is essential for constructing texts. It is also critical for diverse learners, such as English learners, who must understand the rules and forms of the English language.

Grammar instruction is most meaningful and relevant when teachers embed it within authentic writing instruction. Educators suggest focusing on one or two key concepts at a time through the teaching of minilessons (Gallagher, 2006; Kittle, 2008; Smagorinsky, 2008). Minilessons are short, usually ten-minute-long lessons that provide explicit, targeted instruction. Teachers can preview students' writing to see errors they made consistently and then provide a minilesson that addresses particular mistakes. Students can then use the minilesson to make corrections in their writing. By being selective, teachers can target specific errors students make in their writing and remediate them through instruction, rather than decontextualized worksheets or drills.

In addition, while it is important for students to recognize errors, grammar instruction should also focus on teaching students new syntactic structures so they can compose more sophisticated and interesting sentences (Smagorinsky, 2008). In other words, grammar instruction isn't just about fixing mistakes, it is about learning how to craft good writing. Researchers note that instructional methods that focus on students' writing, "while at the same time enhancing their syntactic skills," are effective for improving the quality of students' writing (Graham & Perin, 2007c, p. 21). This provides opportunities for students to gain awareness of how their attention to grammar and sentence structure enhances their writing.

Technology can support grammar and sentence construction in multiple ways. Traditional strategies focus on helping students become meta-analytic and meta-cognitive about grammar and structure. This happens somewhat automatically in online and desktop word processing programs that underline or highlight incorrect grammatical constructions or words that students spell wrong. Unfortunately, because it happens automatically, students often accept changes or make corrections without really thinking about them. A teacher can model how to work with these features more consciously by showing the acceptance or rejection of grammar changes. Teachers can model practice live or through screen-capture recording programs that students can view later. There are also more futuristic technologies—like the social media and text formatting tools mentioned in this section—that are not ubiquitous but will provide new ways to teach and learn grammar and structure.

In chapter 16, Jooyoung Do explains how data-driven learning can help teachers and students engage in grammar instruction. Youngmin Park, Sarah T. Dunton, and Juan M. Ruiz-Hau document in chapter 17 how social media can enrich pattern poetry. Finally, in chapter 18, Charles A. Vogel describes another unique approach to grammar instruction through visual-syntactic text formatting, which arranges phrases and clauses in a visual manner.

 **Jooyoung Do** is an English-as-a-foreign-language teacher at Songpa Middle School in Seoul, Korea. Her pedagogic and research focus is genre-based writing instruction, syllabus and material design, and pedagogic application of corpus linguistics. She received a master's degree in teaching English as a foreign language at the University of Birmingham, United Kingdom, in 2013.

# CHAPTER 16

# Data-Driven Learning
# for Grammar Classrooms

By Jooyoung Do

To understand the meaning and advantages of data-driven learning (DDL), it is important to know what *corpus* and *corpus linguistics* mean. A corpus refers to "a collection of naturally occurring examples of language" (Hunston, 2002, p. 2). A corpus is usually compiled electronically with large amounts of language pieces collected from a wide range of sources, such as newspapers, books, academic lectures, business meetings, and everyday conversations. Corpus linguistics aims to describe linguistic phenomena by using *corpora* (plural form of *corpus*). The range of sources, however, can vary according to the purpose of the corpus. For example, the British National Corpus (http://corpus.byu.edu/bnc) was built to represent current British English and consists of a large number of language samples from a wide range of sources. The TIME Magazine Corpus (http://corpus.byu.edu/time) can be used to track changes over time in American English, and its language samples come from articles in *TIME* published from 1923 to 2006. Corpus linguistics has made significant contributions to describing how people use language in real communications.

Tim Johns (1991), who coined data-driven learning, first suggested the pedagogic application of corpus linguistics. The basic idea behind DDL is that students need to be language researchers to learn a new language as learning can be more effective when students are learning for themselves (Hunston, 2002). With data-driven learning, students are encouraged to discover language rules (or patterns) by themselves. According to Fanny Meunier (2002), the most visible feature of the data-driven learning approach in the classroom is the use of concordance lines. Concordance lines are a set of language pieces (a language piece, here, means a set of consecutive words that form a part of one or more sentences, which has a word or words under investigation in the middle of the set), obtained as a result of a corpus query (made by entering a word or words in the query box of a web-based corpus or a program such as AntConc [www.antlab.sci.waseda.ac.jp/software.html] or WordSmith Tools [www.lexically.net /wordsmith]). Since concordance lines are used to work out the linguistic behavior of the word(s) under investigation (or the key word), these lines are typically presented in the format of *key word in context* (KWIC), as shown in figure 16.1. It should also be noted that these tables do not usually consist of complete sentences, since only a specific number of words on either side of the key word is shown. Different web-based corpora and concordancing programs offer different numbers of words when they return concordance lines as a result, but when you provide those lines for your learners, you can cut out some words to make the lines look less distractive. By looking at these lines, students who already know the typical usage of *any* (that is, *any* in negative declarative sentences and *any* in interrogative sentences) will be able to understand that *any* also has different usage and meanings in different linguistic surroundings (*any* in positive declarative sentences, *any* in comparative sentences, and *any* in phrases such as *any longer*).

| | | |
|---|---|---|
| are interesting to observe. | Any | child under two is given a bottle |
| so the young men went for | any | job they could rather than a farm job |
| state of affairs could not go on | any | longer. Someone had to act soon |
| they hadn't dared to strike | any | more matches—they were just |
| the longest open tradition of | any | of the English links that have |
| complicated. The closing of | any | of them would be a major engineering |
| We work more overtime than | any | other country in Europe, even |
| dry. I don't think there was | any | rain all summer long, was there? |
| just won't come out. Have we | any | stain remover? . . . I thought there |
| at Steve's house. Just turn up | any | time after 12. It'll go on all afternoon |
| hard pressed. There was never | any | time for standing back and appraising |

*Source: Willis, 1998, p. 45.*

Figure 16.1: Sample KWIC concordances of the key word *any*.

One of the advantages of data-driven learning is that it can provide sufficient exposure to authentic language for second and foreign (both are referred to as L2) language learners, who often have limited access to real L2 communication. In addition, by encouraging students to discover patterns among a set of concordance lines on their own, a teacher can help them grow into autonomous learners.

On the other hand, there may be some drawbacks to this approach. Most notably, learners often find it difficult to handle its technical aspects, such as corpora and concordancing software. For this reason, preparing concordance lines in advance and presenting them in a paper-based form to learners can be helpful (Johns, 1991).

This chapter presents both paper- and computer-based data-driven learning strategies to meet the needs of learners at a wide range of levels and suggests practical guidelines for teachers hoping to try this approach in their grammar classrooms.

## How Do I Do It?

Here is an outline of the general procedure to adopt when you are preparing for your initial data-driven learning session.

### Decide What to Teach

The first step in preparing for a data-driven learning session is, not surprisingly, to decide what to teach. However, it is not just about choosing one from a range of grammar items. Even though you may have found that your students are generally weak at using tenses or articles, you can narrow down the scope of instruction by, for example, concentrating on the use of the present progressive for future plans or the definite article when referring to something that has already been mentioned. You can also choose more than one subitem for purposes of comparison, such as present progressive for the future versus present progressive for the present. Dictionaries and grammar reference books will help you find what to choose among several options.

### Collect Language Samples for Instruction

In order to collect language samples, you can use existing corpora or make one of your own. If you are to use an existing corpus open to the public, you can use web-based, free corpora, such as the British National Corpus (http://corpus.byu.edu /bnc) or the Corpus of Contemporary American English (http://corpus.byu.edu/coca), which also provide a user-friendly interface. You can obtain large amounts of concordance lines simply by putting a key word (or key words) in the query box. However, if you find it difficult to find more relevant lines among massive quantities of language data, you can use mediated corpus tools like Just the Word (www.just-the-word.com). You will find this site very useful because it provides concordance lines that have already been arranged based on grammatical categories and typical collocations. For instance, when you want to show your learners how to describe a rainy day using accurate and appropriate English, by just entering *rain* in the query box, you can get numerous frequent and typical usages of *rain* based on two big categories, verbs and nouns.

Alternatively, you can obtain concordance lines from a pedagogic corpus that you have built up on your own. To do this, collect in a computer file classroom written or spoken materials, such as textbooks and transcripts of audiovisual materials from listening and speaking sessions (Willis, 2003). A concordance program like AntLab (www.antlab.sci.waseda.ac.jp/software/html) or WordSmith Tools (www.lexically .net/wordsmith) will sort out the set of concordance lines you need. You will probably be surprised to find that these programs are not very difficult to master once you learn how to use them. AntConc is particularly good for novice users as it is free, and AntConc tutorials are easy to find.

### *Make Materials With the Language Samples Selected*

Once you have collected the set of language samples that you require, you'll need to prepare them for your students. However, it may be necessary to decide first whether you are going to present rules at the beginning or end of the session, since this will influence the form of the materials chosen.

While the type of material in figure 16.1 (page 154) is suitable for learners at an intermediate level or above, you can aim at a lower proficiency level and present only one usage of a grammar item in a single set of lines. Students can also find the features that appear to be described in the lines (inductive learning), or you can give students information about what features they are supposed to find in the lines (deductive learning). For example, you can provide students with a list of concordance lines that have present progressive tense used to describe an action in the near future ("She is arriving later") and ask them to find the common features. By observing the lines, your students can conclude inductively that all these lines have present progressive tense in common and that it is being used to describe what will happen in the near future.

You can make gap-fill materials by erasing a key word or any other words in the concordance lines. Students then guess a missing word based on the surrounding words in each line. This type of activity can be difficult for lower-level students; however, with appropriate guidance, students can use it effectively. Again, you can choose whether or not to mix several usages according to the level of students. To illustrate, figure 16.1 can be modified to make this type of material by erasing all the *any's* in the middle.

A mixture of correct and incorrect lines collected from a *learner corpus* (a corpus compiled with language that learners of the language use) may also be used, for example, on a handout. You can then simply ask your students to correct the sheets. Learner-written corpora (that is, corpora that compile ELs' written work), such as the LUCY corpus (www.grsampson.net/resources.html), will provide useful concordance lines when designing this type of material, since the language of such corpora naturally contains mistakes. Sylviane Granger and Chris Tribble (1998) suggest using a learner corpus alongside a native corpus. A *native corpus* compiles language from native speakers. Learners can compare each set of lines and correct wrong examples. Figure 16.2 shows a sample error-correction activity. Students who have learned that *accept* is not followed by *to* infinitives from their observation of native speaker writing will be able to correct lines two and four in Non-Native Speaker Writing by changing *to* infinitives to *that* clauses with equivalent meanings.

| Native Speaker Writing | |
|---|---|
| not being able to accept | >that fulfillment of life is possible. |
| the act. Hugo cannot accept | >that the party line has changed. |
| mothers and learn to accept | >their traditions. |
| if the peer group doesn't accept | >what the friend is wearing. |
| with their emotions and try to accept | >that diversity. |
| **Non-Native Speaker Writing** | |
| think that women must accept | >that some differences exist. |
| young. He could never accept | >to be inferior. |
| feminists have to accept | >to be treated as men. |
| Johnny will not accept | >the Company's decision. |
| the parents accept | >that new visions of things may |

*Source: Adapted from Granger & Tribble, 1998.*

Figure 16.2: Sample error-correction activity.

## Classroom Example

This section will describe a paper- and computer-integrated data-driven learning session to use with students at various levels.

This sample session was designed for high school students at intermediate level for the purpose of teaching various usages of the word *it*. In the first half of the session, students work out different functions and meanings of *it* by looking through a set of concordance lines on handouts the teacher prepared in advance (table 16.1, page 158). It is important that students check their findings against other sources, such as grammar reference books or dictionaries, to prevent them from making wrong conclusions (Willis, 1998). In the second half of the session, students access a web-based corpus so that they can search for relevant, useful, or interesting concordance lines that they can add to their findings. As students feel more comfortable with this approach, they can explore the corpus with their own queries whenever they have linguistic problems in writing situations.

Table 16.1: Data-Driven Learning Session Outline

| **Setting** |
| --- |
| • Learners: High school students at upper intermediate level and above<br>• Goal: To learn various usages and patterns of it<br>    a.  Referring to an element mentioned before (for example, "It was a brand-new computer.")<br>    b.  Referring to the weather or the time (for example, "It's cold today," "It's time to . . .")<br>    c.  Emphasizing information (for example, "It was Mike who saw the accident.")<br>    d.  Expressing judgment (for example, "It is important that . . . ," "It was difficult for me to . . .")<br>    e.  Expressing possibility (for example, "It is likely that . . . ," "It appears that . . .")<br>• Time of a session: Fifty minutes<br>• Technology: Access to a computer and the Internet<br>• Paper materials: Concordance-line handouts, dictionaries, and thesauruses<br>• Online materials: The Corpus of Contemporary American English (http://corpus.byu.edu/coca) and the *Longman Dictionary of Contemporary English* (www.ldoceonline.com) |
| **Task and Subtasks** |
| • Task: Identify various usages and patterns of it in the concordance lines.<br>• Subtasks:<br>    a.  Identify the meaning of each concordance line, and guess the functions of it.<br>    b.  Classify the lines into several categories based on your findings on it.<br>    c.  Identify a typical pattern surrounding it in each category.<br>    d.  Compare your answers with the information under the entry in the *Longman Dictionary of Contemporary English* or a paper dictionary.<br>    e.  Access the Corpus of Contemporary American English, and find example lines for each category of it. If there are any new usages or patterns of it that you find interesting, try to work out their functions, and again check your understanding against the dictionary.<br>    f.  Share what you have found with the class. |

## Your Turn

The success of data-driven learning sessions depends heavily on the appropriateness of concordance lines, materials, and learning activities, which in turn demands a good deal of preparation time on the part of teachers. Furthermore, take into consideration potential difficulties that learners might face, as well as other practical and technical problems that may occur during a session. Here are some tips that data-driven learning practitioners have suggested regarding these issues.

- Remember that data-driven learning is not a cure-all methodology for grammar instruction. Teachers should complement it with other methodologies, including more communicative types of tasks, such as role-playing games, which can provide a context in which students can use what they have learned from DDL.

- Work in a team to save time and effort in searching for language samples and making materials.

- Organize your session as well as possible, so that you and your students do not get lost in negotiation and interaction over the concordance lines.

- Ensure computers are working properly and that access to the Internet is available before you begin your class.

Your students may want to take time getting used to the data-driven learning approach, because it is based on a wholly different idea of grammar instruction from a more traditional one. Discovering rules among a set of concordance lines is not always easy work, and a data-driven learning session means students need a proper understanding of the basic idea and benefits of this approach. Therefore, you need to explain to your students why it is a task worth the trouble and to keep encouraging them to become language researchers in order to be better writers.

## Useful Resources

Here are some sources that you can refer to when you develop your DDL sessions. They contain topics ranging from the basic ideas and issues of DDL to useful advice and tips for successful implication of DDL.

- "The Pedagogical Value of Native and Learner Corpora in EFL Grammar Teaching," by F. Meunier (2002). In S. Granger, J. Hung, & S. Petch-Tyson (Eds.), *Computer learner corpora, second language acquisition and foreign language teaching* (pp. 119–142). Philadelphia: John Benjamins.

- "Should You Be Persuaded: Two Samples of Data-Driven Learning Materials," by T. Johns (1991). *English Language Research Journal, 4*(1), 1–16.

- "Concordances in the Classroom Without a Computer: Assembling and Exploiting Concordances of Common Words," by J. Willis (1998). In B. Tomlinson (Ed.), *Materials development in language teaching* (1st ed., pp. 44–66). Cambridge, England: Cambridge University Press.

- "Corpora and language teaching: General applications," by S. Hunston (2002). In *Corpora in applied linguistics* (pp. 170–197). Cambridge, England: Cambridge University Press.

- "DDL: Reaching the Parts Other Teaching Can't Reach?" by A. Boulton (2008). In A. Frankenburg-Garcia (Ed.), *Proceedings of the 8th Teaching and Language Corpora Conference, 2008, Lisbon* (pp. 38–44). Portugal: Associação de Estudos e de Investigação Científica do ISLA-Lisboa.

- *Learner English on Computer*, by S. Granger (Ed.) (1998). London: Longman.

 **Youngmin Park** is a doctoral student in education at the University of California, Irvine, specializing in language, literacy, and technology. Previously a high school teacher and teacher trainer in Korea, she has published and presented on topics related to English teaching and learning in English as a foreign language environments.

 **Sarah T. Dunton** graduated from the Commonwealth Honors College at the University of Massachusetts Amherst with a degree in women's studies. She holds a masters of education degree in learning, media, and technology from the University of Massachusetts Amherst. Sarah builds informal learning environments, enhanced with technology and designed to engage girls and women in the STEM fields.

 **Juan M. Ruiz-Hau** is a doctoral student in the educational policy and leadership concentration at the University of Massachusetts Amherst, specializing in higher education. He also holds a master of education degree from the University of Massachusetts Amherst, in the learning, media, and technology concentration. Juan participates in UMass Amherst governance as graduate student senator, conducts research with faculty, and teaches foundational courses on education and social justice.

# CHAPTER 17

# Writing Pattern Poetry on Facebook

By Youngmin Park, Sarah T. Dunton, and Juan M. Ruiz-Hau

Writing in a second language can be challenging. Our classroom observations suggest that one of the most common ways students attempt to learn a second language is to memorize as many words as possible. This is usually through memorizing definitions in their first languages, which makes it easy for those who already have much lexical knowledge in their native language to map words to their definitions.

Vocabulary size is critical for language proficiency, but English-language memorization does not necessarily translate to skillful writing ability. To *know* a word involves more than just recognizing its symbol and reference; it involves understanding its syntactic relations with other words (Lyons, 1977). Students may not use words appropriately in their writing until they understand words' semantic relations, such as synonyms (*huge, gigantic*), antonyms in terms of degree (*alive, dead, pass, fail*), antonyms in a hierarchical order (*big, little*; *hot, cold*), and whole and parts relations (*bicycle, wheels*; *handles, seat*), beyond the simple form and meaning (Schmitt, 2000). In order to increase their syntactic and semantic relational knowledge, students need opportunities to produce output (for example, writing activities) rather than to learn vocabulary words as discrete items.

We recommend writing pattern poems to teachers who want to increase the productive vocabulary knowledge and (eventual) writing abilities of their English language learners and struggling writers. To maximize learning from such writing activities, we further suggest using social media as a forum for sharing students' poems and feedback. Online sites make providing real-time feedback accessible both for teachers and peer students. Immediate feedback, such as through online interactions, scaffolds students' learning by helping them perform tasks at more advanced levels as compared to performing such tasks alone. Social cognitivists describe the difference between individual task performance level and the level at which tasks are performed with a more capable other as the zone of proximal development (Vygotsky, 1978).

Several conceptual frameworks sustain the use of social media as a pedagogical tool: *generative learning, flexibly adaptive instructional design*, and a *contributing student approach* (Collis, 2005; Grabowski, 2004; Schwartz, Lin, Brophy, & Bransford, 1999). As with other constructivist theories, *generative learning* rejects the characterization of learners as passive recipients of information. Instead, learners actively participate in their learning process as contributors to the meaningful interpretation of knowledge (Grabowski, 2004). In *flexibly adaptive instructional design*, students obtain a deep understanding of various disciplines through problem-based and open-ended project-based learning (Schwartz et al., 1999). This design helps foster the development of tacit problem-solving, collaboration, and communication skills that implicitly help student interactions toward learning. Through the *contributing student approach*, participants become content developers and suppliers by engaging in online exercises to create and edit media as a form of learning activity (Collis, 2005).

This chapter aims to provide teachers with a number of poem patterns and valuable vocabulary and grammar teaching points. Additionally, it discusses approaches that maximize the effects of writing pattern poems through a nontraditional medium—such as social networking sites—for educational purposes.

## How Do I Do It?

We first share practical experiences gained from English as a second language classes. Using patterns, low English proficiency high school students felt motivated to write their own poem (table 17.1). Students left the class with a sense of accomplishment and were excited about this writing activity. While writing pattern poetry, these English learners were able to acquire and develop vocabulary knowledge as well as other language skills such as grammar and syntactic knowledge.

Despite patterns having fixed formats, students are able to express their ideas or thoughts in limitless ways. Because teachers provide forms, students are able to concentrate on expressing their thoughts and feelings instead of worrying about structure. For example, on the first day of school, teachers can have students describe themselves using one of the patterns (for example, an acrostic or an alphabetic poem). When reading informational texts, classrooms can use some patterns to summarize what students have learned (for example, an alphabetic poem or a *who, what, where, when, why, how* poem). Most patterns can also convey short narrative stories. We offer examples of such patterns and student writing in the next section.

How can social networks enrich pattern poetry writing? Among a number of social networks, we selected Facebook, primarily based on its popularity and ubiquity. Not only does Facebook have a great number of users, but it also meets the aforementioned instructional design principles. This social medium can facilitate the learning process by promoting active participation, collaboration, and opportunities for spontaneous learning, as well as authentic learning experiences (Mazman & Usluel, 2010).

## Classroom Example

Vicki Holmes and Margaret Moulton (2001) use poetry to teach and reinforce grammar and writing conventions, such as structure, vocabulary, punctuation, and parts of speech. The poetry patterns in table 17.1 are appropriate for teaching and learning vocabulary and sentence generation in English classes of various levels from elementary school to college (Kim, 2007; Lee, 2005; Park & Yu, 2009). The table also indicates patterns and teaching points; each poem's focus: exploring diverse words, exercising parts of speech, generating sentences, or combining two or more of these skills; and parts of speech or learning goals. Since there are more than twenty patterns, at varying levels of complexity, teachers have a variety to choose from as appropriate for learning goals and students' learning levels.

Table 17.1: Examples of Pattern Poems

| Poems | Teaching Points | | | Detailed Teaching Points |
|---|---|---|---|---|
| | **Vocabulary** | **Parts of Speech** | **Sentence** | |
| **Acrostic** | | | | Spelling |
| **Adjective poem** | X | X | | Adjective after linking verbs |
| **Alphabetic poem** | | X | X | Order of letters in the alphabet |
| **Blotz poem** | X | X | | Alliteration |
| **Catalog poem** | | X | X | Nouns, verbs, phrases, and classification |

Continued on next page →

| Poems | Teaching Points | | | Detailed Teaching Points |
|---|---|---|---|---|
| | Vocabulary | Parts of Speech | Sentence | |
| Contrast poem | X | X | X | Simple and compound sentence structure, negation, and linking verbs followed by adjectives or *but* |
| Diamante | X | X | | Synonyms and antonyms, adjectives, participles, and thesis and antithesis |
| Five senses poem | X | | X | Sensory verbs, basic sentence structure, phrases, and metaphors and similes |
| Haiku | X | | | Syllabication, spelling, imagery, and conciseness of expression |
| "I like" poem | X | | X | Simple and compound sentence structure, conjunction, using *but*, negatives, and active verb |
| "I wish" poem | | | X | Structures following *wish*, tense, and noun clauses |
| Simile poem | X | | X | Similes, analytical thinking, and possessive pronouns |

*Source: Adapted from Park & Yu, 2009.*

Figure 17.1 presents a sample pattern and student work. The pattern calls for specific parts of speech on specific lines. Such patterns serve as *recipes* (Holmes & Moulton, 2001). Teachers do not need to create recipes using ready-made patterns. Students can *cook* their poems by just following a recipe and adding their thoughts.

| Pattern | Example |
|---|---|
| Line 1. (noun) | Mankind |
| Line 2. (adjective) (adjective) | Smart, intelligent |
| Line 3. (participle) (participle) (participle) | Eating, thinking, talking |
| Line 4. (nouns—4 words) | Town, family, habitat, pack |
| Line 5. (participle) (participle) (participle) | Eating, hunting, screaming |
| Line 6. (adjective) (adjective) | Wild, fierce |
| Line 7. (noun—a synonym or related word of the first line) | Beast |

*Source: Holmes & Moulton, 2001.*

Figure 17.1: Sample pattern poem and student work.

## Your Turn

Search for online examples or glean them from *Writing Simple Poems: Pattern Poetry for Language Acquisition* (Holmes & Moulton, 2001). Pattern poetry activities using Facebook can be set up and managed as described in the following section.

### Page Creation and User Invitation

Facebook supports user-defined groups. Teachers can open a private group and invite students to join. If students want to keep their private Facebook accounts separate from class, they can use a different email account for this group. The users who join the group will be notified of any updates for that group via email or the Facebook app, giving them access to the updated posts anytime with their web-browsing devices.

### Class Objectives and Guidelines

As in the traditional classroom, the teacher needs to make class objectives and activities clear. Examples will help guide students' work. For lectures in the classroom, teachers commonly use PowerPoint, which they can upload onto the group page using Add File. To ensure students can access lecture notes with any device, teachers can save PowerPoint files as images (for example, as a JPEG or GIF), a universal format for display purposes, and post them on Facebook. We recommend using a separate photo album for each activity, so users can easily locate class notes.

### Supporting Materials

Facebook's rich-media cross-compatibility offers participants the capability to share original work on a number of channels: text-only, sound, video (when linked to a video repository such as YouTube or Vimeo), or a combination thereof. Teachers can use multiple resources to motivate students who are more visual learners and not as inspired by text-only instruction. Students can also post videos or pictures relevant to their works. Teachers can repurpose and use these web products, which students create throughout the course, for learning in other contexts.

### Student Work

As an individual or a group, students create poems per the class notes or teacher-posted multimedia. Figure 17.2 shows student comments to the teacher's guideline. With Facebook, poems generated through individual or group exercises can evolve from online text-only formats to more dynamically rich media. Students, for example, are able to record and post themselves reading or acting out their poetry. Capturing these uniquely aesthetic aspects of performance could potentially generate tremendous learning opportunities for participants. Another advantage of using Facebook is that students can collaborate synchronously and asynchronously (through in-class and out-of-class exercises). Students can use previous comments as springboards to post, edit, and repurpose for other user-generated material whenever students want to. The opportunities for content generation give students a sense of accomplishment and contribution to the learning environment, increasing confidence in the learning process.

### Discussion

All student-generated material is subject to peer evaluation, commentary, and review on Facebook. A variety of communication routes are available: simply clicking Like, sharing interesting posts, adding a comment, messaging, and using Facebook and video chat. Peer feedback in writing instruction has been proven to play a critical role in learning (Graham & Perin, 2007c). Online discussion especially encourages those who are unwilling to voice their thoughts and ideas in class to become involved in the feedback process. One concern in peer feedback or group writing is miscorrection that nonexpert classmates may not correct or modify (Holt, 1992). However, as Facebook sends user notifications to the users regarding all updates, teachers can easily detect any possible issues and mediate.

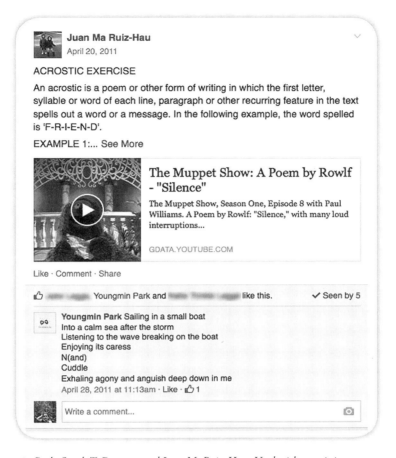

Source: *Youngmin Park, Sarah T. Dunton, and Juan M. Ruiz-Hau. Used with permission.*

Figure 17.2: Screenshot of Literacy Lure group on Facebook.

## *Assessment*

Teachers can use Facebook for assessment in multiple ways. First, teachers can recognize whether and how students actively participate in class by reviewing students' activity. This is possible because Facebook logs users' activities with time stamps. Another simple way to assess students' learning is to ask questions through posts, with student responses as comments. Additionally, by using online surveying services such as SurveyMonkey, instructors and participants can generate questions, post on Facebook, then share results. Instructors can then post responses as comments or status updates. Attempting to reach English learners can help increase their academic success and lower dropout rates. In particular, these students need support to increase their literacy skills, including vocabulary, grammar, and writing. Our online literacy group uses poetry as a hook for students to improve their literacy skills. As a platform of literacy activities, Facebook offers these students the benefits of a traditional content- and learning-management system in an intuitive, user-friendly environment. When partnered with a comprehensive instructional approach and instructor support, Facebook provides an accessible and affordable infrastructure for students to communicate, meet, share information, and learn from one another. Finally, as technology continues to permeate all aspects of life, engaging with learners in an online, media-rich environment helps students develop critical literacy skills on digital channels: skills they will continue to use well into the future.

While this new medium has great potential for improved learning outcomes, many people may see the possible risks of social networking for educational purposes. Students may be willing to shed the perception of privacy in favor of pleasure and expression. Cautious implementation is necessary to avoid any possible risks that may be associated with using social media. Facebook supports the control of privacy in terms of items posted, users, and groups. Teachers should be aware of such features and use them to protect their students' privacy.

**Charles A. Vogel, PhD,** is an instructor in secondary social sciences and communications for Eagle County School in Eagle, Colorado. He has thirty-eight years of classroom experience. In 1991–1992, the Colorado Council for the Social Studies named him the Outstanding Educator of the Year. He continues to research and develop methods in literacy instruction, specializing in the use of visual-syntactic text formatting, and reading and writing formats utilizing computer technology. Charles has a doctorate in curriculum and instruction from the University of Denver.

# CHAPTER 18

# Visual-Syntactic Text Formatting

By Charles A. Vogel

The explicit teaching of grammar in U.S. schools has been replaced with instruction in the writing process. In support of this approach, studies have suggested that the explicit teaching of grammar, where students recognize parts of speech or learn the rules for punctuation, only reduces the quality of writing for most students (Hillocks, 1984). Nevertheless, students must master sophisticated text structures in order to be skilled writers.

Grammar instruction has been problematic primarily because grammar rules and sentence structure have been taught in isolation, without applying them in free writing. In contrast to teaching grammar rules in isolation, research has supported the use of sentence-combining activities as an effective means to improve sentence variety with students of varying abilities (Graham & Perin, 2007b). By having students first manipulate phrases and clauses prescriptively, they can then model the practiced structures in their own writing. The success of such instruction depends on the direct application of syntax—that is, in the standard organization of words into the phrases and clauses that comprise sentences and paragraphs.

Using an algorithm, visual-syntactic text formatting (VSTF) arranges these phrases and clauses in a cascading fashion, which students may then read from the top of a computer screen to the bottom. This is similar to the old practice of sentence diagramming, in which students cluster the parts of a sentence and highlight their function and purpose.

Unlike normal reading from block text, visual-syntactic text formatting makes visible the sentence structures, grammatical usages, and unifying devices writers use and whose patterns change according to the writing genre. In figure 18.1, for example, we see visual-syntactic text formatting applied to a famous passage about reading drawn from Francis Bacon's *The Essays*. This pattern effect was found to be significant in a quasi-experimental design used to test reading comprehension in middle school students in Orange County, California. An unintended outcome was that student scores in the experimental group improved significantly when compared to the control group in standardized tests of English usage and grammar. It was theorized that students could easily attend to the visual arrangement of syntactic components, allowing them to transfer that knowledge to improving recognition of grammatical forms (Park, Warschauer, Farkas, & Collins, 2012). The conclusions drawn from that study confirm results of prior studies in Eagle County, Colorado (Vogel, 2002).

> Some books
>    are to be tasted,
> others
>       to be swallowed,
>    and some few
>       to be chewed
>    and digested;
> that is
>    some books
>       are to be read
>          only in parts;
> others
>    to be read,
>       but not curiously;
> and some few
>    to be read wholly
>       and with diligence and attention.

Figure 18.1: Visual-syntactic text formatting applied to the writing of Francis Bacon.

Walker Reading Industries (Walker, Schloss, Fletcher, Vogel, & Walker, 2005) developed visual-syntactic text formatting. The primary tool that converts traditional text into visual-syntactic text formatting is the online computer program ClipRead. Any electronic text loaded into this computerized tool will be automatically converted to visual-syntactic text formatting. This allows the writing instructor to project models of exemplary writing in the classroom or evaluate them individually online. Most importantly, students can convert their own texts.

In essence, ClipRead serves as a syntactic and grammatical editing device. This is because poor writing tends to lack the regular features that create the highlighting effect. On the other hand, regularity in the form of useless redundancies also stands out dramatically when given the algorithmic treatment. When using the ClipRead tool, which analyzes for regularity, poor writing shows up as chaotic. As students add correct grammatical forms and recast sentences to add variety, concision, and clarity, they can visually see these improvements to the architecture of the text with every edit.

# How Do I Do It?

The first roadblock to syntax instruction was the inability of my students to dialogue with me about grammar or syntax. They were familiar with the parts of speech and a few punctuation rules, and that was about it. However, explicit grammar instruction—vocabulary included—is important and can benefit the struggling writer if applied to a writing task in real time rather than isolation (Graham & Perin, 2007b, 2007c).

Prior to instruction, I had converted lessons into visual-syntactic text formatting for projection to the whole group, starting with simple sentence structures. The cascading words highlighted the complete subject and predicate combinations that could be elaborated, modified, and compounded. The idea was to exhaust the possibilities for simple sentences before moving on to compound sentences, then to complex sentences, and so on. As an example, the preamble to the U.S. Constitution (figure 18.2) is an elaborated simple sentence ("We . . . ordain"), having the rhetorical power of the compounded infinitive form, with each infinitive following the lead of "to form a more perfect union" (U.S. Const. pmbl.).

I accompanied each explicit lesson with sentence-combining exercises for assisted and independent practice. The combining activities achieved two goals: (1) they prepared students to pare down their own writing for conciseness, and (2) they allowed practice in using the syntactic forms under scrutiny. Moreover, sentence-combining activities have been shown to be more effective than free writing in the enhancement of student writing (Hillocks, 1984; Nordquist, 2013).

At the conclusion of a syntax learning cycle, students would take a prescriptive test relating to the prescribed sentence structure. The test asked them to write a simple sentence with a compound adjective modifying the appositive, restating the object of the adverbial phrase. (Answer: Joe went into the **bar**, a *vile* and *smoky* <u>place</u>.) Three points were allocated for fulfilling the requirements of the request: one point for using the adverbial phrase *into the*

**Preamble
  to the Constitution**

We the people
  of the United States,
 in order
  to form
   a more perfect union,
  establish justice,
   insure domestic tranquility,
  provide
   for the common defense,
    promote the general welfare,
  and secure
   the blessings of liberty
    to ourselves
  and our posterity,
do ordain
  and establish this Constitution
   for the United States
    of America.

Figure 18.2: Grammatical structure of the preamble to the U.S. Constitution.

*bar,* another for the appositive "*place*," and the third point for the compound adjective "*vile and smoky.*"

---

### Sentence-Combining Activity

Combine the sentences into a single clear sentence with at least one participial phrase.

- I stood on the roof of my apartment building at dawn.

- I watched the sun rise through crimson clouds.

**Sample combination:** Standing on the roof of my apartment building at dawn, I watched the sun rise through crimson clouds.

*Source: Adapted from Nordquist, 2013.*

---

After students became comfortable identifying and modeling sentence structures, I introduced them to the notion of rhetoric. The art of rhetoric in writing lies in how regular sentence structures convey novelty, humor, emotion, influence, and form—in brief, writing qualities associated with particular genres with attention to the rhetorical characteristics specific to each. While experimenting with various genres using visual-syntactic text formatting, we discovered that writing for history or science demanded differing syntaxes for rhetorical effect. For example, history texts commonly use parallel structures to build *cause-and-effect* relationships for the reader. In science, the writer would *sequence* the steps for photosynthesis with the use of subordinate clauses. Writing within the different genres became the most daunting task for my students, as until then, they were used to only one genre—narratives that used story grammars. To best display the syntax and grammar associated with genre writing, I used exemplars from great writing or public speeches converted in visual-syntactic text formatting for analysis.

Great writing still utilized the standard syntaxes—simple, compound, complex, and compound-complex sentences with various phrase forms. Then, we examined the intentions of the writer. If the intentions were exposition, description, or explanation, the best writers manipulated sentence structure to maximize the rhetorical effect. It was here that students were required to stretch their abilities, for students had to stay within the syntax requirements but use their own word choice and topic. These mirrored exercises gave students extended practice of writing at the rhetorical level but within the limits the sentence structures set. It also gave them practice at writing technically within various genres.

During the course of writing instruction, students used their newly found syntactic knowledge by writing compositions and essays that varied in purpose and structure. It was here that the ClipRead tool became essential editing for composing and polishing writing.

The six steps for the process were the following.

1.  After writing a rough draft, the student analyzed it with the instructor or with the whole class to get immediate recommendations for revision, depending on the writer's confidence and his or her comfort level. (Student papers were projected to facilitate a whole group discussion. If class sizes are large, small-group peer reviews are more timely, using the "print" feature of the VSTF to provide a hard copy of the assignment for small-group analysis.)

2.  The first edit focused on eliminating redundancies by combining concepts similar to the sentence-combining exercises students used to practice various syntaxes.

3.  The second edit built in transitions and syntaxes, unifying ideas and adding sentence variety within the general organization of the composition.

4.  The third edit was aimed at rhetorical heft, recasting wording to establish a desired effect.

5.  The fourth edit focused on word choice and provided the writer with a second chance at concision.

6.  The fifth edit allowed for a whole-group examination of the piece.

By using the ClipRead tool (figure 18.3) during all the various edits, students were able to see their revisions literally transform the shape of their writing in real time. Moving text, building parallel structure and subordination, and adding transitions and rhetorical features became an evolutionary experience for them.

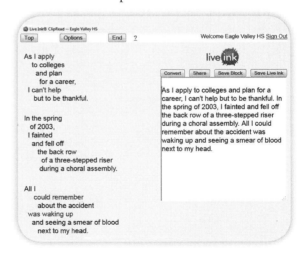

*Source: Carson Jay Preytis. Used with permission.*

Figure 18.3: ClipRead text converted for editing.

# Classroom Example

The overall lesson student writers learned was that serious writing begins with spontaneity but is polished and revised into something much better before it is completed. So many students have commented that for them, the initial splurge, their first draft, scratched out in pursuit of a grade, is all the time and energy they devote to writing in general. However, by following what is essentially a tiered set of drafts, students became aware that drafting leads to crafting a superior product. Figure 18.4 shows the response of a student experienced in the use of VSTF training.

According
    to Roman tradition,
the city of Rome
    was founded
        by a Romulus
after he fought
    and killed his brother
    Remus.

As legend
    would have it
Romulus and Remus
    were abandoned
        as infants,
only to be found,
    adopted,
    and raised
        by a she-wolf named
        Lupa.

Having grown up
    as wolves,
the boys
    developed
        a fierce sense of unity
        and strength in
        numbers,
or as many
    would describe it,
        a wolf-pack mentality.

In reality,
    shortly after the founding
    of Rome,
    its Neolithic society

and geographical location
    made it vulnerable
        to conquest
    by a mysterious people,
        the Etruscans.

Although enslaved
    for nearly a hundred
    years,
the Romans
    were heavily influenced
    by Hellenistic Stoicism,
a philosophy
    which taught the
    Romans
    to be a fatalistic
        emotionally hard,
        duty-oriented people.

Hard fought freedom
    came about
due to this cultural change
    among the Latin
        speaking peoples.

The Roman love
    of freedom
molded the Romans
    into a military society
    and a Republic
in order
        to defend themselves
    and govern Rome
based on their
    stoic sense of duty.

This collective sense
    of duty
was embodied
    in the Roman seal,
an Eagle
    carrying a fasces,
    or a bundle of sticks.

One stick
    Could be easily snapped,
whereas a bundle
    was impossible
        to snap simultaneously.

Until the rise
    of Christianity
        displaced Stoicism
    as the principal moral
    influence
    of Rome,
    and over-extension
        made the Empire
        impossible
            to govern effectively,
    the Romans
        were an unstoppable
        military machine,
duty-bound
    to controlling
        the entire
        Mediterranean.

*Source: Slater Christopher Sabo. Used with permission.*

Figure 18.4: Student response to an essay question.

# Your Turn

The use of visual-syntactic text formatting will be an invaluable tool in both a reading and writing context. It is often said that good readers learn from their reading to be good writers (Rijlaarsdam et al., 2012). That is the position taken with this strategy. The difference with visual-syntactic text formatting is that the substance of good writing is grammatically visible and regularized, which student writers can model. How far a teacher wishes to extend this modeling of course depends on the student audience. Visual-syntactic text formatting has been used as a reading platform from grade 3 to the college level. In addition, students of high- and low-level abilities benefit from the format (Walker et al., 2007).

The first step for any teacher wishing to use this writing instruction is to contact Walker Reading Technologies (www.liveink.com). Instructors may request a free trial to the ClipRead tool or the web-based version, WebClipRead.

After receiving the ClipRead tool online, the writing instructor can build lessons using Internet examples in the public domain. It is important to store examples and assignments to a folder as LIV files (for example, Steinbeck.liv). To convert text, highlight and copy an example from the Internet, open the ClipRead tool, and click the cursor in the writing field. The text will appear in its converted form; from there, you can save examples to a folder. Then, to access the example, one simply has to open the online ClipRead tool and access the file. There are numerous options available for presentation. You can alter font size and background coloring, for example. It is helpful if the instructor has access to classroom projectors for whole-class presentations. Any interactive board technology adds power to the presentations, since one can highlight, underline, and modify the text manually for effect.

The last step in the process is for student writers to use ClipRead to analyze and modify their own writing through the various drafting steps. Once they open their rough drafts into the ClipRead tool, students can modify the writing in real time, as the words and the shape of the text change with each revision. The student writer must remember to save his or her writing after each session, or he or she will lose that day's revisions. Students can email or save LIV files to a flash drive for sharing purposes. Additionally, they can print off converted text in traditional block-text format after they've completed their drafts.

Visual-syntactic text formatting has opened new avenues to graphically demonstrate the wide variety of sentence structures to students through teacher modeling. The editing function provides authentic practice in drafting, refining, and publishing student writing—writing that is polished and above all structured with syntactic sophistication. Moreover, regardless of grade level, visual-syntactic text formatting expands the palette for teachers and students alike to use grammar with intention and purpose.

# PART VII | Editing and Revising

Revision is an integral part of the writing process; however, teachers often struggle with how to engage students in revision that is meaningful to their growth as writers. Revision is not simply about fixing mistakes but understanding root issues driving writing errors, which is challenging and complex work for both teachers and students (Shaughnessy, 1976).

Many teachers engage students in peer review opportunities to facilitate the revision process. Peer review promotes collaboration and cooperative learning. Students benefit from peer review, as it is often easier for students to identify problems in peers' writing than in their own. Additionally, students gain insight and a deepened understanding of writing. It also provides opportunities for students to analyze and reflect on how they communicate their ideas.

Peer review, however, can be difficult to implement in classrooms. First, logistically, teachers must consider how they physically arrange the classroom, and how students will be engaged during the process and in the quality of their work. Second, we often forget to teach students how to provide feedback. This leads to students providing either generic feedback (for example, "This is good") or feedback focused solely on editing or mechanical issues (for example, "Fix punctuation"). The third problem is that students don't often know how to use feedback they receive in their revisions. They end up either ignoring the suggestions or making the changes without really understanding the rationale for the revision. These issues make the process of peer review challenging for teachers and students. Despite these challenges, teachers need to conceptualize effective pedagogical practices that will engage students in revision opportunities.

Software tools have made revision and editing extremely simple. One can turn on Microsoft Word and enable Track Changes, for example. One could then write on another person's document, either by directly making changes or by adding comments for suggested revisions. The original author could then see those changes and accept or reject them. Teachers can also use platforms such as Google Docs, which allow students to see in real time the revisions teachers are making. Such editing and revision is an important part of the collaborative writing process.

All too often, we see this step as leading to an outcome—the paper has been revised or has edits on it—rather than understanding the data that are now available for helping students understand the revising and editing process. Finally, a third strategy revolves around writing spaces and online writing communities. These spaces provide opportunities for revision, editing, and feedback to come from an entire community of writers.

New technology easily allows revision to be an integral part of the writing process. Teachers can use these online tools to create a community of writers and to help students identify their strengths and weaknesses as writers.

Katie Stover and Chase Young open this section in chapter 19 by documenting specific online spaces and digital tools that can be used for peer feedback. Lisa Holmes and Dawn Reed describe how digital peer review can also be done on student blogs in chapter 20. Matthew T. Pifer's chapter concludes this section with an explanation of how online writing centers can support writing instruction.

**Katie Stover** is an assistant professor in the Education Department at Furman University in Greenville, South Carolina. Katie's research interests include critical literacy, writing for social justice, digital literacy, and teacher education. She has a doctorate in curriculum and instruction with a concentration in urban literacy from the University of North Carolina at Charlotte. Follow her on Twitter @kstover24.

**Chase Young** is an assistant professor at Texas A&M University in Corpus Christi, Texas. He is a former primary grades teacher and literacy coach. Chase loves transforming dated classroom strategies and making them awesome. He received his doctorate in reading education from the University of North Texas. To learn more about Chase's work, visit his website, www.thebestclass.org.

# CHAPTER 19

# Using 21st Century Technology
# to Edit and Revise

By Katie Stover and Chase Young

In response to emerging 21st century technologies, students need to be prepared to read, write, and communicate in new ways. New digital tools change the way we produce, distribute, and communicate text, which changes the writing process (Lankshear & Knobel, 2003; Yancey, 2009). Specifically, writing in the 21st century classroom has shifted from a single author writing for the teacher as the audience to collaborative writing for authentic audiences within and beyond the four walls of the classroom (Merchant, 2005). Web 2.0 applications offer a myriad of digital networking tools designed to promote collaboration among Internet users (Laru, Naykki, & Jarvela, 2012).

Jennifer Bogard and Mary McMackin (2012) discuss the use of a recursive writing process in which third graders create digital storyboards of personal narratives and use a podcast to record their narrations and obtain peer feedback. Brian Morgan and Richard Smith (2008) describe the use of a wiki for student-created multimedia research reports. With the wider communication space that the Internet provides, writers can more readily interact with others to create, share, and receive feedback.

Students can use digital spaces to publicly or privately revise and edit their writing. When students write for an authentic audience, they are more likely to reflect on the clarity, purpose, and significance of their writing. According to Donald Murray (1999), "The writer has to keep an eye open for the audience, standing back and making sure that what is being said and re-said on the page is clear to the reader" (p. 226). Rather than the first piece of writing being their last (Murray, 1999), students are motivated to develop their writing when given opportunities to collaboratively revise and edit using digital tools. With peer revision and editing, students offer one another feedback to help clarify, organize, and develop details and assist with spelling, punctuation, and grammar. This enhances the writing by allowing the writer to step back and obtain a fresh perspective on his or her piece. As Georgia Heard (2002) states, "We need to invite young writers into the world of revision through invitations and tools that make revision concrete and tangible" (p. x). Web 2.0 applications can offer students digital tools that allow them to envision their writing in new ways and obtain meaningful feedback.

VoiceThread is an online multimedia presentation tool that enables students to upload images, documents, and videos. VoiceThread allows students to present information in a range of ways, collaborate with their peers, and ultimately increase participation in the learning process (Gillis, Luthin, Parette, & Blum, 2012). The potential uses of VoiceThread in educational settings are endless. Afton Gillis and colleagues (2012) discuss its use in creating expressive and receptive learning activities in the early childhood setting. Katie Stover (2012) explores the use of Voice-Thread to publish first graders' collaborative writing projects with a wider, more authentic audience to build awareness of social justice issues. Wood, Stover, and Kissel (2013) explore the use of VoiceThread to publish sixth-graders' online book reviews and found poetry. While VoiceThread offers users an online space to publish a written product, teachers can also use it as a tool to foster collaboration during the writing process.

## How Do I Do It?

Students begin by uploading a digital photo of their writing to the computer. After setting up an account on VoiceThread, students click Create to begin a new project and upload the image of their writing. The student can then use the Comment feature either to record him- or herself reading his or her writing or leave a message for the reader. For instance, the writer may want specific feedback related to developing an effective lead or enhancing word choice. Viewers can use the Comment feature to add praise or ask questions to clarify something. (Visit **go.solution-tree.com /technology** to view an example.) Another aspect of VoiceThread that allows the user and viewer to communicate and collaborate is the interactive doodle feature. Doodling allows the users to draw right on the media while simultaneously commenting. Like the Comment feature, this tool is easy to use and allows both the creator and viewer to circle errors or mark the text.

## Classroom Example

Cathy Tecza introduced her second graders to VoiceThread by showing examples of published VoiceThreads from the website. She shared a mathematics strategy and story retellings to demonstrate its versatility. She also shared writing of her own that she posted on a VoiceThread and showed students how others commented on it and added their compliments and suggestions. Next, she made an anchor chart of different kinds of comments that would be useful to the writer (figure 19.1).

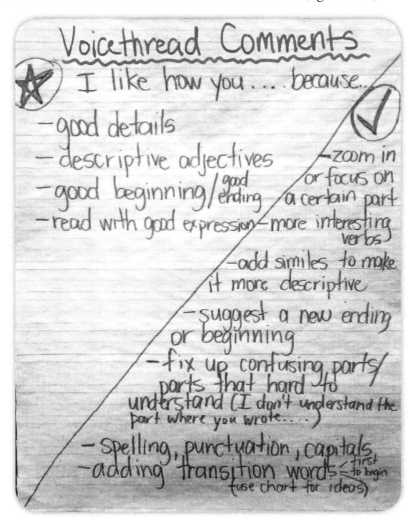

*Source: Cathy Tecza. Used with permission.*

Figure 19.1: VoiceThread comment anchor chart.

During writing workshop, students uploaded completed drafts of their work to VoiceThread. One student posted an excerpt of his writing titled "How to Be a Good Friend" for peer feedback (figure 19.2, page 188).

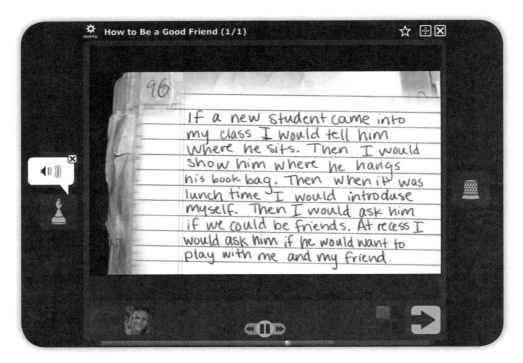

*Source: Kennedy Chumley. Used with permission.*

Figure 19.2: A sample VoiceThread.

The writer's peers recorded the following responses.

> **Liam:** I think it is thoughtful how you saved a seat for a new friend. I also think you should add more detail to where he should sit and hang his book bag.

> **Destiny:** I like how you said all the different places you'd help the new friend. You need to fix all of the 'thens' [underline each *then* using the Doodle feature]. Use different words like next, finally, and then only once.

> **Jose:** My favorite part was when you said that you showed him where to hang the book bag. Maybe you could change the beginning to a question like, "Do you know how to be a good friend?"

The writer reflected on this feedback and referred to a chart of transition words to change all the *thens*. He also decided to revise the first sentence to a question. See figure 19.3 for the final draft. Using effective leads was something Cathy had discussed with her students during several minilessons. After incorporating these revisions, the writer stated that the piece of writing "would not have been as interesting if I didn't make the changes they said. They helped me think of things to fix." When asked to reflect on the activity, Liam, one of the peer editors, noted, "I liked listening to his story and telling him how he could fix it. It's neat how you can write on it like a SMART Board." Destiny stated, "I was a little nervous saying it on the microphone, but it was fun. At first it was hard to think of something, but then I thought of what you taught us and that gave me some ideas of what to tell him he could fix." These comments suggest students' engagement in the use of VoiceThread to revise their writing and demonstrate application of meaningful learning of effective writing strategies.

*Source: Second-grade student. Used with permission.*

Figure 19.3: Revised writing sample on VoiceThread.

## Your Turn

Before incorporating VoiceThread into your writing workshop, be sure to first familiarize yourself with the website. You may want to begin by creating your own as an example for your students. Additionally, it would be beneficial to demonstrate the steps for taking digital images of the writing, saving them to the computer, uploading them to VoiceThread, and recording yourself reading the piece using the Comment feature. By scaffolding the experience for your students, you can avoid confusion later on. Once you have modeled how to create a VoiceThread, it is important to allow your students time to explore the website and the many possibilities this web 2.0 application offers before beginning on their specific writing project.

The use of these digital tools for peer feedback in the classroom enhances the revision process for students. According to Murray (1999), exposure to peer feedback will help the writer "become a more apt critic of writing, not to mention a better revisionist" (p. 219). Students begin to see that writing is never perfect the first time, and revision can be a positive experience that improves the writing. Twenty-first century revision methods provide a safe place where students can construct, nurture, and share their masterpieces.

Visit **go.solution-tree.com/technology** to download more information about how to use VoiceThread.

 **Lisa Holmes** is an English teacher at Okemos High School in Okemos, Michigan. Lisa is interested in the development and delivery of digital literacy programming. She has a master's degree in the humanities with a focus in feminist and border studies from California State University. You can follow Lisa on Twitter @MSHolmesOHS.

 **Dawn Reed** is an English teacher at Okemos High School in Okemos, Michigan, and a codirector of the Red Cedar Writing Project at Michigan State University. She engages in teacher research focused on writing instruction and digital literacies. She has a master's degree in rhetoric and writing from Michigan State University. You can follow Dawn on Twitter @dawnreed.

# CHAPTER 20

# Peer Review in a Digital Space

By Lisa Holmes and Dawn Reed

Multiple researchers support co-composing, collaborative writing, peer editing, and review as important strategies for the development of writing skills (Ito et al., 2010; Kist, 2010; National Writing Project, 2010; Shanahan, 2004; Slater, 2004). These acts of social writing and editing take place in most classrooms, of course, but it is our belief that the digital environment creates unique opportunities for composition and revision. Digital peer review—a regular, ongoing process of posting student work online for peer evaluation—improves student writing, sharpens literary analysis skills, and fosters critical thinking. Because this work takes place in digital social environments, where pairs of students, small groups, and whole classes can collaborate, every student engaged in digital peer review can access every other student's work, peer reviews, and teacher comments. This allows students access to both the authentic audiences and social learning opportunities consistently stressed in research as crucial factors in students' writing progress (Ito et al., 2010; Kist, 2010; Slater, 2004).

We have found that our collection of student feedback through comments and surveys supports this research base anecdotally. Although any pedagogical change is bound to create a certain amount of dissent, our experience is that student support for digital peer review is overwhelmingly positive. An anonymous survey of Lisa's Advanced Placement literature students, for instance, reveals that 93 percent of respondents believe that the consistent practice of digital review helps them become better writers (Advanced Placement Literature, class survey, April 2013). Although some report feeling embarrassed by so much of their work appearing in a public forum, and some mention anxiety about potentially hurting a classmate's feelings with critical comments, when asked specifically in the survey to rate these two areas as concerns, only 25 percent of students said that they worry "a lot" about hurting someone's feelings, and 12.5 percent said that it embarrasses them "a lot" to have peers view most of their work.

One of the more valuable aspects of the survey was that students were able to leave comments to explain their ratings: one student who mentioned feeling anxious about having to post most of his or her work online commented, "There seems to be a lot of competitiveness in students, which is only natural as we are in competition for everything. Together we need to move past this competitive spirit to improve everyone's work." This comment suggests that the student understood and valued the collaborative, peer-mentoring nature of peer review regardless of the years of prior indoctrination in a competitive system. Comments like "It does force me to put a little more effort into my work since I know my peers are reading it" were common; clearly, the authentic audience really does matter to students. Students responding to the survey reflected thoughtfully in the comments section about the power of having many readers' points of view and many examples of how to approach the same assignment.

## How Do I Do It?

Successful digital peer review, like any other classroom strategy, isn't something that happens without preparation. Before moving into digital spaces and asking students to do their first peer reviews—whether these will be for an essay, a literary forum, a multimedia composition, or some other kind of work—we give examples of high- and low-quality peer reviews and discuss with students why one is helpful and the other is not. We stress to students that high-quality peer review is:

- **Analytical**—A good peer reviewer thinks critically about the work and offers very specific, detailed remarks about how well the different parts of the work contribute to the overall functioning of the whole piece.

- **Challenging**—A good peer reviewer opens doors instead of closing them, suggesting possible solutions to problems, offering new directions for thought, posing interesting questions, and so on.

- **Respectful**—A good peer reviewer doesn't attack the work or its author but also doesn't shy away from justified criticism, because failing to point out errors and challenge less-rigorous thinking is condescending.

Often, after modeling, we go through a peer review session as a collaborative group and review the process through class discussion. This review takes place through discussion and, at times, through an entire class peer review in an online space. At this point, students are ready to try their own peer reviews.

Student writing groups work together in a digital space, such as Google Drive, Blogger, Spruz (an online social networking forum), or Eli Review (a digital peer review system). Students can use each of these tools to conduct digital peer review. Teachers can set up peer review in a variety of ways: students may respond to something specific such as content or style or respond more holistically. Writers may also be encouraged to leave their own questions and areas of focus for their peer reviewers.

We leave careful feedback about the quality of the first few peer reviews that students write. In this open-access environment, students are thus able to consider many examples of how to attempt peer review and have access to many examples of our feedback. Their generally rapid progress during the first few rounds of peer review is gratifying—but our primary goal is not simply to teach students to be better critics of one another's work. It is to hone communication skills. Ultimately, we want growth in peer reviews to translate into growth in other areas, including each student's own writing. This is just what we *have* seen: we have been impressed with how eager students are to learn from one another once they are receiving criticism and advice that they truly value, and this work translates into their own refined thinking and writing.

One of the uses for the forums set up on our Spruz classroom sites is the analysis of literature. These forums can be set up in a variety of ways depending on a teacher's objective, but a typical assignment might be for all students to initially post their own responses to a single prompt based on a common piece of literature. Afterward, threaded discussions of these original posts will take place, with students providing analytical commentary on the original post and then on one another's ideas in a constant effort to (as we are always urging) move the conversation forward. Observation of site statistics shows us that students often hop from thread to thread, reading conversations that may or may not be closely related to their own conversations. In other words, they are not necessarily gathering ideas for their own responses but are simply curious about their peers' ideas. In some classes, such as American literature, this means that students have as many as 150 peers' ideas to consider. This rich conversation, we believe, plays a large role in their rapid progress in analyzing literature.

## Classroom Example

Advanced Placement students use digital peer review on their blogs. These blogs contain close readings of nonfiction articles; practice open-prompt essays; short, reflective, synthesis pieces about the course material; and analytical pieces about course readings. In this online space, students benefit from access to nearly eighty examples of each assignment, and students are assigned the work of three peers to review for each assignment. In the following example, John is reviewing a peer's close-reading essay on the writer's blog.

> *John.* October 2, 2012, at 8:30 p.m.
>
> This is a high-quality analysis of Cuban's blog post. In your paragraph about diction, you do a good job of identifying the pejorative elements of his writing, including, as you say, "meltdown" and (financial) "bubble." One thing I might add in this section would be the use of honorific diction, as Cuban glorifies new learning institutions as "flexible" and "innovative," and mentioning this would help to make your paragraph stronger. I like how you point out the juxtaposition of traditional versus new style learning institutions that Cuban uses, as he tries to point out the flaws of our modern, debt-ridden college education system.
>
> In your paragraph about details you talk about how he uses quite a bit of rhetoric about "bubbles" instead of actual numbers, which I think seems very correct. However, I think this might represent a gap in Cuban's knowledge about the statistics of our college education system, as even though he speaks from experience, he seems to make slightly wild claims that students just cannot get jobs right out of traditional colleges. He leaves out the stories of all the kids that have gotten jobs straight out of college, and for whom college has been a good investment. This might show how he is twisting the facts in order to meet his own personal beliefs.
>
> *Source: John Groetsch. Used with permission.*

Students working in small groups on peer review assignments are responsible for reading one another's reviews and proceeding with the same kind of ongoing conversation about the work under consideration as we require in other peer review assignments. Here, Neha offers her own perspective and also comments on what she agrees with in another peer reviewer's work.

> *Neha.* October 29, 2012, at 5:02 p.m.
>
> Overall good job, you have a lot of strong examples! When I started reading your essay, I felt like I was bombarded with examples in your diction paragraph. Don't get me wrong, examples are great but maybe choose fewer examples and take the time to explain each one. I think it's really cool you were able to find figurative language in your article, because normally you don't find that in news articles. I think your figurative language paragraph is extremely strong, you have great examples and you analyze them well. I do agree with Grace that your last paragraph is somewhat disconnected from the rest of the essay so maybe try to make that connection more clear. Overall this is a strong essay!
>
> *Source: Neha Buch. Used with permission.*

Finally, as these teacher comments on Haley's work indicate, students do attend to the comments of peer reviewers and benefit from their advice:

*Ms. Holmes.* November 4, 2012, at 4:13 p.m.

> You do a good job here using warrants that justify your examples—this was a concern for your peer reviewers last month and I see that you have given it some thought in this month's essay. In your thesis, though, you don't make a clear statement about what the overall meaning of *Gatsby* is—and this causes problems later on, in your final paragraphs when you are trying to tie Daisy's conflict to the book's theme. What you really end up doing is just showing how Daisy's conflict drives the book's plot—and this is not at all the same as showing how her conflict sheds light on Fitzgerald's message.

We are encouraged to find that through this constant process of writing, reviewing, and reading feedback from multiple sources, our students are improving rapidly—as readers, as writers, and as critical thinkers.

Visit **go.solution-tree.com/technology** to download additional classroom examples.

## Your Turn

As we establish our goals for growth in analytical thought, peer response, and writing, we've found various digital spaces to support students in their skill development. Teachers can base some decisions about which tools to use for writing with a focus on revision on costs of using the tool, but we also seriously consider learning objectives, student population, and skill level. As you start your own practice of moving peer review into an online space, consider your goals and objectives for peer response, which tool you'll select, and how you'll incorporate the peer review. To start, you might want to investigate Google Drive and a blog space like Blogger or WordPress: each of these is free and none require any special skills to use. They both offer unique capabilities as a tool for online learning.

Digital peer review focuses our practice as English teachers on the 21st century communication skills necessary for authentic communication today and prepares our students for tomorrow's job market. Given the structure of the modern workplace and the prevalence of team-based work, digital peer review is a skill students are likely to use in their careers. This chapter, in fact, was composed primarily online in Google Drive using a process of digital collaboration and peer review. As professionals responsible for teaching tomorrow's writers the skills they will need to express themselves in a digital world, we feel it's necessary to consider the transitions in communication and to make the necessary transitions in our own pedagogies.

 **Matthew T. Pifer** is an associate professor of English at Husson University in Bangor, Maine, where he is the director of the writing center, and editor of the university's literary magazine, *Crosscut*. In addition to his administrative and teaching responsibilities, Matthew pursues research in both composition and American literature. Matthew has a blog called the "American Scholar" at http://associateprofessorpifer.wordpress.com.

CHAPTER 21

# Effective Revision and Editing Strategies

By Matthew T. Pifer

As stressed in the college and career readiness anchor standards (CCRA) in the Common Core State Standards for English language arts, students need to develop effective revision and editing strategies to prepare for college-level writing expectations.

> Develop and strengthen writing as needed by planning, revising, editing, rewriting, or trying a new approach. (CCRA.W.5; NGA & CCSSO, 2010, p. 18)

Toby Fulwiler (2003), among others, stresses that revision functions as the primary means by which "both thinking and writing evolve, mature, and improve" (p. 157). Yet, the means by which students develop and reinforce these revision and editing strategies remain elusive. Too often, students are left to revise in a vacuum, receiving little guidance as they decipher their instructors' textual marks and marginal comments. This lack of guidance can result in students simply moving around commas or replacing words with little sense of the rhetorical implications of their choices. Often, students complete a draft, receive a grade, and feel—as their instructors might—that their work is done. Yet, it is at this point that the work of both teaching writing and learning to write has begun. To help students develop conscious rhetorical strategies, we need to close the feedback loop, linking our revision and editing suggestions back to class instruction as well as to the standards and abilities students have already experienced.

To help implement a developmental sequence that takes advantage of the CCSS and CCRA scaffolding, I recommend creating an online writing center or course-specific online writing lab that supports the three components of the instructional process:

(1) developing clear writing assignments, (2) implementing effective writing pedagogies, and (3) creating thoughtful assessments that facilitate skill transfer and lifelong learning. Supporting this process can prepare instructors to provide the type of
feedback that will help students become more effective writers, teaching them at the
same time to use technology effectively to engage in the writing process. As noted in
the CCSS, students will need to:

> Use technology, including the Internet, to produce and publish writing
> and to interact and collaborate with others. (CCRA.W.6; NGA & CCSSO,
> 2010, p. 18)

## How Do I Do It?

To develop online writing spaces and help facilitate students' revision and editing
practices, I use Google Sites (figure 21.1) that, in addition to linking to the other
writing-center materials, includes a description of how the lab functions, a chat
group to allow for synchronous discussions with teachers or students who are working within a particular online lab, and a set of lab-specific writing resources, including videos, assignment sheets, and instructional tips and guidelines. This information and the associated online space allow me to collaborate with instructors, tutors,
and students, providing feedback during each of the three stages in the instructional
process—a process that provides the framework necessary to coach students as they
develop effective revision and editing strategies.

### Developing Clear Writing Assignments

At the beginning of each semester, I ask all instructors to submit a copy of their
writing assignments to the writing center. Once I receive these, I upload them to
the appropriate online lab and review how clearly the instructors have articulated
the learning objectives, purpose and audience, and evaluation criteria, all of which
allow the instructor to effectively assess a student's performance. During this stage,
I provide constructive feedback either through email, the chat group, or face-to-face
meetings. After this collaboration, I upload the corrected assignment sheets to the
Writing Assignment Sheets page, using the information to prepare the peer writing
tutors to assist students enrolled in these classes. By reviewing these assignments,
I can intercede on the students' behalf, suggesting that faculty members consider
creating authentic writing tasks that link to students' previous learning and encourage the ongoing development and refinement of effective writing practices, central
among these being revision and editing.

# Husson University Writing Center

## Discipline-Specific Writing Labs

Located here are resources for the writing labs developed for each of the disciplines.

**Purpose:**

The purpose of the writing labs is to assist faculty in effectively integrating writing into their courses. This is a collaborative effort in which experts from different disciplines come together to create writing assignments that will help students

1. build upon previous knowledge they have about writing well and
2. transfer their knowledge between different academic and professional contexts.

In general effective writing assignments share the following characteristics:

1. The requirements of each writing task should be clearly explained on the assignment sheet. This explanation should include the purpose of the task, its audience, the criteria required to complete it effectively, and a description of how the task will be evaluated. The explanation should clearly relate this writing task to the stated course objectives that the instructor has articulated on the course policy statement. The aim is to create authentic, inquiry-based writing requirements.

For this reason, instructors should not only create writing assignments that link to a course objective but they should also have students write those to an identifiable audience. For example, a chemistry instructor might have students write a description of an experiment for third graders, describing both how to conduct the experiment and why that experiment matters.

2. The writing task needs to be taught during class. Teaching writing in a course that is not devoted to it can no doubt be difficult. However, writing that relates to course objectives can be used to assess how well students have learned those objectives. Sometimes a *sustained* writing task--rather than multiple choice, short answer, or essay tests--is the only way to assess our students' ability to think critically, for instance.

In addition to teaching the writing task during the class, including for instance, a clear and accurate description of genre conventions, instructors need to talk about writing using similar terminology such as the following:

   a. Discuss writing as a process, which includes the creation of a topic, completion of research, planning, drafting, revision, and proofreading and editing.

   b. Note that writing well begins with global issues, such as developing a thesis and organizing the sections of the essay into a logical sequence using effective transitional strategies. After the global, content-level issues have been addressed, students should consider local-level concerns, such as grammar and mechanics.

   c. After the global- and local-level issues have been addressed, students should proofread and edit before turning in their final draft. Editing, for instance, is not the same activity as revising, and maintaining this distinction, among the others, is not merely semantics. Revision requires rethinking and radically altering versions of a document to support and illustrate an argument more effectively. Editing, on the other hand, is a mere polishing of an already coherent document.

3. The instructor who has assigned and taught the writing task must evaluate it, providing relevant feedback that will help students learn. The evaluation *of* and feedback provided *on* a writing task should not only justify the grade. Instead, the aim should be to explain to students (1) what they have done well (2) and what they need to do to improve. This explanation should go beyond mere discussion of sentence-level concerns, such as how to use commas and semi-colons. Instead the discussion should revolve around criteria that relate to the stated course objectives. To help provide relevant feedback, instructors might use rubrics that use consistent terminology and contain the specific skills and abilities students should be exploring and refining.

4. Instructors should think of writing as part of the learning process, and modify their expectations accordingly. Student will not mastery writing in one semester; in many cases, proficiency requires several semesters of sustained practice, as students acquire new knowledge and learn to use it to address a number of different issues. Most often, students need to understand the course material before they can write convincingly about it. Viewing student writing as "completed" can cause inappropriate stress for both instructors and students, undermining the educational process.

**Comments**

**Matthew Pifer**

Add a comment

*Source: Matthew T. Pifer. Used with permission.*

Figure 21.1: Online writing space using Google Sites.

### *Implementing Effective Writing Pedagogies*

When instructors attempt to incorporate writing into their courses, they either find it challenging due to the content they must cover, or they are not certain how to teach writing. Through the online lab, I and the writing tutors can provide instructional tips, convenient handouts, informational videos, or online workshops that align with the specific objectives or standards we are attempting to teach and assess.

We should remember that if instructors assign writing but fail to teach or comment on it, given the content demands of their courses, they create two difficulties.

1.   If a writing task is not linked to specific course objectives and therefore fails to be stressed in the course content, then students will have little chance of understanding what they should be learning from completing the task.

2.   When an instructor does not provide useful feedback on an assigned writing task, discussing the student's performance in relation to express learning objectives, then the student is likely to learn very little.

Evaluating student writing performances can often devolve, due to time constraints and other institutional pressures, into merely justifying grades rather than providing the feedback necessary to inform students' revision and editing strategies. The online writing center or lab is perhaps most effective during this phase of a student's writing process. If teaching writing, as Fulwiler (2003) claims, "is teaching rewriting," then focusing our efforts on revision and editing can help students learn the strategies necessary to write more effectively in a wide variety of contexts (p. 157).

### *Creating Thoughtful Assessments*

The online writing lab can shape the types of assessments instructors develop by offering supplemental instruction and informed writing resources. Because of this support, instructors can design assessments that function less to justify grades and more to suggest areas students should continue to develop, which could help create a "system of assessments" rather than a series of unlinked snapshots of students' *past* performances (Conley, 2014). This system promotes ongoing and self-directed learning, such as that seen in the implementation of student writing portfolios or student-centered learning groups. For example, when students submit a writing portfolio at the end of a writing course or marking period, instructors can score it not merely to evaluate the completed tasks but also, and perhaps more importantly, to identify unresolved issues. Once these issues have been identified, instructors can suggest strategies their students can use to refine their portfolios in preparation for subsequent submissions. The online writing lab can provide many of the resources necessary to support this assessment process, helping students engage in the iterative activities necessary to improve their writing skills—activities, one should note, that more accurately emulate authentic writing behaviors. Such collaborations require little additional resources and can lead to the proficiency-based assessment encouraged by the CCSS.

With this framework in place, the online writing lab can provide support for a wide range of writing activities, including coaching students to revise and edit their drafts effectively.

## Classroom Example

I used the online writing lab within the online writing center to collaborate with our chemistry department to structure clearer writing assignments. In my efforts to encourage both writing across the curriculum (WAC) and writing in the disciplines (WID), I solicited writing assignments from the faculty. In response to this request, the chemistry faculty submitted a writing assignment in which they required their students to develop a topic dealing with any issue related to chemistry and present it in written form. In completing this summary, students were required to adhere to the following restrictions.

- This is not a reflection paper or book report—it's a condensation of the original article, but shorter and in different words.

- Try not to quote the text, and limit paraphrasing unless absolutely necessary (that is, unless there's no other way to say it).

- Don't add any opinion or new examples.

- Don't use expressions like "This passage says . . ." or "According to the author . . ."

My concern with this writing task was twofold: (1) it was not well contextualized in that it did not provide students with the purpose such writing serves, and (2) it presented arbitrary criteria as though they were normative rules without articulating the rhetorical justification for instituting them. In relation to the first point, students participating in the chemistry writing lab expressed frustration with this assignment, often describing it as busywork. In relation to the second, students noted the contradiction of requiring a condensation of an article while both restricting personal opinion and quotations and limiting paraphrasing. Given these guidelines, students found it almost impossible to write anything. Students were being asked to develop a topic relevant to chemistry, find an article supporting that topic, and summarize it without quoting, paraphrasing, or examining how the article commented on that topic. These restrictions inhibited their efforts by placing them in an untenable situation. After reading the assignment sheet, students were unable to define the rhetorical context, such as the intended audience or the exigencies that informed the writing task. Because of this confusion, students reverted to vague generalizations, with little consideration of the detailed information relevant to the topic.

As illustrated in figure 21.1 (page 201), students can use Google Groups on the lab page to collaborate with writing consultants as they work through the revision and editing of their drafts. Instructors can also participate in or review these discussions to assess student learning. This type of collaboration, as Andrea Lunsford (2011) notes, extends the classroom, allowing students to engage more fully and realistically in the kinds of practice required to compose an effective text.

Using the chemistry writing lab, I found it easier to connect with the chemistry instructors to collaborate on developing outcomes for the writing assignment that more clearly related to the learning objectives of the course and to those skills students had learned in their previous writing courses. I was also able to help the instructors select models that clarified these outcomes, providing students with a better idea of how summaries function in chemistry as part of larger research projects.

Guided by our collaboration, I created assignment-specific workshops, such as "How to Summarize" and "Using APA Formatting Guidelines," to help the chemistry instructors teach writing while still attending to required course content. Finally, developing these materials helped the instructors create rubrics for evaluating student performance, rubrics that provided coherent criteria that allowed students to identify and build on their strengths and weaknesses.

Having implemented more effective writing assignments and associated pedagogical strategies, students were better prepared to work with the writing tutors to revise and edit their drafts. To ensure that these consultations not only guided revision and editing but also encouraged students to take responsibility for their learning, my tutors and I heeded the typical, and now canonical, advice about writing consultations, advice Harry Denny (2005) relates after he completed an e-consultation pilot between the Stony Brook University Writing Center and a nearby high school.

> We . . . agreed that the tutors would avoid evaluative responses (ostensibly "correcting" and grading students' performances). As a result, the tutors' responses posed open-ended questions related to argument and paragraph development, yet the students, teachers, and administrator wanted more directive evaluation. In spite of our conversations and readings about the tutoring process, the high school participant instructors had expected the tutors to serve as initial respondents to student papers—a sort of dialog that the high school participants found absent in the tutors' response. (p. 2)

Denny's observations highlight the conflict between *minimalist tutoring* (Brooks, 2011) and *directive tutoring* (Shamoon & Burns, 2011). A minimalist, or *pens-off approach*, is understood as the most effective approach to use when tutoring, primarily because it ensures that the writing tutor will not appropriate the student's text, an act that is all too common in any form of writing instruction. For instance, on several occasions, I have observed my colleagues rewrite a student's thesis. The student may appear thankful for the help, but reappropriating a thesis she did not develop is very difficult and ultimately counterproductive. Still, as Linda Shamoon and Deborah Burns (2011) argue, directive tutoring (or expressly reworking a student's essay) can help inexperienced writers address a gap in their knowledge by having more effective writing practices modeled for them. When I observe my writing tutors, they often default into a mixed approach, having a conversation with students about their writing at one moment and modeling how to articulate a point the next. Even though I initially trained them to use the minimalist approach, as Harry Denny (2005) and Jeff Brooks (2011) describe, I have found that mixing the strategies is more effective. The online environment seems to be a particularly appropriate venue for this combined approach.

Using the Google Docs commenting feature, writing tutors can emulate the transition from minimal to directive tutoring often observed during a physical writing consultation. Such an exchange is nearly impossible through email, where comments become monologues rather than dialogues. Using email, an open comment such as "What is your topic sentence in this paragraph?" is of little use. However, using the synchronous comment function in Google Docs, or a similar resource, allows a student to respond to such a question and immediately practice alternative approaches. As when teaching grammar, locating this particular type of discussion within the context of a student's own writing allows him or her to experience the improvements and thus become more aware of how a particular revision or editing strategy functions to improve the clarity not only of the document but also of his or her thinking.

Teachers can store information from these consultations for later review and analysis and use it to track student progress. Tracking students' progress by collecting their writing process work provides the evidence needed to fulfill mandated learning assessments. In particular, an online writing lab can play a central role in monitoring our students' fulfillment and the continued development of the skills that the CCSS outline.

## Your Turn

For most schools, the resources available to create a physical writing center are limited. However, schools can use Google Sites or a similar software solution as an online writing space with little cost, space, or staffing requirements. In many cases, a director and a few committed faculty or capable students can run the online environment, at least initially. To implement this type of space, you might consider the following four steps.

1. Using the institutional mission or standards, such as those articulated in the CCSS and CCRA or *Framework for Success in Postsecondary Writing* (O'Neill, Adler-Kassner, Fleischer, & Hall, 2012), develop specific writing objectives, writing outcomes from each course, and plans for assessing student learning. Articulate this information in a document that you can include on the online writing center or course-specific online writing lab. This information will create the framework for the development of writing assignments, teaching pedagogies, and assessments.

2. Select peer tutors and train them using Christina Murphy and Steve Sherwood's (2011) *The St. Martin's Sourcebook for Writing Tutors* or a similar resource. One benefit of peer tutors is that they will learn more about writing as they work with their fellow students. For this reason, the use of rolling tutors or the writing center or lab as part of a composition course can increase its institutional value.

3. Using Google Sites or a similar resource, such as Blogger or WordPress, develop a parent writing center site, and include course-specific labs on separate pages. In addition to functioning as a writing reference, this site will also help centralize your writing discussions and serve to create a community of practice.

4. Assess the performance of your writing center by gathering a variety of information about how students who use the service fare in their writing courses. Neal Lerner (2011) discusses relevant research methods in "Writing Center Assessment: Searching for the 'Proof' of Our Effectiveness."

Once implemented, an online writing space can be instrumental in promoting effective writing practices throughout the institution. Such a space can achieve this aim because it centralizes writing support for both faculty and students. In doing so, it facilitates informed discussions about the role writing plays in our students' academic and professional success.

# PART VIII | Assessment

Teachers know that students need frequent opportunities to write and receive feedback; however, for many teachers, the constant demands of responding to students' writing can become tedious and time consuming. Teachers can also become discouraged when they do not see their evaluations and assessments contributing to students' writing development. How do teachers provide feedback and assess students' writing in ways that lead to positive growth in writing? How do teachers develop criteria for responding to and assessing students' writing?

Research recommends that teachers focus on specific elements of writing and provide targeted feedback (Graham et al., 2012). Kelly Gallagher's (2006) work supports this idea. He recommends that teachers should be readers during the writing process and uses the analogy of a coach providing support throughout a game or practice. For writing instruction, this means the teacher provides feedback and suggestions throughout students' writing process rather than solely at the end, when students submit a final draft. One way to do this is to implement teacher-led conferences at various points of the process, so that students can focus their attention on specific aspects of their writing.

Another strategy for providing meaningful feedback is through writing portfolios. Many educators advocate for the use of portfolios as a way to document and chart student growth as writers over time. This option allows students to select the pieces of writing that best demonstrate their abilities. Portfolios provide students with a voice and a sense of ownership over their writing, which can contribute to them becoming more metacognitive about their writing. Graham and colleagues (2012) suggest that teachers can encourage students to self-monitor and self-evaluate by answering, "Did I meet the goals I developed for my writing? If not, what changes should I make to meet my goals?" (p. 16). Writing assessments should be formative; they need to contribute to students' growth as writers, allowing students to become more reflective on their strengths and weaknesses.

There are at least four areas in which technology affects or can affect assessment: (1) automated scoring, (2) massive open online courses, (3) alternative forms of assessment, and (4) digital portfolios.

First, automated scoring is a controversial topic in the literature and in policy discussions and decisions. However, that does not mean we should ignore it. We should continue to find ways to explore such tools and the promise they offer. Second, a popular new tool is the massive open online course. Some courses have hundreds of thousands of students. One successful strategy for instructors handling student loads that are very high is peer revision. Instructors find that most peer revision is as useful as sole instructor feedback, provided modeling is performed and multiple assessments are offered. A third strategy is to explore alternative forms of assessment. Assessment can come through audio and video as easily and quickly as it can come through written text. A final area in which technology affects assessment is, as we have already seen, the digital portfolio. Digital portfolios allow for measured growth as they provide an opportunity to observe a student's complete body of work over an extended period of time.

The use of technology to support the assessment of the entire student is both easy and important. It is easy because teachers can facilitate it through cloud computing—or places that host all of a student's material regardless of the physical location of the student. And it is important because it provides an accurate portrayal of students as writers.

Deborah-Lee Gollnitz begins the section in chapter 22 by addressing the affordances and constraints of using automatic essay-scoring software. In chapter 23, Andy Schoenborn explains how teachers can use digital tools to provide feedback on student writing. Jeremy Hyler documents how digital portfolios can be used to measure students' growth and development as writers in chapter 24.

 **Deborah-Lee Gollnitz, PhD,** is a curriculum coordinator at Birmingham Public Schools in Michigan. She started teaching in the mid-1970s, left to pursue a business career, and returned to teaching in the mid-1990s. Teaching both business technology and English, she found her passion in writing instruction. Deb holds a bachelor's degree and master of business administration from Bryant University in Rhode Island and an educational specialist degree and a doctorate from Oakland University in Michigan. To learn more about her work, visit http://doctordeborah.wordpress.com, or follow her on Twitter @DebGollnitz.

# CHAPTER 22

# Automated Essay-Scoring Software

By Deborah-Lee Gollnitz

Writing instruction includes assessment at multiple phases of the writing process. Students need formative assessment to help them determine the next steps in a task. Teachers need formative assessment to help them develop meaningful lessons and just-in-time activities that scaffold student learning. As classroom teachers work to differentiate learning, assessment begins to take on a different look. No longer is it sufficient to assess all students' writing at the same time. Each writer needs different assistance at different times; each needs specific feedback. Teachers use assessment to develop lessons for whole-class and individual instruction, and students use assessment to revise their writing.

Response to student writing serves as a scaffold. Teachers can give formative feedback during the writing process to guide students as they revise text (Burnett & Kastman, 1997). As an integral part of the way we teach writing, assessment rarely stands alone as a summative measure of student performance. Rather, we intuitively ask students to do something with the assessment results. In other words, we want them to use our feedback. We also want them to internalize what they learn through that feedback so that they can become self-regulated and ask themselves deeper questions about their own work.

As a form of assessment, feedback leads to revision. When students receive feedback from another person, they have to decide what to do with it. Sometimes they agree with the suggestions, and sometimes they don't. In either case, in order for the feedback to serve as a learning tool, students must have time to think about it and do something with it (Brookhart, 2008, 2012). Teachers need to provide that time in the classroom if they are writing comments on students' papers and returning them in hard copy.

Vygotsky (1978) suggests that a learner's highest possible performance occurs when he or she receives assistance to achieve the next highest level of a learning goal. Assessment in the form of good feedback scaffolds learning for students by providing not only things to think about when writing but also resources to aid in the writing task. Elements of good feedback include reliability, consistency, clarity, timeliness, and specificity to individual work (Brookhart, 2012; Goodwin & Miller, 2012; Hattie, 2012a; Lalor, 2012; Wiggins, 2012). By responding to frequent and consistent feedback, students engage in experiences that develop memory and recall of learning for use in future contexts (Foertsch, 1995). Writing instruction illustrates the importance of assessment as an integral part of teaching and learning.

Writing teachers know the demands of the work involved in providing effective feedback, but they can leverage technology to help with this task. Automated essay-scoring (AES) software can tirelessly provide consistent feedback, along with resources for immediate resolution of problems with grammar, spelling, punctuation, and word usage. This software is comprised of several different computer programs in a single suite that together provide feedback on multiple traits of writing during the composing process. Commenting on the basics of writing can take a great deal of a teacher's attention away from the real work of developing strong writers. At the same time, if not well developed, these skills can hamper a student's progress in becoming a good writer. By coupling automated essay scoring technology with a teacher's expertise for dialogue around constructs of writing, students can experience the best possible assessment scenario that supports writing instruction.

Automated essay scoring technology gives writers full access to writing resources 24-7, with more detailed suggestions for editing than word processing software gives. These programs also compare student writing against thousands of anchor papers that have been scored by humans using specific rubrics. Teachers and students can access the rubrics and sample essays scored at each level of proficiency for a given writing prompt. Teachers can use resulting holistic scores as predictors of effectiveness.

English teachers tend to have challenges with the software adoption. For instance, it can be cumbersome to use the software for personally created assignments, and some teachers find that the assignments built into the software do not suit their classroom needs. For less technologically savvy teachers, creating assignments online and tracking student use of the software can be a challenge. Some teachers report that the rules of grammar or the structure of a particular mode of writing that is promoted through the software does not align with their own teachings or preferences. However, software is not the end of the story. Teachers continue to be the most important element in the writing classroom. Guidance, encouragement, and dialogue among students and teachers lead to critical thinking about written language. Technology is one additional tool to assist in the process and can be valuable, freeing up time for teachers to help students with writing forms, structures, meaning, and critical supports for their ideas.

As the United States tests for the Common Core State Standards approach, software is being evaluated, compared, and reviewed. Examples of these reviews include the work of Mark Shermis and Ben Hamner (n.d.) and Hyojung Lim and Jimin Kahng (2012). The national tests will be administered electronically, and many vendors are working to establish a good delivery system. In the meantime, teachers can embrace technology as one more tool in the toolbox of instruction to help students learn and grow into the writers we want them to become.

Two groups are preparing the assessments that will be electronically delivered. Sample ELA assessment tasks are available on two websites: the Smarter Balanced Assessment Consortium (www.smarterbalanced.org/sample-items-and-performance-tasks) and the Partnership for Assessment of Readiness for College and Careers (http://practice.parcc.testnav.com). Depending on which group a particular state is aligned with for assessment, the online environments will vary slightly. In both platforms, students are asked to identify phrases within text that support specific arguments. Reading and writing assessment are merged in the sample tasks. The writing portions provided on both websites offer a glimpse of what can be expected of students. Students will read and compose responses to challenging texts. The samples focus on literature, with copy for reading and analysis on the left side of the screen and a text box for responding on the right side of the screen. Students need to be familiar with navigating multiple open screens within the electronic assessment environment, understand how to compose and revise in a text box within a testing screen, and understand that submission of text is their final draft. Using technology as a writing tool during the learning process will help prepare students for these online assessments.

## How Do I Do It?

There are a few important elements to look for in student writing. For example:

- A strong sense of purpose for the written piece
- Appropriate style and voice for the purpose and audience
- Clarity of meaning
- Coherence and unity
- Grammar and overall mechanics
- General language use

For the most part, by the time students are enrolled in a high school composition class like the ones I taught, they understand the need to think about their writing from the global perspective of purpose and audience. My students had good ideas, and they worked hard to get those ideas into a meaningful piece of writing. Sometimes, however, those last two bullet points distracted me. After years of working to find the most efficient and effective way to give student feedback on the conventions of writing, I realized that technology could make my life easier.

Web-based programs, such as those from the Educational Testing Service (www.ets.org) and Vantage Learning (www.vantagelearning.com), serve as scoring tools for typed essays. They are available at a per-student fee with a sliding scale that offers discounts for subscriptions based on greater numbers of students using the software. The pricing varies widely depending on the platform and provider. Subscriptions allow each student to create an account. Teachers also create accounts and establish classes. Students join classes when teachers are ready, and they access and complete assignments through the website.

Some free software packages are also available. The University of Kansas provides downloadable software, the Kansas Writing Instruction and Evaluation Tool (KWIET), that scores student writing as a means to prepare students for state testing. (See www.ksassessments.org for more information.) LightSide (http://lightsidelabs.com) is developing other free software. LightSide is a group that originally developed software for large-scale testing and is working to bring the tool to classroom teachers.

All of the samples I have reviewed have the same basic steps. To get started, teachers set up a class and students create accounts. They create assignments directly in the web-based program. Teachers can create:

- Extended writing assignments on topics of choice
- Quick-write assessments using built-in writing prompts
- Prompts that address their own learning targets

For longer, independent writing assignments with student-selected topics, an automated essay-scoring program serves a different purpose than it does for in-class assignments that use one prompt. In the case of individual essays, students use the software for feedback to guide their revision and editing processes. Students can access the software online anytime, allowing students to work from home at any time of day and to submit as many drafts for feedback as necessary. Generally, the writer creates a document and then copies and pastes the text into a textbox on the webpage. Within minutes, if not immediately, the site generates a report. In this case, the program assesses the mechanics, grammar, and language elements, and the student has the opportunity to bring his or her writing to the highest possible level before a teacher reads it.

Students see highlighted areas of their writing that need attention, and details of what to investigate for improvement are available through linked writing handbooks. Figure 22.1 is an example of the kind of analysis students see on the screen when using Criterion, an Educational Testing Service product. Visit www.riversidepublish ing.com to learn more about Criterion.

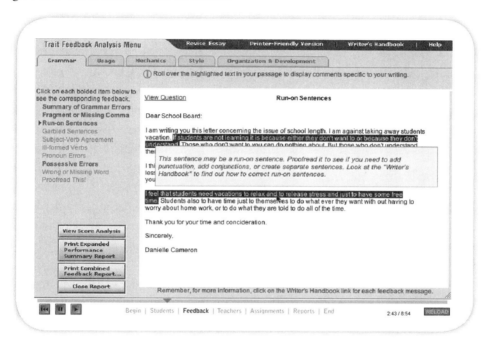

*Source: Copyright © Educational Testing Service. www.ets.org. Reprinted by permission of Educational Testing Service, the copyright owner, and no endorsement of any kind of this publication by Educational Testing Service should be inferred.*

Figure 22.1: Trait feedback analysis.

Because this software is designed for use with informational text, the feedback results are based on standard written English and not poetic or metaphoric language. Students are asked to apply rules of writing and to consider the applicability of those rules within the context of their own work. Figure 22.1 is a perfect example of the need for the writer to consider those rules of grammar that might apply to this high-lighted text. The pop-up text suggests that the statement over which it appears may be a run-on sentence. The implication is that punctuation may be needed. The sentence includes a short introductory prepositional phrase that is not followed by a comma. By referring to the handbook and digging deeper into the intended meaning of the sentence and the intent of the introductory phrase, the writer is asked to make decisions.

The program does not correct the text for the writer as might happen through autocorrect features or suggested corrections available in word processing software. The students themselves make decisions about the best way to edit their work and are making judgments on how to best convey the meaning they want to express. They also make judgments about the quality of their writing. Depending on how the teacher perceives the assignment, this step might be the beginning of revision around needed support for a claim or around the organization of the text. Automated essay-scoring software allows the writer to manage copyediting, freeing up time for dialogue about the meaning of text.

As educators, we may have viewed automated essay-scoring software as a piece of technology that attempts to do the work of a human reader. Certainly, this software cannot replace the teacher, but it can assist with assessment and add to the learning experience for developing writers. As a sole source of gathering information on student writing progress through a testing scenario, AES software may not be the best answer. As noted from the feedback example provided in figure 22.1 (page 215), some of the flagged errors are not really errors; they are writer choices. When used in conjunction with a human reader as the second reviewer, then it is possible that the software can cut the cost of administering large-scale writing assessments that require calibrated double scoring of every student essay. There are other drawbacks, of course. The technology needs to be reliable and accessible, which in itself can be cost prohibitive. Moving into the future, as Common Core State Standards testing moves into an electronic environment, more school districts will find ways to be equipped. The dialogue will undoubtedly change where the use of AES software is concerned as that scenario becomes reality.

Using AES software as a formative assessment tool, students take responsibility for drawing on previous instruction to improve their work. By using the prompts that are built into the software, students can learn from sample essays. For instance, one assignment taken from the database might be designed to allow students to write for an unlimited amount of time, save their work to finish writing later, review exemplar essays, review the feedback, submit the essay multiple times, and see a predictive holistic score. In this case, students can use all of the tools available to revise their writing. Feedback reports show writers how well they have performed, and the process of revising serves as a learning activity. Again, students make the decision about when to submit a final copy of their writing for teacher review. Students are actually going through a self-assessment process with the help of the technology.

## Classroom Example

When using automated essay-scoring software for quick-write assessments that are a snapshot of student progress, built-in prompts make the most sense. Some of these programs allow timed writing of thirty minutes. In these cases, students create a short writing sample without opportunities to review feedback and submit a revised composition. They submit the essay one time and receive a holistic score. Figure 22.2 shows a sample of this type of assessment in the Criterion software. In this example, students see the feedback to learn from it but do not use the feedback for editing.

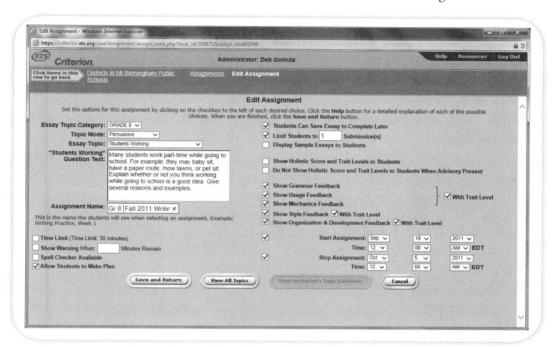

*Source: Copyright © Educational Testing Service. www.ets.org. Reprinted by permission of Educational Testing Service, the copyright owner, and no endorsement of any kind of this publication by Educational Testing Service should be inferred.*

Figure 22.2: Sample writing prompt from Criterion.

In this scenario, the technology delivers one prompt to an entire district of students at one grade level with the same rubric, calendar for completion, amount of writing time, feedback, and unbiased scorer. Teachers can quickly review the essays and scores to verify the validity of the automated essay-scoring results. The work of scoring a common writing assessment is greatly diminished, yet progress-monitoring data on overall performance become readily available. If a teacher feels a particular score is not accurate, he or she should have the option of grading the essay manually. Some school districts ask that all students complete these short writing assessments two to three times each year. The data are used as one more piece of information to add to the dialogue during team meetings that are focused on improving student learning.

## Your Turn

Most automated essay-scoring software producers are willing to provide trial periods. Vendor sites are numerous, and vary in capability, application, and cost. (Visit **go.solution-tree.com/technology** to download links to a number of vendor sites.) One sample of an online essay scorer that can be used immediately for short writing prompts can be found on the Pearson website (www.pearsonschool.com/index .cfm?locator=PS1f8e). Other publishers of textbooks are offering these online tools as an embedded piece of their curriculum materials. Look at Holt, Rinehart, and Winston for a description of their service (http://my.hrw.com/support/hos/host_FAQ _Fall_2006.html) or Houghton Mifflin Harcourt for their latest English language arts program, which will embed a writing and editing space known as myWriteSmart (http://finance.yahoo.com/news/houghton-mifflin-harcourt-announces-cutting -133000743.html). A web search for "online writing assessment" or "automated essay-scoring software" will produce many results for organizations, corporations, and universities that are involved in creating new software to meet the increased need for these tools. During a trial period, use the prompts that are built into the software and that provide exemplar essays for the students to review. Here are six suggested steps to consider.

1.  Create an assignment to collect baseline data. Elect the options that give students access to the feedback, and ask them to use the feedback tools to correct errors. Give them one class period to do this work so that you can watch the process. Pay particular attention to how the students interact with the software and what they do with the holistic scores that result. My colleagues and I have watched students working toward an improved score or decreased number of errors, almost as if they were playing a computer game.

2.  Use the data that result from the writing session to develop a starting point for your own instruction. Review the software's reports. (Visit **go.solution-tree.com/technology** to view sample reports.) Some of these reports are described at sites like Vantage Learning .com (www.vantagelearning.com) in a downloadable brochure or explained through video orientation, as through the Riverside Publishing website (www.riversidepublishing.com/products/criterion). The details of surface errors can include the number of instances of such things as run-on sentences, repetitive word use, or comma errors, and reports containing this information can be the foundation of classroom instruction and differentiation.

3.  Pull small groups of students and deliver minilessons that target the specific areas of writing that need attention.

4.  Develop review lessons for whole-class instruction as necessary and move to a new level of instruction in those traits in which students are showing higher levels of mastery. Differentiated instruction is easier when data are available immediately.

5.  Make use of the online tools that allow you to provide your own feedback directly to the student within the online window. These features make commenting on student work very convenient, and students can read the comments easily, unlike the scribbled comments many of us make in the margins of student papers.

6.  Before the trial ends, allow students to use the software for a topic of choice. Pull away all of the parameters, and ask them to find ways to make the software work for them. For instance, don't set a limit on the number of submissions allowed on one assignment. Students may actually choose to submit their work for review many more times than you would allow during an assessment. Also, provide the opportunity for students to write on different topics or to get feedback on different modes of writing that are self-selected. Be sure they understand that using the software for creative prose will not produce the most meaningful results. Ask students to tell you what they are experiencing as they explore the software. They will enjoy finding fault with the flagged errors. Your job, then, is to ask why they believe text that may not need correcting was flagged. Here is where the dialogue about writer choice can begin.

While teachers know what is best for students, we also know that technology is moving very quickly. The newest technologies offer many more options for student learning and for assessment to foster learning. Automated essay-scoring software is just one of those tools. Many districts use these technologies for student learning and assessment. The Smarter Balanced Assessment Consortium and the Partnership for Assessment of Readiness for College and Careers tests around the Common Core State Standards will use these technologies, so it is in our best interest as educators to move with the times and still maintain the very important role of developing strong classroom discourse around writing.

 **Andy Schoenborn** is an English teacher at Mt. Pleasant Public Schools in Mt. Pleasant, Michigan. He is also a teacher consultant for Central Michigan University's Chippewa River Writing Project and frequently conducts workshops related to literacy and technology. Andy focuses his work on progressive literacy methods, including student-centered critical thinking, digital collaboration, and professional development. Follow him on Twitter @aschoenborn.

# CHAPTER 23

# Authentic Writing Through Digital Feedback

By Andy Schoenborn

The decision to move to digital feedback is a practical one, in order to meet students where they are—online. Most students find information with relative ease by using the smartphones, computers, and tablets already around them. They regularly consider responses to their ideas through text messages, Facebook posts, discussion threads, YouTube videos, and other forms of digital technology. They—and we—don't often think of it, but students receive written digital feedback on a daily basis, although it is usually not the kind that we value in the classroom. Students are used to efficient personal feedback that feels like dialogue instead of a set of instructions to follow. As Ken Robinson (2011) notes, "The pervasiveness of digital technology changes the whole equation for education and for the role of teachers" (p. 76). By embracing technology and modeling constructive digital feedback, we can make this change a manageable shift for students.

The fundamentals of giving effective feedback remain, but we should consider, as Troy Hicks (2009) notes, that:

> When we ask students to be writers in this age, we are inherently asking them to be digital writers. Therefore, our pedagogy needs to acknowledge this shift and adopt a perspective that honors digital writing and integrates it into our classrooms. (p. 11)

A move to incorporate digital writing must also include a shift in the delivery of effective feedback. In this way, we can honor student writers when they are able to receive what Grant Wiggins (2012) describes as "helpful feedback [that] is goal-referenced; tangible and transparent; actionable; user-friendly; timely; ongoing; and consistent" (p. 10). Using the flexibility, privacy, and multimodality of Google Drive and the web-based office suite Google Docs, learners enter into a productive feedback loop, thereby increasing their confidence as writers.

Creating authentic writing experiences for students builds confidence in them as they begin to *know* what it means to be a writer. Jeff Anderson (2011) explains: "The knowing comes through the flow of student-teacher transactions, through students' observation . . . through students' talking, collecting, imitating, writing, experimenting, revising, editing, and reflecting" (p. xiii). Digital feedback increases the flow of interactions between students, peers, and teachers. Ashley, a student of mine, can attest to its usefulness:

> [Digital feedback] makes me want to revise my work, because I don't have to find the paper and I don't have to struggle to read the handwriting. I just have to go on to the computer and look at the comments; I can comment back, converse with the teacher, and ask them what they are talking about. It makes me inspired to go back and correct my work. (A. Montgomery, personal communication, November 13, 2012)

Ashley's reflection suggests a learning opportunity in which writing instruction using digital feedback intrinsically motivates her to engage in the writing process. The Harvard Writing Project (2000) supports her reflection, noting, "Feedback improves [students'] writing, as well as providing them with a more satisfying writing experience" (p. 1). Digitizing feedback increases the willingness of young writers to incorporate it in their revisions.

## How Do I Do It?

The attraction to digital writing comes from its productivity, efficiency, and collaborative nature. Its usefulness lies in its accessibility, speed of communication, and possibilities for differentiation. As with any tool, we should be excited about the success our students experience through its use. The primary goal of instructors who use digital-based components in the classroom should be to use these tools to encourage student growth. Google Drive is the best tool to encourage this, and on the first day of any new trimester, I introduce students to it and my classroom website (www .mphsroom202.weebly.com). Here I direct them to the Getting Started tab, where students have the option of working at their own pace or following my instructions to set up a Google account (see figure 23.1). Once all the students have their accounts, I ask them to use the form on the same page to share their email address with me in order to open the lines of communication.

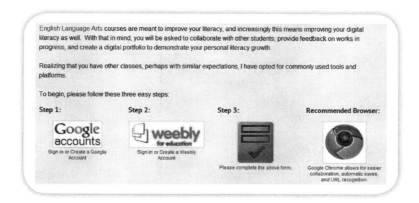

*Source: Andy Schoenborn. Google and the Google logo are registered trademarks of Google Inc. Used with permission.*

Figure 23.1: Getting Started instructions.

Fridays in my classroom are tech days. On these days, we take advantage of one of the five computer labs available at my high school, and I sign up for a computer lab weekly for our digital writing workshops. When my students create a new Google Doc, I ask them to click the blue Share button, add my Gmail address to the "Invite people" text box, and allow for permission to edit.

Once students share their essays, the digital essays are automatically sent to the Shared with Me tab on the left-hand column of the Google Drive homepage. Here, I organize all of the essays by moving them into folders. Then, I am able to respond to student writing by clicking on the document, highlighting a portion of text, selecting Insert, choosing Comment, and typing in the dialogue box that appears to the right. Figure 23.2 shows the menu in Google Drive.

Much in the same way that feedback reduces friction in the writing process, Google Docs, with its commenting feature, essentially removes the stumbling blocks for writers and focuses attention on the improvement of writing, as good feedback is meant to do. Beyond using feedback to augment the teaching and learning of writing, technology-facilitated feedback demonstrates to learners that they can use technology to become more efficient and productive as they become more proficient writers.

*Source: Google Drive. Google and the Google logo are registered trademarks of Google Inc. Used with permission.*

Figure 23.2: Sharing feature on Google Drive.

## Classroom Example

In my classroom, students find personal peer editing, the revision history function, and hyperlinks useful for creating the authenticity found in digital writers today. Personal peer editing gives student writers control over who views their pieces during the composing stage and allows them to think through their choices as writers. The revision history function lets students easily go back and track their changes while acting as a visual reference for them to see the writing process unfold. Using hyperlinks in comment boxes directs students to web pages, rubrics, and video tutorials for support with writing mechanics.

### Personal Peer Editing

The Comment function gives the peer editor pinpoint control when offering feedback. He or she can highlight specific words, sentences, or phrases and insert comments and clarifying questions to which the author is able to reply within a comment thread.

Soon after creating and titling a new document, students share their piece with a peer and me. I agree with Thomas Newkirk (2009) and "find it easier, and more congenial, to respond to a student's paper after it has received feedback from a peer, and I often echo a comment that has already been made" (p. 146). Once peers have commented on the work (figure 23.3), I am better able to supply precision feedback or offer affirmation to the feedback students have supplied by replying to a comment.

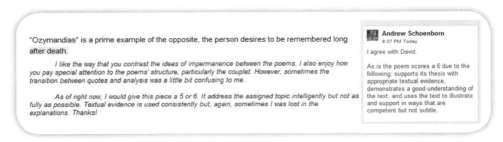

*Source: David Dai. Google and the Google logo are registered trademarks of Google Inc. Used with permission.*

Figure 23.3: Digital feedback using Google Docs.

### Revision History

For many students, collaborative writing unfortunately means either taking charge of a group task or allowing someone else to do the majority of the thinking. The assessed piece that results from this type of collaboration is usually not equally distributed for those who have done most of the intellectual lifting. Created as a productivity tool, Google Docs, with its revision history function (figure 23.4), irrefutably tracks each edit as students write a piece. This feature inspires confidence among educators and holds students accountable for doing their share.

More importantly, students are able to visualize their improvements and reflect on their rhetorical choices as a piece develops. Although students may not reflect on their writing without prompting, using this feature allows for thoughtful discussion points during workshop conferences. The ability to see when revisions were made and how much (or how little) was actually revised helps young writers understand that revision is more than editing.

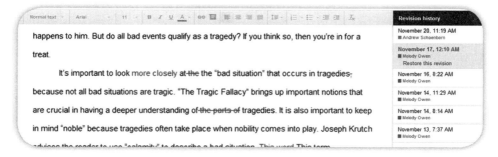

*Source: Ashley Montgomery. Google and the Google logo are registered trademarks of Google Inc. Used with permission.*

Figure 23.4: Revision history using Google Docs.

### Hyperlinks

Sometimes feedback takes more explanation than teachers can comfortably insert into a comment thread. For example, students may forget to use Modern Language Association (MLA) format in their papers. When this happens, I share a link to a short video that walks students through the process. When they use the link, I encourage them to open a window containing their paper side-by-side with a window playing the video, and ask them to follow along with the video. It takes five minutes or less to watch a description of the adjustments they need to make, and they can do so while maintaining their focus on the writing itself.

When patterns emerge locally, usually due to grammatical or mechanical issues, I direct them via hyperlink (figure 23.5) to online writing sources. In this way, students learn to become more autonomous editors of their own papers. Furthermore, they are practicing skills necessary to search for writing help from multiple sources, a desirable trait for college and career readiness.

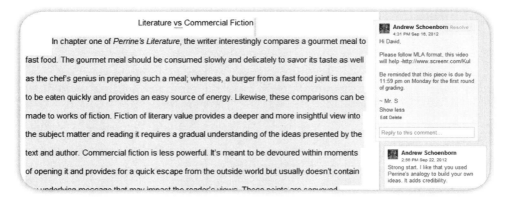

*Source: David Dai. Google and the Google logo are registered trademarks of Google Inc. Used with permission.*

Figure 23.5: Hyperlinks using Google Docs.

## Your Turn

At its core, feedback on writing, digital or otherwise, "should be presented hierarchically, in what Nancy Sommers, Sosland Director of Expository Writing, calls a 'scale of concerns'—from *global* (problems with thesis, structure, analysis, or, as we have already seen, style) to *local* (problems with sentences and formatting)" (Harvard Writing Project, 2000). Borrowing from Sommers's scale of concerns, I keep the following in mind when giving digital feedback.

- Read through the entire piece before inserting comments.

- Focus comments on patterns of representative strengths and weaknesses.

- Use a respectful tone, and search for what is right and effective.

- Ask questions and respond as a reader, not an evaluator.

- Personalize final comments using two positives and one suggestion.

After a piece of student writing is finished, I read it through and offer summative feedback at the end, focused on its strengths and weaknesses, to encourage growth in the student writer. In the words of *Harvard Writing Project Bulletin* editor, Kerry Walk (Harvard Writing Project, 2000), "The best final comments take student writers seriously, conveying an understanding of what they were trying to do and making concrete suggestions for how it might be done more effectively" (p. 7). To this end, and borrowing from Walk's format for final comments, I created a template (table 23.1) to ensure each student receives useful and strategic digital feedback.

Table 23.1: Feedback Template

| Feedback | Example |
|---|---|
| **Start with a greeting.** | "Hi, Sarah." |
| **Restate the overarching ideas.** | "As a reader, I find it is clear that your paper is about . . ." |
| **Share two strengths of the piece.** | "I enjoyed the vivid imagery used in the introduction, because it helped to generate interest. Also, I liked how you weaved your transitions in without losing the flow of the piece." |
| **Share a large weakness of the piece.** | "I wonder, though, if you could blend your use of quotations in by leading into the quote instead of just placing it between sentences." |
| **Add concluding remarks.** | "As is, the piece scores 8 out of 10 due to the comments and rubric." |
| **Close.** | "Thank you for sharing!—Mr. S" |

Visit **go.solution-tree.com/technology** to download a reproducible version of this table.

Using Google Docs to insert comments and encourage the flow of student-to-teacher dialogue is a fine starting point for those who are venturing into the digital feedback arena. Students appreciate the timeliness of the feedback, and as students—as well as instructors—get familiar with the digital process, they find, as my student Melody did, that:

> Digital feedback is a lot easier to communicate with the instructor. It helps me as a writer to know what [they] are looking for and what I should be doing. It is easier for [them] to teach me different writing skills. And oftentimes, I insert a comment myself, because it helps me to see what I thought. (M. Owen, personal communication, November 13, 2012)

Sharing feedback digitally has proven useful and effective in my classroom, but when students read the same voice it can lose its intended impact. Additionally, as a writing instructor, I want to introduce voices, minilessons, and digital resources as part of the commentary. Google Docs helps teachers through the use of personal peer editing, revision history, and hyperlinks in addition to our individual feedback.

Our digital lives, including those of writers and editors, have received a boost of encouragement from the technology-facilitated feedback opportunity that Google Drive offers. Students find it refreshing, because as my student David puts it, "You're not limited to the space on the paper, it's clearer, and it feels more professional because it's typed, and you have a constant interface to work in" (D. Dai, personal communication, November 13, 2012). The stage is set for the elimination of nearly infinite email loops, the removal of indecipherable educator scrawl, and the processing of feedback from only one source at a time. Digital feedback paves the way for authentic writing to happen.

 **Jeremy Hyler** is a seventh- and eighth-grade English teacher at Fulton Middle School in Middleton, Michigan. In addition, he is a teacher consultant for the Chippewa River Writing Project. He delivers professional development on the Common Core State Standards and is coauthor of *Create, Compose, Connect!: Reading, Writing and Learning with Digital Tools*. To learn more about Jeremy's work, visit his website, http://jeremyhyler40.wordpress.com, or follow him on Twitter @Jeremybballer.

CHAPTER 24

# Measuring Student Growth
# With Digital Portfolios

By Jeremy Hyler

Using writing portfolios is not a new method for collecting student work over the school year. Richard Koch (2010), director of Michigan Portfolios (www.michigan portfolios.org), notes that:

> Portfolios compiled from classroom work can show what students are able to do far better than tests. Portfolios can make it possible for all stakeholders to see how our learners are doing. Portfolios can make it possible for schools to "showcase" the best their students can do and also to "document growth" over time powerfully and helpfully. (p. 1)

English language arts teachers need a way to measure individual students adequately in a subject that encompasses so many aspects, including thesis statements, grammar, sentence structure, tone, voice, and audience. As new waves of assessments continue to swirl around us in what seems to be a never-ending vortex, writing portfolios are one of the best means to measure student growth in an English language arts classroom. Digital portfolios possess the potential to be powerful assessment tools, especially when students are required to meet criteria and guidelines of the CCSS:

> Use technology, including the Internet, to produce and publish writing and present the relationships between information and ideas efficiently as well as to interact and collaborate with others. (CCRA.W.6; NGA & CCSSO, 2010, p. 18)

Kathleen Yancey (1999) explains portfolios in the following way:

> The one model [holistically scored] essay is replaced by a set of texts,
> so that: a single draft becomes two drafts; two drafts becomes two
> drafts accompanied by some authorial commentary; two drafts plus
> commentary become an undetermined number of multiple final drafts
> accompanied by a "reflection," and this set of texts becomes the new:
> *portfolio assessment.* (p. 486)

Classrooms manage digital portfolios electronically or through an online cloud space. They are not only easier to manage than hard-copy portfolios but also more convenient, and there are multiple tools and websites to use for collecting student work. Students can place multiple modes of writing in an online space. For instance, students can share word clouds, digital movies, brainstorming maps, digital book trailers, speeches, and so on. Dànielle Nicole DeVoss, Elyse Eidman-Aadahl, and Troy Hicks (2010) note, "E-portfolios allow for texts that are richly textured and layered, with elements of print pieces, spoken pieces, visuals, and various digital composing processes across the work" (p. 109). Students become more motivated to complete their work because of the potential for an increased audience, which gives them more of a vested interest in it. Students may even share their writing through blog posts and Wikispaces, or they may share their portfolio with future teachers to read through them.

With so many tools at a teacher's disposal and so many ways to use tools to measure students' growth, it can be difficult to know where to start the digital portfolio process and how exactly the students will be measured. However, the most important aspect of the portfolio is how students reflect on their work. Peter Elbow (1994) argues that:

> The most important part of the portfolio is an essay that introduces,
> explores, and explains the pieces in the portfolio and talks about what
> the student has learned from these pieces of work. This self-reflexive
> writing provides a kind of meta-discourse that leads to new under-
> standing and enriches fragile, incipient insights. (p. 2)

In the past, the teacher collected student work and placed it in a folder. However, digital portfolios are more than a folder of memories of what students have written. They can be a place where students write, edit, revise, reflect, and more importantly, grow as writers. This chapter focuses on the use of digital portfolios in a middle school classroom using Wikispaces. Specifically, we examine how to use a digital portfolio to measure student growth. Teachers can adapt many of the suggestions for other grade levels and other tools.

# How Do I Do It?

Teachers should look for positive changes and growth with digital portfolios in specific areas—for example:

- Organization

- Style and design

- Attribution (or citing sources)

- Sentence structure

- Attention to spelling accuracy

- Depth of reflection

- Understanding and utilization of the digital nature of the space

By having students create, revise, and store their writing in cloud-based collaborative spaces, websites, or other social media sites for school, teachers are meeting CCRA.W.6 (NGA & CCSSO, 2010, p. 43) and W.8.10:

> Write routinely over extended time frames (time for research, reflection, and revision) and shorter time frames (a single sitting or a day or two) for a range of discipline-specific tasks, purposes, and audiences. (NGA & CCSSO, 2010, p. 44)

The Common Core allows for flexibility in what technology I can use in my classroom, and my personal preference is Wikispaces. Wikispaces is very user-friendly and is easy to sign up for, whether you are a teacher or a student. Wikispaces also offers a free upgrade if you are using the space for education. In addition, security is never an issue, which is important for parents, teachers, and students. Whether you are a teacher or a student user, you need to sign up by creating a username and a password. As an administrator, you will have control over who can be part of this collaborative space.

Administrators approve each member who requests to join. Again, students have to create a username and password to access the classroom wiki and to have access to their student page, where they will archive their work. Figure 24.1 (page 232) shows a classroom wiki dashboard on which the administrator manages members. One can invite, remove, or upgrade a member's status. Wikispaces also has an excellent help section (www.help.wikispaces.com).

Once each student is granted access, I ask him or her to create a page. On this page, the student writes an eight- to ten-sentence biography and includes an appropriate image that represents him or her and the following three subheadings—(1) narrative, (2) informational, and (3) argumentative—per the CCSS.

Figure 24.1: Managing members on a wiki.

Under each heading, students put their writing artifacts for those particular genres we cover in class. As you can see in figure 24.2, a seventh grader completed his biography and each genre heading at the beginning of the year. From here, the student takes over responsibility of his or her wiki. Even though each student is responsible for updating the page when necessary, I give them instructions on how to complete their reflections for each assignment and meet with them throughout each marking period.

## Classroom Example

Because my school is on marking periods, I prefer to have students update their pages halfway through and at the end of each marking period.

During the reflection process, I ask students to choose a piece of writing they have worked on during the given marking period and to complete a one-page reflection sheet. Part of their grade at the end of each marking period is based on the work they post in their portfolios and their completed reflection. Furthermore, I have them complete an overall reflection on their assignments at the end of the school year. Visit http://wp.me/p1rSoi-iW or **go.solution-tree.com/technology** to find the reflection questions I give to my students at the end of each marking period and at the end of the year.

What's Up! My name is _____ or as most call me JIMMY! I am 12 years old and was born in Alma on July 20, 1999. I am a huge Michigan fan. I also like the Tennessee Volunteers, the Duke Blue Devils, the UConn Huskies and the Oregon Ducks. I like to read statistical sports books and creepy especially Jonathan Rand. My favorite athlete is Kema Walker from the University of Connecticut or better known as UCONN. Though I like to read Jonathan Rand my fave author is Mike Lupica. I also like to write about sports stuff that goes on in my life like this spring (late March) when the Fulton HS basketball team went to the state finals and played at the Breslin Center. One thing few people know about me is that when I get a job I want to be drawing logos for pro or college teams (if I'm not playing for them).

**NARRATIVE:**

DAY IN A SENTENCE: Losing the state title in my favorite sport was a bitter ending to an amazing experience ☹

**INFORMATIONAL:**

**ARGUMENATIVE:**

*Source: Caleb Walden. Used with permission.*

Figure 24.2: Sample student wiki.

By having my students reflect on their writing within the portfolio, I am not just handing an assignment back for them to look at the grade and toss the paper into a folder and forget about it. Instead, students begin to develop a mentality that they can make themselves better English students, especially when it comes to narrative, informational, and argumentative writing. By the end of their seventh-grade year, students in my class begin to critically assess their own writing and start to think of ways they can make pieces better. In addition to critically assessing their writing, my students also begin using reflection as a way to reinforce their revision and editing. Throughout this constant cycle of writing, I tell them that their writing is never done. In the future, I intend to expand on the use of digital portfolios by setting up guidelines for my students to use in responding to each other's portfolios. As you can see in figure 24.3 (page 234), the student has added each genre heading and has pieces of writing underneath each heading showing a completed portfolio.

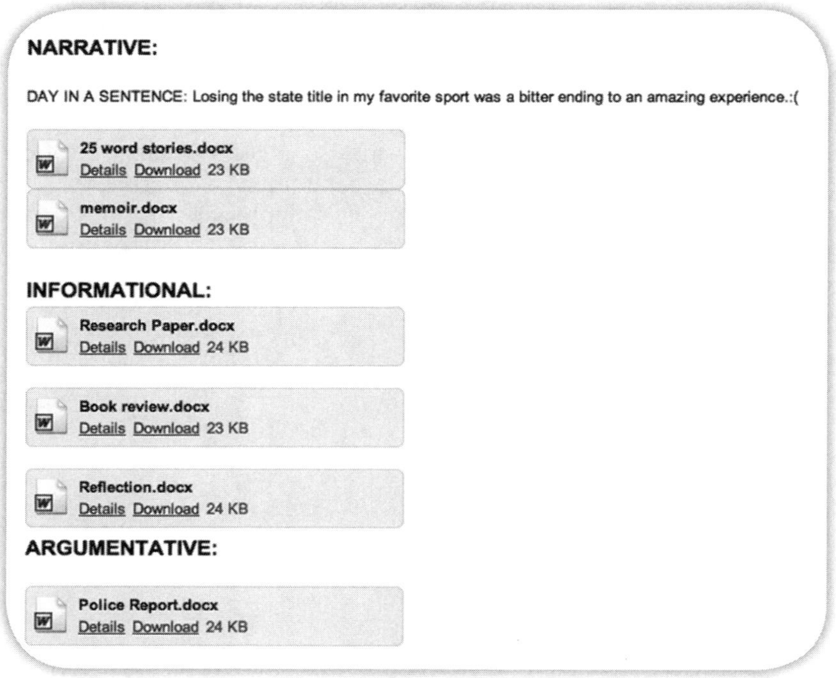

**NARRATIVE:**

DAY IN A SENTENCE: Losing the state title in my favorite sport was a bitter ending to an amazing experience.:(

**25 word stories.docx**
Details Download 23 KB

**memoir.docx**
Details Download 23 KB

**INFORMATIONAL:**

**Research Paper.docx**
Details Download 24 KB

**Book review.docx**
Details Download 23 KB

**Reflection.docx**
Details Download 24 KB

**ARGUMENTATIVE:**

**Police Report.docx**
Details Download 24 KB

*Source: Caleb Walden. Used with permission.*

Figure 24.3: Completed student wiki.

## Your Turn

There are many different approaches to digital portfolios, and all of them can develop growth in our writers and create an environment where the students are confident in their writing skills.

After you choose the tool that best fits the needs of everyone, I encourage you to play, play, play! Take the time to know the ins and outs of the site, tool, or platform you are using. Helen Barrett has a robust website about digital portfolios that is worth exploring (http://electronicportfolios.com). Whenever I introduce a new digital tool to my students, I always give them one or two days to play around on it. Anyone planning on using a wiki in his or her classroom should take time over the summer to get things prepared prior to launching it. It will take careful planning and some frontloading. For example, Wikispaces has various colors you can use to emulate your school colors. Furthermore, you can see things through the eyes of the student by creating a student account. This will enable you to answer questions better and understand some of the issues students might have when they use the wiki.

Along with familiarizing yourself with how to use a wiki, it is important to think about how you want your students' portfolios to look and how you want them organized. Although I suggest giving the student his or her own page and dividing it into narrative, informational, and argumentative writing per the CCSS, teachers can also divide it into units of study, marking periods, or semesters. In my opinion, student reflection is key to the success of the portfolios. Developing a reflection sheet for each assignment is helpful, or alternatively, students can reflect on specific assignments after the marking period or semester. As noted previously, create a student account for yourself to help model a wiki for students to ensure they're clear on expectations for the portfolio. Along with Helen Barrett's website, you can also visit the National Writing Project's Digital Is website (http://digitalis.nwp.org), where a National Writing Project colleague discusses digital portfolios and provides a student example. Visit **go.solution-tree.com/technology** to access live links to the websites in this book.

When deciding on the artifacts students will place in their portfolios, you should consider if the students get to choose what they put in their portfolio or if you will control this aspect. In my experience, if students are allowed to choose the artifacts, they take more ownership of their portfolio, which increases their motivation.

Overall, teachers have a lot of decisions to make in order to be successful with digital portfolios. Kicking off the school year by introducing digital portfolios can set the stage for teachers and students. This tool can assist teachers and students in being more organized and can empower all parties to have easy access to writing, listening, and speaking.

The use of digital portfolios is a progressive means for evaluating student work and demonstrating growth. Not only is this tool assistive to the teacher, but it also provides students with an opportunity to take greater ownership of their work and become reflective about their growth as writers. Digital portfolio tools are just one of the many 21st century options that are redefining the way education can be personalized. Although digital portfolios are only one tool in the toolbox, it is one with a wide range of exciting possibilities.

# References and Resources

Aguilar, E. (2011, February 18). Motivating students: Writing for an audience [Web log post]. Accessed at www.edutopia.org/blog/motivating-student-writers-audience-elena-aguilar on January 30, 2013.

Allington, R. L. (2001). *What really matters for struggling readers: Designing research-based programs*. New York: Longman.

Altieri, J. (2014, May). *Creating powerful content connections: Developing readers, writers, and thinkers in Grades K–3. Paper presented at the annual conference of the International Reading Association*. New Orleans, LA.

Alvermann, D. E. (2003). *Seeing themselves as capable and engaged readers: Adolescents and re/mediated instruction*. Naperville, IL: Learning Point Associates.

Alvermann, D. E. (2008). Why bother theorizing adolescents' online literacies for classroom practice and research? *Journal of Adolescent and Adult Literacy, 52*(1), 8–19.

Anderson, J. (2011). *10 things every writer needs to know*. Portland, ME: Stenhouse.

ASCD EDge. (2013). *5 ways you (yes YOU!) should be integrating digital citizenship into your classes*. Accessed at http://edge.ascd.org/_5-Ways-You-yes-YOU-Should-Be-Integrating-Digital -Citizenship-Into-Your-Classes/blog/6264447/127586.html on December 13, 2013.

Atwell, N. (1998). *In the middle: New understandings about writing, reading, and learning* (2nd ed.). Portsmouth, NH: Boynton/Cook.

August, D., & Shanahan, T. (Eds.). (2008). *Developing reading and writing in second-language learners: Lessons from the Report of the National Literacy Panel on Language-Minority Children and Youth*. New York: Routledge.

Ausubel, D. P. (1960). The use of advance organizers in the learning and retention of meaningful verbal material. *Journal of Educational Psychology, 51*(5), 267–272.

Barbeiro, L. F. (2011). What happens when I write? Pupils' writing about writing. *Reading and Writing, 24*(7), 813–834.

Barrett, H. (2011). *Digital storytelling*. Accessed at http://electronicportfolios.org/digistory /index.html on March 21, 2014.

Barton, D., & Hamilton, M. (1998). *Local literacies: Reading and writing in one community*. New York: Routledge.

Baumann, J. F., & Thomas, D. (1997). "If you can pass Momma's tests, then she knows you're getting your education": A case study of support for literacy learning within an African American family. *The Reading Teacher, 51*(2), 108–120.

Bereiter, C., & Scardamalia, M. (1987). *The psychology of written composition*. Mahwah, NJ: Erlbaum.

Bernardini, S. (2004). Corpora in the classroom: An overview and some reflections on future developments. In J. M. Sinclair (Ed.), *How to use corpora in language teaching* (pp. 15–38). Philadelphia: Benjamins.

Bernasconi, N., & Desler, G. (n.d.). *The Digital ID Project helps districts meet Internet safety: Digital citizenship legal mandates*. Accessed at www.google.com/search?q=The+Digital+ID +Project+helps+districts+meet+Internet+safety%3A+Digital+citizenship+legal+mandates .&oq=The+Digital+ID+Project+helps+districts+meet+Internet+safety%3A+Digital +citizenship+legal+mandates.&aqs=chrome..69i57.1841j0j7&sourceid=chrome &es_sm=93&ie=UTF-8 on January 16, 2014.

Biancarosa, G., & Snow, C. E. (2004). *Reading next: A vision for action and research in middle and high school literacy—A report to Carnegie Corporation of New York*. Washington, DC: Alliance for Excellent Education.

Bogard, J. M., & McMackin, M. C. (2012). Combining traditional and new literacies in a 21st -century writing workshop. *The Reading Teacher, 65*(5), 313–323.

Boulton, A. (2008). DDL: Reaching the parts other teaching can't reach? In A. Frankenberg-Garcia (Ed.), *Proceedings of the 8th Teaching and Language Corpora Conference, 2008, Lisbon* (pp. 38–44). Lisbon, Portugal: Associação de Estudos e de Investigação Científica do ISLA-Lisboa.

Britton, J. (1970). *Language and learning*. London: Lane.

Brookhart, S. M. (2008). *How to give effective feedback to your students*. Alexandria, VA: Association for Supervision and Curriculum Development.

Brookhart, S. M. (2012). Preventing feedback fizzle. *Educational Leadership, 70*(1), 24–29.

Brooks, J. (2011). Minimalist tutoring: Making the student do all the work. In C. Murphy & S. Sherwood (Eds.), *The St. Martin's sourcebook for writing tutors* (4th ed., pp. 128–132). Boston: Bedford.

Brown, J., Bryan, J., & Brown, T. (2005). Twenty-first century literacy and technology in K–8 classrooms. *Innovate, 1*(3).

Bruffee, K. A. (1973). Collaborative learning: Some practical models. *College English, 34*(5), 634–643.

Bruffee, K. A. (1984). Collaborative learning and the "conversation of mankind." *College English, 46*(7), 635–652.

Burnett, R. E., & Kastman, L. M. (1997). Teaching composition: Current theories and practices. In G. Phye (Ed.), *Handbook of academic learning: Construction of knowledge* (pp. 265–305). San Diego, CA: Academic Press.

Calkins, L. M. (1994). *The art of teaching writing* (2nd ed.). Portsmouth, NH: Heinemann.

Canada Writes. (2012). *Lynda Williams: Writing that flies*. Accessed at www.cbc.ca/books/canada writes/2012/10/lynda-williams-writing-that-flies.html on January 22, 2014.

Castek, J., & Beach, R. (2013). Using apps to support disciplinary literacy and science learning. *Journal of Adolescent and Adult Literacy, 56*(7), 554–564.

Cerratto Pargman, T. (2003). Collaborating with writing tools: An instrumental perspective on the problem of computer-supported collaborative activities. *Interacting With Computers, 15*(6), 737–757.

Cherry, L. (2000). *The great Kapok tree: A tale of the Amazon rain forest.* Orlando, FL: Harcourt.

Coker, D., & Lewis, W. E. (2008). Beyond writing next: A discussion of writing research and instructional uncertainty. *Harvard Educational Review, 78*(1), 231–250.

Coleman, J. M., Bradley, L. G., & Donovan, C. A. (2012). Visual representations in second graders' information book compositions. *The Reading Teacher, 66*(1), 31–45.

Collis, B. A. (2005). The contributing student: A blend of pedagogy and technology. *The Next Wave of Collaboration,* 7–12.

Common Sense Media. (2013a). *Lesson: Cyberbullying—Crossing the line (6–8).* Accessed at www .commonsensemedia.org/educators/lesson/cyberbullying-crossing-line-6-8 on January 15, 2014.

Common Sense Media. (2013b). *Lesson: Writing good emails (K–2).* Accessed at www.common sensemedia.org/educators/lesson/writing-good-emails-k–2 on January 15, 2014.

Conley, D. T. (2014). *Getting ready for college, careers, and the Common Core: What every educator needs to know.* San Francisco: Jossey-Bass.

Cox, C. (2007). *Teaching language arts: A student-centered classroom* (6th ed.). New York: Pearson.

Cunningham, P. M., & Allington, R. L. (2007). *Classrooms that work: They can all read and write* (4th ed.). Boston: Pearson.

Davey, B. (1983). Think aloud: Modeling the cognitive processes of reading comprehension. *Journal of Reading, 27*(1), 44–47.

Delpit, L. D. (1988). The silenced dialogue: Power and pedagogy in educating other people's children. *Harvard Educational Review, 58*(3), 280–298.

Delpit, L. D. (2006). Lessons from teachers. *Journal of Teacher Education, 57*(3), 220–231.

Denny, H. (2005). Confessions of first-time virtual collaborators: When college tutors mentor high school students in cyberspace. *The Writing Lab Newsletter, 29*(10), 1–5.

Desler, G. (2013a, February 13). *Upstanders, not bystanders* [Video file]. Accessed at http://digital-id .wikispaces.com/Focus+1+-+Stepping+Up on January 16, 2014.

Desler, G. (2013b, October 30). *Digital ID: Citizenship in the 21st century* [Video file]. Accessed at http://prezi.com/arvby3sos0el/digital-id-citizenship-in-the-21st-century on November 25, 2013.

Desler, G., Tsukamoto, M., & Elk Grove Unified School District. (n.d.). *I'm American too: A story from behind the fences* [Video file]. Accessed at www.secctv.org/time-of-remembrance.html on November 25, 2013.

DeVoss, D. N., Eidman-Aadahl, E., & Hicks, T. (2010). *Because digital writing matters: Improving student writing in online and multimedia environments.* San Francisco: Jossey-Bass.

Dewey, J. (1916). *Democracy and education: An introduction to the philosophy of education.* New York: Macmillan.

Dewey, J. (1938). *Experience and education.* New York: Macmillan.

Doering, A., Beach, R., & O'Brien, D. (2007). Infusing multimodal tools and digital literacies into an English education program. *English Education, 40*(1), 41–60.

Duke, N. K. (2000). 3.6 minutes per day: The scarcity of informational texts in first grade. *Reading Research Quarterly, 35*(2), 202–224.

Duke, N. K., & Bennett-Armistead, V. S. (2003). *Reading and writing informational text in the primary grades: Research-based practices.* New York: Scholastic Teaching Resources.

Duke, N. K., Caughlan, S., Juzwik, M. M., & Martin, N. M. (2012). *Reading and writing genre with purpose in K–8 classrooms.* Portsmouth, NH: Heinemann.

Duplichan, S. C. (2009). Using web logs in the science classroom. *Science Scope, 33*(1), 33–37.

Durkin, J. (1981). What is the value of the new interest in reading comprehension? *Language Arts, 58*(1), 23–43.

Ede, L., & Lunsford, A. (1984). Audience addressed/audience invoked: The role of audience in composition theory and pedagogy. *College Composition and Communication, 35*(2), 155–171.

Elbow, P. (1973). *Writing without teachers.* New York: Oxford University Press.

Elbow, P. (1994). Will the virtues of portfolios blind us to their potential dangers? In L. Black, D. A. Daiker, J. Sommers, & G. Stygall (Eds.), *New directions in portfolio assessment: Reflective practice, critical theory, and large-scale scoring* (pp. 40–55). Portsmouth, NH: Boynton/Cook.

Elk Grove Unified School District. (2005). *I'm American too: Stories from behind the fence.* Accessed at www.secctv.org/time-of-remembrance.html on January 15, 2014.

Emig, J. (1971). *The composing process of twelfth graders* (Research Rep. No. 13). Champaign, IL: National Council of Teachers of English.

Engstrom, M. E., & Jewett, D. (2005). Collaborative learning the wiki way. *TechTrends, 49*(6), 12–15, 68.

Fang, Z. (2010). *Language and literacy in inquiry-based science classrooms, grades 3–8.* Thousand Oaks, CA: Corwin Press.

Fetters, C. (2010). *An exploration of reading strategy instruction using science expository text in grades 2–5.* Unpublished doctoral dissertation, Louisiana State University, Baton Rouge.

Figg, C., & McCartney, R. (2010). Impacting academic achievement with student learners teaching digital storytelling to others: The ATTTCSE Digital Video Project. *Contemporary Issues in Technology and Teacher Education, 10*(1), 38–79.

Flanders, N. (1970). *Analyzing teaching behavior.* Reading, MA: Addison-Wesley.

Fleischer, C., & Andrew-Vaughan, S. (2009). *Writing outside your comfort zone: Helping students navigate unfamiliar genres.* Portsmouth, NH: Heinemann.

Fletcher, R. (1993). *What a writer needs.* Portsmouth, NH: Heinemann.

Fletcher, R. (2006). *Boy writers: Reclaiming their voices.* Portland, ME: Stenhouse.

Fletcher, R., & Portalupi, J. (2001). *Writing workshop: The essential guide.* Portsmouth, NH: Heinemann.

Flower, L. (1979). Writer-based prose: A cognitive basis for problems in writing. *College English, 41*(1), 19–37.

Flower, L. (1981). Revising writer-based prose. *The Journal of Basic Writing, 3*(3), 62–74.

Flower, L., & Hayes, J. R. (1980). The cognition of discovery: Defining a rhetorical problem. *College Composition and Communication, 31*(1), 21–32.

Foertsch, J. (1995). Where cognitive psychology applies: How theories about memory and transfer can influence composition pedagogy. *Written Communication, 12*(3), 360–383.

Friedman, T. L. (2005). *The world is flat: A brief history of the twenty-first century.* New York: Farrar, Straus and Giroux.

Fulwiler, T. (2003). Provocative revision. In C. Murphy & S. Sherwood (Eds.), *The St. Martin's sourcebook for writing tutors* (2nd ed., pp. 157–169). Boston: Bedford.

Gallagher, K. (2006). *Teaching adolescent writers*. Portland, ME: Stenhouse.

Garmer, A. (2010, November 10). Digital and media literacy: A plan of action [Web log post]. Accessed at www.knightcomm.org/digital-and-media-literacy-a-plan-of-action on November 20, 2013.

Gere, A. R. (Ed.). (1985). *Roots in the sawdust: Writing to learn across the disciplines*. Urbana, IL: National Council of Teachers of English.

Gillis, A., Luthin, K., Parette, H. P., & Blum, C. (2012). Using VoiceThread to create meaningful receptive and expressive learning activities for young children. *Early Childhood Education Journal, 40,* 203–211.

Goodwin, B., Lefkowits, L., Woempner, C., & Hubbell, E. (2011). *The future of schooling: Educating America in 2020*. Bloomington, IN: Solution Tree Press.

Goodwin, B., & Miller, K. (2012). Good feedback is targeted, specific, timely. *Educational Leadership, 70*(1), 82–83.

Grabowski, B. L. (2004). Generative learning contributions to the design of instruction and learning. In D. H. Jonassen (Ed.), *Handbook of research on educational communications and technology* (2nd ed., pp. 719–743). Mahwah, NJ: Erlbaum.

Graham, S., Bollinger, A., Booth Olson, C., D'Aoust, C., MacArthur, C., McCutchen, D., et al. (2012). *Teaching elementary school students to be effective writers: A practice guide* (NCEE 2012-4058). Washington, DC: National Center for Education Evaluation and Regional Assistance. Accessed at http://ies.ed.gov/ncee/wwc/pdf/practice_guides/writing_pg_062612.pdf on November 22, 2013.

Graham, S., Harris, K., & Mason, L. (2005). Improving the writing performance, knowledge, and self-efficacy of struggling young writers: The effects of self-regulated strategy development. *Contemporary Educational Psychology, 30*(2), 207–241.

Graham, S., & Perin, D. (2007a). A meta-analysis of writing instruction for adolescent students. *Journal of Educational Psychology, 99*(3), 445–476.

Graham, S., & Perin, D. (2007b). What we know, what we still need to know: Teaching adolescents to write. *Scientific Studies of Reading, 11*(4), 313–335.

Graham, S., & Perin, D. (2007c). *Writing next: Effective strategies to improve writing of adolescents in middle and high schools—A report to Carnegie Corporation of New York*. Washington, DC: Alliance for Excellent Education. Accessed at www.a114ed.org/files/WritingNext.pdf on November 20, 2013.

Granger, S. (Ed.). (1998). *Learner English on computer*. London: Longman.

Granger, S., & Tribble, C. (1998). Learner corpus data in the foreign language classroom: Form-focused instruction and data-driven learning. In S. Granger (Ed.), *Learner English on computer* (pp. 199–209). New York: Addison-Wesley.

Graves, D. H. (1983). *Writing: Teachers and children at work*. Portsmouth, NH: Heinemann.

Graves, D. H., & Sunstein, B. S. (Eds.). (1992). *Portfolio portraits*. Portsmouth, NH: Heinemann.

Guthrie, J. T., & Davis, M. H. (2003). Motivating struggling readers in middle school through an engagement model of classroom practice. *Reading and Writing Quarterly, 19*(1), 59–85.

Gutiérrez, K. D., Baquedano-López, P., Alvarez, H., & Chui, M. M. (1999). *Building a culture of collaboration through hybrid language practices. Theory Into Practice 28*(2), 87–93.

Guthrie, J. T., Hoa, A. L. W., Wigfield, A., Tonks, S. M., Humenick, N. M., & Littles, E. (2007). Reading motivation and reading comprehension growth in the later elementary years. *Contemporary Educational Psychology, 32*(3), 282–313.

Guthrie, J. T., & Wigfield, A. (2000). Engagement and motivation in reading. In M. L. Kamil, P. B. Mosenthal, P. D. Pearson, & R. Barr (Eds.), *Handbook of reading research* (Vol. 3, pp. 403–422). Mahwah, NJ: Erlbaum.

Gutiérrez, K. D. (2008). Developing a sociocritical literacy in the third space. *Reading Research Quarterly, 43*(2), 148–164.

Gutiérrez, K. D., Baquedano-López, P., & Turner, M. G. (1997). Putting language back into language arts: When the radical middle meets the third space. *Language Arts, 74*(5), 368–378.

Hall, L. R. (2007, February 4). About me [Web log post]. Accessed at http://harleyspaws.blog spot.com/2007/02/about-me.html on November 2, 2013.

Hancock, M. (2011, August 3). *Preparing our children for global digital citizenship success.* Accessed at www.ikeepsafe.org/educational-issues/preparing-our-children-for-global-digital-citizenship -success on November 20, 2013.

Hansen, J. A. (2007). First grade writers revisit their work. *Young Children, 62*(1), 28–33.

Haring-Smith, T. (1994). *Writing together: Collaborative learning in the writing classroom.* New York: HarperCollins.

Harvard Writing Project. (2000). *Harvard Writing Project Bulletin: Special issue—Responding to student writing.* Accessed at www.usfca.edu/uploadedFiles/Destinations/Office_and_Services /Academic_Support/Learning_and_Writing_Center/HWP.responding.pdf on October 23, 2012.

Harvey, S. (1998). *Nonfiction matters: Reading, writing, and research in grades 3–8.* Portland, ME: Stenhouse.

Harvey, S., & Goudvis, A. (2007). *Strategies that work: Teaching comprehension for understanding and engagement* (2nd ed.). Portland, ME: Stenhouse.

Hattie, J. (2012a). Know thy impact. *Educational Leadership, 70*(1), 18–23.

Hattie, J. (2012b). *Visible learning for teachers: Maximizing impact on learning.* London: Routledge.

Heard, G. (2002). *The revision toolbox: Teaching techniques that work.* Portsmouth, NH: Heinemann.

Heath, S. B. (1983). *Ways with words: Language, life, and work in communities and classrooms.* New York: Cambridge University Press.

Herrell, A. L., & Jordan, M. (2012). *50 strategies for teaching English language learners* (4th ed.). Columbus, OH: Pearson.

Hicks, T. (2009). *The digital writing workshop.* Portsmouth, NH: Heinemann.

Hillocks, G. (1984). What works in teaching composition: A meta-analysis of experimental treatment studies. *American Journal of Education, 93*(1), 133–170.

Hillocks, G., Jr. (1986). *Research on written composition: New directions for teaching.* Urbana, IL: ERIC Clearinghouse on Reading and Communication Skills.

Holmes, V. L., & Moulton, M. R. (2001). *Writing simple poems: Pattern poetry for language acquisition.* New York: Cambridge University Press.

Holt, M. (1992). The value of written peer criticism. *College Composition and Communication*, *43*(3), 384–392.

Hore, R. (2007, June 22). *Righteous anger (*Okal Rel Saga*, part two): Review by Ronald Hore.* Accessed at www.umanitoba.ca/outreach/cm/vo113/no22/righteousanger.html on May 12, 2013.

Hunston, S. (2002). *Corpora in applied linguistics.* Cambridge, England: Cambridge University Press.

International Reading Association. (2009). *IRA position statement on literacy and technology.* Newark, DE: Author. Unpublished draft.

International Reading Association, & National Council of Teachers of English. (1996). *Standards for the English language arts.* Urbana, IL: Authors. Accessed at www.ncte.org/library/NCTE Files/Resources/Books/Sample/StandardsDoc.pdf on January 16, 2014.

International Reading Association, & National Council of Teachers of English. (2010). *Standards for the assessment of reading and writing* (Rev. ed.). Newark, DE: Authors.

International Society for Technology in Education. (2007). *International Society for Technology in Education standards.* Washington, DC: Author. Accessed at www.iste.org/docs/learning-and-leading-docs/nets-s-standards on January 15, 2014.

Ito, M., Baumer, S., Bittanti, M., Boyd, D., Cody, R., Herr-Stephenson, B., et al. (2010). *Hanging out, messing around, and geeking out: Kids living and learning with new media.* Cambridge, MA: MIT Press.

Johns, T. (1991). Should you be persuaded: Two samples of data-driven learning materials. *English Language Research Journal, 4*, 1–13.

Juniper, D. K. (2013, May 12). Reality skimming: The Okal Rel universe [Web log post]. Accessed at http://okalrel.org/reality-skimming on March 1, 2014.

Kaiser Family Foundation. (2010). *Generation M2: Media in the lives of 8- to 18-year-olds.* Menlo Park, CA: Author. Accessed at www.kff.org/entmedia/upload/8010.pdf on November 20, 2013.

Kajder, S., & Swenson, J. (2004). Digital images in the language arts classroom. *Learning and Leading with Technology, 31*(8), 18–22.

Kamil, M. L., Iterator, S. M., & Kim, H. S. (2000). The effects of other technologies on literacy and literacy learning. In M. L. Kamil, P. B. Mosenthal, P. D. Pearson, & R. Barr (Eds.), *Handbook of reading research* (Vol. 3, pp. 771–788). Mahwah, NJ: Erlbaum.

Kim, K. (2007). English and American poetry teaching based on pattern poetry writing. *English Literature Education, 11*(1), 5–22.

Kist, W. (2010). *The socially networked classroom: Teaching in the new media age.* Thousand Oaks, CA: Corwin Press.

Kittle, P. (2008). *Write beside them: Risk, voice, and clarity in high school writing.* Portsmouth, NH: Heinemann.

Kittle, P., & Hicks, T. (2009). Transforming the group paper with collaborative online writing. *Pedagogy: Critical Approaches to Teaching Literature, Language, Composition, and Culture, 9*(3), 525–538.

Kiuhara, S., Graham, S., & Hawken, L. (2009). Teaching writing to high school students: A national survey. *Journal of Educational Psychology, 101*(1), 136–160.

Kluger, J. (2012, September 6). *We never talk any more: The problem with text messaging.* Accessed at www.cnn.com/2012/08/31/tech/mobile/problem on November 20, 2013.

Koch, R. (2010, April 16). Portfolios in a digital age [Web log post]. Accessed at www.michigan portfolios.org on November 22, 2013.

Koda, K. (2005). *Insights into second language reading: A cross-linguistic approach*. Cambridge, England: Cambridge University Press.

Koschmann, T. D. (Ed.). (1996). *CSCL: Theory and practice of an emerging paradigm*. Mahwah, NJ: Erlbaum.

Kress, G. (2003). *Literacy in the new media age*. London: Routledge.

Labbo, L. D. (2006). Literacy pedagogy and computer technologies: Toward solving the puzzle of current and future classroom practices. *Australian Journal of Language and Literacy, 29*(3), 199–209.

Lacina, J. & Griffith, R. (2012). Blogging as a means of crafting writing. *The Reading Teacher, 66*(4), 316–320.

Lalor, A. D. (2012). Keeping the destination in mind. *Educational Leadership, 70*(1), 75–78.

Lane, B. (1993). *After the end: Teaching and learning creative revision*. Portsmouth, NH: Heinemann.

Lankshear, C., & Knobel, M. (2003). *New literacies*. Buckingham, England: Open University Press.

Larson, L. C., & Miller, T. N. (2011). 21st century skills: Prepare students for the future. *Kappa Delta Pi Record, 47*(3), 121–123.

Laru, J., Naykki, P., & Jarvela, S. (2012). Supporting small-group learning using multiple web 2.0 tools: A case study in the higher education context. *Internet and Higher Education, 15*(1), 29–38.

Lawless, K. A., & Pellegrino, J. W. (2007). Professional development in integrating technology into teaching and learning: Knowns, unknowns, and ways to pursue better questions and answers. *Review of Educational Research, 77*(4), 575–614.

Leander, K. M. (2008). Toward a connective ethnography of online/offline literacy networks. In J. Coiro, M. Knobel, C. Lankshear, & D. J. Leu (Eds.), *Handbook of research on new literacies* (pp. 33–66). Mahwah, NJ: Erlbaum.

Lee, S. (2005). Making writing pleasant: Pattern poetry. *Young English Learners, 18*, 25–28.

LeLoup, J. W., & Ponterio, R. (2003). *Second language acquisition and technology: A review of the research*. Washington, DC: Center for Applied Linguistics. Accessed at www.cal.org /resources/digest/0311leloup.html on November 20, 2013.

Lerner, N. (2011). Writing center assessment: Searching for the "proof" of our effectiveness. In C. Murphy & S. Sherwood (Eds.), *The St. Martin's sourcebook for writing tutors* (4th ed., pp. 199–214). Boston: Bedford.

Leu, D. J., Jr., Kinzer, C. K., Coiro, J., & Cammack, D. (2004). Toward a theory of new literacies emerging from the Internet and other information and communication technologies. In R. B. Ruddell & N. Unrau (Eds.), *Theoretical models and processes of reading* (5th ed., pp. 1570–1613). Newark, DE: International Reading Association.

Leu, D., McVerry, G., O'Byrne, I., Kiili, C., Zawilinski, L., Everett-Cacopardo, H., et al. (2011). The new literacies of online reading comprehension: Expanding the literacy and learning curriculum. *Journal of Adolescent and Adult Literacy, 55*(1), 5–14.

Leu, D. J., O'Byrne, W. I., Zawilinski, L., McVerry, J. G., & Everett-Cacopardo, H. (2009). Comments on Greenhow, Robelia, and Hughes: Expanding the new literacies conversation. *Educational Researcher, 38*(4), 264–269.

Lever-Duffy, J., & McDonald, J. B. (2008). *Teaching and learning with technology* (3rd ed.). Boston: Allyn & Bacon.

Lewis, C., & Fabos, B. (2005). Instant messaging, literacies, and social identities. *Reading Research Quarterly*, *40*(4), 470–501.

Lim, H., & Kahng, J. (2012). Review of Criterion. *Language Learning and Technology*, *16*(2), 38–45. Accessed at http://llt.msu.edu/issues/june2012/review4.pdf on January 13, 2013.

Lott, D. (2009, June 17). *Lynda at Bridges* [Video file]. Accessed at www.youtube.com /watch?v=80lDH7o8aCI on January 22, 2014.

Lunsford, A. (2011). Collaboration, control, and the idea of the writing center. In C. Murphy & S. Sherwood (Eds.), *The St. Martin's sourcebook for writing tutors* (4th ed., pp. 70–76). Boston: Bedford.

Luscombe, B. (2010, October 18). Working moms' kids turn out fine, 50 years of research says. *Time*. Accessed at http://healthland.time.com/2010/10/18/working-moms-kids-turn-out -fine-50-years-of-research-says/#ixzz12jg4KSof on February 3, 2014.

Lyons, J. (1977). *Semantics I*. Cambridge, England: Cambridge University Press.

Macrorie, K. (1970). *Uptaught*. New York: Hayden Books.

Marjanovic, O. (1999). Learning and teaching in a synchronous collaborative environment. *Journal of Computer Assisted Learning*, *15*(2), 129–138.

Martinez, G. (2007). English language learners: What every teacher should know. *Maryland Association for Supervision and Curriculum Development Journal*, 29–34.

Marzano, R. J., Pickering, D. J., & Pollock, J. E. (2001). *Classroom instruction that works: Research-based strategies for increasing student achievement*. Alexandria, VA: Association for Supervision and Curriculum Development.

Mazman, S., & Usluel, Y. (2010). Modeling educational usage of Facebook. *Computers and Education*, *55*(2), 444–453.

McGrail, E., & Davis, A. (2011). The influence of classroom blogging on elementary student writing. *Journal of Research in Childhood Education*, *25*(4), 415–437.

Meadows, D. (2003). Digital storytelling: Research-based practice in new media. *Visual Communication*, *2*(2), 189–193.

Merchant, G. (2005). Electric involvement: Identity performance in children's informal digital writing. *Discourse: Studies in the Cultural Politics of Education*, *26*(3), 301–314.

Merchant, G. (2009). Literacy in virtual worlds. *Journal of Research in Reading*, *32*(1), 38–56.

Meskill, C., & Mossop, J. (2000). Technologies use with learners of ESL in New York State: Preliminary report. *Journal of Educational Computing Research*, *22*(3), 265–284.

Meunier, F. (2002). The pedagogical value of native and learner corpora in EFL grammar teaching. In S. Granger, J. Hung, & S. Petch-Tyson (Eds.), *Computer learner corpora, second language acquisition and foreign language teaching* (pp. 119–142). Philadelphia: Benjamins.

Miller, L. C. (2010). *Make me a story: Teaching writing through digital storytelling*. Portland, ME: Stenhouse.

Miller, S., & Pennycuff, L. (2008). The power of story: Using storytelling to improve literacy learning. *Journal of Cross-Disciplinary Perspectives in Education*, *1*(1), 36–43.

Moje, E. B., Ciechanowski, K. M., Kramer, K., Ellis, L., Carrillo, R., & Collazo, T. (2004). Working toward third space in content area literacy: An examination of everyday funds of knowledge and discourse. *Reading Research Quarterly*, *39*(1), 38–70.

Moll, L., Amanti, C., Neff, D., & Gonzalez, N. (1992). Funds of knowledge for teaching: Using a qualitative approach to connect homes and classrooms. *Theory Into Practice*, *31*(2), 132–141.

Moore, R. A. (2004). Reclaiming the power: Literate identities of students and teachers. *Reading and Writing Quarterly, 20*(4), 337–342.

Moore, R. A., & Seeger, V. (2009). *Dear sincerely*: Exploring literate identities with young children and preservice teachers through letter writing. *Literacy Research and Instruction, 48*(2), 185–205.

Morgan, B., & Smith, R. D. (2008). A wiki for classroom writing. *The Reading Teacher, 62*(1), 80–82.

Murphy, C., & Sherwood, S. (Eds.). (2011). *The St. Martin's sourcebook for writing tutors* (4th ed.). Boston: Bedford.

Murray, D. (1999). *Write to learn* (6th ed.). Fort Worth, TX: Harcourt Brace.

Nash-Ditzel, S., & Brown, T. (2012). Freedoms in the classroom: Cultivating a successful Third Space for literacy growth. *Language and Literacy, 14*(3), 95–111.

National Center for Education Statistics. (2012). *The nation's report card: Writing 2011* (NCES 2012-470). Washington, DC: U.S. Department of Education, Institute of Education Sciences.

National Council of Teachers of English. (1985). *NCTE position statement*. Urbana, IL: Author. Accessed at www.ncte.org/positions/statements/grammarexercises on June 10, 2014.

National Council of Teachers of English. (2008a). *NCTE position statement*. Urbana, IL: Author. Accessed at www.ncte.org/positions/statements/21stcentdefinition on November 20, 2013.

National Council of Teachers of English. (2008b). *Writing now: A policy research brief produced by the National Council of Teachers of English*. Urbana, IL: Author. Accessed at www.ncte.org/library/NCTEFiles/Resources/Magazine/Chron0908Policy_Writing_Now.pdf on November 20, 2013.

National Governors Association Center for Best Practices & Council of Chief State School Officers. (2010). *Common Core State Standards for English language arts and literacy in history/social studies, science, & technical subjects*. Washington, DC: Authors. Accessed at www.corestandards.org/assets/CCSSI_ELA%20Standards.pdf on January 15, 2014.

National Writing Project (2010). *Because digital writing matters: Improving student writing in online and multimedia environments*. San Francisco: Jossey-Bass.

Newkirk, T. (2009). *Holding on to good ideas in a time of bad ones: Six literacy principles worth fighting for*. Portsmouth, NH: Heinemann.

Nexus International School. (2013). *Cultural crossovers*. Accessed at https://sites.google.com/a/nexus.edu.my/cultural-crossovers/home on November 22, 2013.

Nielsen, J., & Pernice, K. (2010). *Eyetracking web usability*. Berkeley, CA: New Riders Press.

Noel, S., & Robert, J. (2004). Empirical study on collaborative writing: What do co-authors do, use, and like? *Computer Supported Cooperative Work, 13*, 63–89.

Nordquist, R. (2013). *What is sentence combining and how does it work?* Accessed at http://grammar.about.com/od/grammarfaq/f/faqsentcomb.htm on April 14, 2013.

Notess, G. R. (2005). Casting the net: Podcasting and screencasting. *Online, 29*(6), 43–45.

Nystrand, M. (1987). The role of context in written communication. In R. Horowitz & S. J. Samuels (Eds.), *Comprehending oral and written language* (pp. 197–214). San Diego, CA: Academic Press.

Ohler, J. B. (2010). *Digital community, digital citizen*. Thousand Oaks, CA: Corwin Press.

OkalRelsDaughter. (2013, February 17). *ABC's of the Okal Rel Universe* [Video file]. Accessed at www.youtube.com/watch?v=r46pwotuR5c on January 22, 2014.

Okal Rel Universe. (2013). In *Wikipedia*. Accessed at http://en.wikipedia.org/wiki/Okal_Rel_Universe on November 22, 2013.

Olshansky, B. (2006). Artists/writers workshop: Focusing in on the art of writing. *Language Arts*, *83*(6), 530–533.

O'Neill, P., Adler-Kassner, L., Fleischer, C., & Hall, A. M. (2012). Symposium: On the framework for success in postsecondary writing. *College English, 74*(6), 520–553.

Organisation for Economic Co-operation and Development. (1996). *The knowledge-based economy*. Paris: Author. Accessed at www.oecd.org/dataoecd/51/8/1913021.pdf on November 20, 2013.

Ormrod, J. (2008). *Extrinsic versus intrinsic motivation*. Accessed at www.education.com/reference /article/extrinsic-versus-intrinsic-motivation on January 30, 2013.

Oud, J. (2009). Guidelines for effective online instruction using multimedia screencasts. *References Services Review*, *37*(2), 164–177.

Park, Y., Warschauer, M., Farkas, G., & Collins, P. (2012). *The effects of visual-syntactic text formatting on adolescents' academic development*. Unpublished manuscript.

Park, Y., & Yu, J. B. (2009). Vocabulary teaching and learning through pattern poetry writing. *Journal of Research in Curriculum Instruction*, *13*(2), 299–321.

Partnership for 21st Century Skills. (2009). *P21 Framework definitions*. Accessed at www.p21 .org/documents/P21_Framework_Definitions.pdf on November 20, 2013.

Partnership for 21st Century Skills. (2013). *Skills framework collaboration and communication*. Accessed at www.p21.org/overview/skills-framework/261 on November 22, 2013.

Pearson, P. D., & Gallagher, M. C. (1983). The instruction of reading comprehension. *Contemporary Educational Psychology*, *8*(3), 317–344.

Pearson, P. D., & Tierney, R. J. (1984). On becoming a thoughtful reader: Learning to read like a writer. In A. C. Purves & O. Niles (Eds.), *Becoming readers in a complex society* (pp. 144–173). Chicago: National Society for the Study of Education.

Peregoy, S. F., & Boyle, O. F. (2013). *Reading, writing, and learning in ESL: A resource book for teaching K–12 English learners* (6th ed.). Boston: Pearson.

Pitcher, S., Martinez, G., Dicembre, E. A., Fewster, D., & McCormick, M. K. (2010). The literacy needs of adolescents in their own words. *Journal of Adolescent and Adult Literacy*, *53*(8), 636–645.

Prensky, M. (2001). Digital natives, digital immigrants: Part 1. *On the Horizon*, *9*(5), 1–6.

Prince, G. (1982). *Narratology: The form and functioning of narrative*. Berlin, Germany: Mouton.

Pritchard, R., & Honeycutt, R. (2006). The process approach to writing instruction: Examining its effectiveness. In C. MacArthur, S. Graham, & J. Fitzgerald (Eds.), *Handbook of writing research* (pp. 275–290). New York: Guilford Press.

Purcell-Gates, V. (1997). *Other people's words: The cycle of low literacy*. Cambridge, MA: Harvard University Press.

Purcell-Gates, V., Duke, N. K., & Martineau, J. A. (2007). Learning to read and write genre-specific text: Roles of authentic experience and explicit teaching. *Reading Research Quarterly*, *42*(1), 8–45.

Quillen, I. (2011, June 15). Educators evaluate learning benefits of iPad. *Education Week*, *4*(3), 38, 40–41.

Rasinski, T. V., & Padak, N. D. (2008). *Evidence-based instruction in reading: A professional development guide to comprehension*. New York: Pearson.

Ribble, M., & Bailey, G. (2007). *Digital citizenship in schools*. Eugene, OR: International Society for Technology in Education.

Rijlaarsdam, G., Van den Bergh, H., Couzijn, M., Janssen, T., Braaksma, M., Tillema, M., et al. (2012). Writing. In E. Anderman, P. H. Winne, P. A. Alexander, & L. Corno (Eds.), *Handbook of educational psychology* (pp. 189–227). New York: Routledge.

Rish, R. M. (2011). Engaging adolescents' interests, literacy practices, and identities: Digital collaborative writing of fantasy fiction in a high school English elective class (Doctoral dissertation, Ohio State University). *Dissertation Abstracts International, A, 73.*

Rish, R. M., & Caton, J. (2011). Building fantasy worlds together with collaborative writing: Creative, social and pedagogical challenges. *English Journal, 100*(5), 21–28.

Robinson, K. (2011). *Out of our minds: Learning to be creative* (Rev. ed.). Oxford, England: Capstone.

Roblyer, M. D., & Doering, A. H. (2013). *Integrating educational technology into teaching* (6th ed.). Boston: Pearson.

Roscoe, R. D., & Chi, M. T. H. (2008). Tutor learning: The role of explaining and responding to questions. *Instructional Science, 36*(4), 321–350.

Rosenbaum, S. (2011). *Curation nation: How to win in a world where consumers are creators.* New York: McGraw-Hill.

Scarcella, R. C. (2003). *Accelerating academic English: A focus on the English learner.* Oakland: Regents of the University of California.

Schmitt, N. (2000). *Vocabulary in language teaching.* New York: Cambridge University Press.

Schultz, K. (1997). "Do you want to be in my story?": Collaborative writing in an urban elementary classroom. *Journal of Literacy Research, 29*(2), 253–287.

Schwartz, D., Lin, X., Brophy, S., & Bransford, J. D. (1999). Toward the development of flexibly adaptive instructional designs. In C. M. Reigeluth (Ed.), *Instructional-design theories and models: A new paradigm of instructional theory* (Vol. 2, pp. 183–213). Mahwah, NJ: Erlbaum.

Seaman, M. (2008). Birds of a feather?: Communities of practice and knowledge communities. *Curriculum and Teaching Dialogue, 10*(1–2), 269–279.

Shamoon, L. K., & Burns, D. H. (2011). A critique of pure tutoring. In C. Murphy & S. Sherwood (Eds.), *The St. Martin's sourcebook for writing tutors* (4th ed., pp. 133–148). Boston: Bedford.

Shanahan, C. (2009). Disciplinary comprehension. In S. E. Israel & G. G. Duffy (Eds.), *Handbook of research on reading comprehension* (pp. 240–260). New York: Routledge.

Shanahan, T. (2004). Overcoming the dominance of communication: Writing to think and learn. In T. L. Jetton & J. A. Dole (Eds.), *Adolescent literacy research and practice* (pp. 59–74). New York: Guilford Press.

Shaughnessy, M. P. (1976). Diving in: An introduction to basic writing. *College Composition and Communication, 27*(3), 234–239.

Shermis, M. D., & Hamner, B. (n.d.). *Contrasting state-of-the-art automated scoring of essays: Analysis.* Accessed at www.scoreright.org/NCME_2012_Paper3_29_12.pdf on January 19, 2013.

Silverman, S. (2005). Getting connected: My experience as a collaborative Internet project coordinator. In R. A. Karchmer, M. H. Mallette, J. Kara-Soteriou, & D. J. Leu, Jr. (Eds.), *Innovative approaches to literacy education: Using the Internet to support new literacies* (pp. 103–120). Newark, DE: International Reading Association.

Slater, W. H. (2004). Teaching English from a literacy perspective: The goal of high literacy for all students. In T. L. Jetton & J. A. Dole (Eds.), *Adolescent literacy research and practice* (pp. 40–58). New York: Guilford Press.

Smagorinsky, P. (2008). *Teaching English by design: How to create and carry out instructional units.* Portsmouth, NH: Heinemann.

Smith, M. W., & Wilhelm, J. D. (2002). *Reading don't fix no Chevys: Literacy in the lives of young men.* Portsmouth, NH: Heinemann.

Stahl, G., Koschmann, T., & Suthers, D. (2006). Computer-supported collaborative learning: An historical perspective. In R. K. Sawyer (Ed.), *The Cambridge handbook of the learning sciences* (pp. 409–426). New York: Cambridge University Press.

Standley, M., & Ormiston, M. (2010). *Digital storytelling with PowerPoint* (2nd ed.). Eugene, OR: Visions Technology in Education.

Stover, K. (2012). *Digital collaborative literacy, critical literacy, and writing for social justice: A case study of meaningful learning in a first grade classroom.* Unpublished doctoral dissertation, University of North Carolina at Charlotte. Accessed at http://search.proquest.com on November 22, 2013.

Sweeney, S. (2010). Writing for the instant messaging and text messaging generation: Using new literacies to support writing instruction. *Journal of Adolescent and Adult Literacy, 54*(2), 121–130.

Sylvester, R., & Greenidge, W. (2009). Digital storytelling: Extending the potential for struggling writers. *The Reading Teacher, 63*(4), 284–295.

Temple, C., Ogle, D., Crawford, A. N., & Freppon, P. (2008). *All children read: Teaching for literacy in today's diverse classrooms* (2nd ed.). Boston: Pearson Education.

Thesen, A., & Kara-Soteriou, J. (2011). Using digital storytelling to unlock student potential. *New England Reading Association Journal, 46*(2), 93–100.

Thomas, A. (2008). Community, culture, and citizenship in cyberspace. In J. Coiro, M. Knobel, C. Lankshear, & D. J. Leu (Eds.), *Handbook of research on new literacies* (pp. 671–697). New York: Routledge.

Thornton, J. S. (2013). The 4E Wiki Writing Model: Redefining collaboration for technological relevance. *Curriculum and Teaching Dialogue, 15*(1–2), 49–62.

Todorov, T. (1981). *Introduction to poetics.* Minneapolis: University of Minnesota Press.

Tomlinson, C., & Strickland, C. (2005). *Differentiation in practice: A resource guide for differentiating curriculum, grades 9–12.* Alexandria, VA: Association for Supervision and Curriculum Development.

Tomlinson, C. A. (1999). *The differentiated classroom: Responding to the needs of all learners.* Alexandria, VA: Association for Supervision and Curriculum Development.

Tompkins, G. (2005). *Process posters: Making the writing process visible.* Upper Saddle River, NJ: Merrill/Prentice Hall.

Tompkins, G. E. (2010). *Literacy for the 21st century: A balanced approach* (5th ed.). Boston: Pearson.

United States Department of Health and Human Services. (2006). *Research-based web design & usability guidelines.* Washington, DC: U.S. Government Printing Office.

University of Houston. (2014). *Educational uses of digital storytelling: About digital storytelling.* Accessed at http://digitalstorytelling.coe.uh.edu/page.cfm?id=27&cid=27 on March 20, 2014.

U.S. Const. pmbl.

Vogel, C. A. (2002). *A program evaluation of the Live Ink format.* Unpublished doctoral dissertation, University of Denver.

Vygotsky, L. S. (1978). *Mind in society: The development of higher psychological processes* (M. Cole, V. John-Steiner, S. Scribner, & E. Souberman, Eds.). Cambridge, MA: Harvard University Press.

Walker, R. C., Schloss, P., Vogel, C. A., Gordon, A. S., Fletcher, C. R., & Walker, S. (2007, October). *Visual-syntactic text formatting: Theoretical basis and empirical evidence for impact on human reading.* Paper presented at the IEEE Professional Communications Conference, Seattle, WA.

Walker, S., Schloss, P., Fletcher, C. R., Vogel, C. A., & Walker, R. (2005). Visual-syntactic text formatting: A new method to enhance online reading. *Reading Online, 8*(6).

Wallace, C. (2000). Storytelling: Reclaiming an age-old wisdom for the composition classroom. *Teaching English in the Two-Year College, 27*(4), 434–439.

Warschauer, M. (2006). *Laptops and literacy: Learning in the wireless classroom.* New York: Teachers College Press.

Wenger, E. (1998). *Communities of practice: Learning, meaning, and identity.* Cambridge, MA: Cambridge University Press.

Wheeler, S., & Wheeler, D. (2009). Using wikis to promote quality learning in teacher training. *Learning, Media and Technology, 34*(1), 1–10.

Wiggins, G. (2012). 7 keys to effective feedback. *Educational Leadership, 70*(1), 10–16.

Wilder, L. I. (1963). *Little house on the prairie.* New York: HarperCollins Children's Books.

Wiley, M. (2000). The popularity of formulaic writing (and why we need to resist). *English Journal, 90*(1), 61–67.

Williams, L. (2012, December 15). I promised my dolls [Web log post]. Accessed at http://okalrel.org/i-promised-my-dolls on January 24, 2013.

Willis, D. (2003). *Rules, patterns and words: Grammar and lexis in English language teaching.* Cambridge, England: Cambridge University Press.

Willis, J. (1998). Concordances in the classroom without a computer: Assembling and exploiting concordances of common words. In B. Tomlinson (Ed.), *Materials development in language teaching* (1st ed.) (pp. 44–66). Cambridge, England: Cambridge University Press.

Wollman-Bonilla, J. (2000). *Family message journals: Teaching writing through family involvement.* Urbana, IL: National Council of Teachers of English.

Wood, K., Stover, K., & Kissel, B. (2013). Using digital VoiceThreads to promote 21st century learning. *The Middle School Journal, 44*(4), 58–64.

Writing in Digital Environments Research Center Collective. (n.d.). *Why teach digital writing?* Accessed at http://english.ttu.edu/kairos/10.1/binder2.html?coverweb/wide/index.html on November 20, 2013.

Yancey, K. B. (1999). Looking back as we look forward: Historicizing writing assessment. *College Composition and Communication, 50*(3), 483–503.

Yore, L. D., & Treagust, D. F. (2006). Current realities and future possibilities: Language and science literacy—Empowering research and informing instruction. *International Journal of Science Education, 28*(2–3), 291–314.

# Index

### Rebuilding the Foundation
**_Edited by Timothy V. Rasinski_**
Teaching reading is a complex task without a simple formula for developing quality instruction. Rather than build on or alter existing models, this book considers how educators and policymakers might think about rebuilding and reconceptualizing reading education, perhaps from the ground up.
**BKF399**

### Contemporary Perspectives on Literacy series
**_Edited by Heidi Hayes Jacobs_**
Today's students must be prepared to compete in a global society in which cultures, economies, and people are constantly connected. The authors explain three "new literacies"—digital, media, and global—and provide practical tips for incorporating these literacies into the traditional curriculum.
**BKF441, BKF235, BKF236, BKF415**

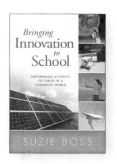

### Bringing Innovation to School
**_By Suzie Boss_**
Activate your students' creativity and problem-solving potential with breakthrough learning projects. Across all grades and content areas, student-driven, collaborative projects will teach students how to generate innovative ideas and then put them into action.
**BKF546**

### What Principals Need to Know About Teaching and Learning Writing
**_By Ruth Culham_**
Discover practical strategies for supporting and assessing writing instruction in all content areas while equipping teachers with instructional practices that emphasize this critical skill, which students need to adapt to the demands of the CCSS and thrive in the 21st century.
**BKF557**

Solution Tree | Press

a division of
Solution Tree

Visit solution-tree.com or call 800.733.6786 to order.

# Wait! Your professional development journey doesn't have to end with the last pages of this book.

We realize improving student learning doesn't happen overnight. And your school or district shouldn't be left to puzzle out all the details of this process alone.

**No matter where you are on the journey, we're committed to helping you get to the next stage.**

Take advantage of everything from **custom workshops** to **keynote presentations** and **interactive web and video conferencing**. We can even help you develop an action plan tailored to fit your specific needs.

*Let's get the conversation started.*

Call 888.763.9045 today.

solution-tree.com